JAMES & CONRAD

SOUTH ATLANTIC
MODERN LANGUAGE ASSOCIATION
AWARD STUDY

James

&

Conrad

Elsa Nettels

THE
UNIVERSITY OF GEORGIA
PRESS
ATHENS

Library of Congress Catalog Card Number: 76–2897
International Standard Book Number: 0–8203–0408–5

The University of Georgia Press, Athens 30602

Set in 11 on 13 point Caledonia type
Printed in the United States of America

TO MY FATHER AND MOTHER

Contents

Preface

In this study of the fiction and criticism of Henry James and Joseph Conrad I seek to analyze the relationship between the two writers and their work and to illuminate the distinctive contributions made by each writer to the development of the novel in the nineteenth and twentieth centuries. The friendship of James and Conrad, extending over a period of nearly twenty years, during which they corresponded, sent each other their works, and wrote critical essays about each other, is one justification for a study of this kind. Another is that from the outset reviewers and critics have noted resemblances between James's and Conrad's fiction and their ideas about the art of fiction, although no one has hitherto pursued the comparison beyond the scope of a short essay.

The first chapter of this study traces the course of the relationship between James and Conrad and estimates its importance to both writers. The evidence, I believe, does not prove conclusively that Conrad was James's disciple in the sense that he consciously imitated James's methods or developed his themes. Differences in the temperament, cultural traditions, and personal histories of the two writers are reflected in fundamental differences in their fiction. Conrad's statements about James, however, indicate that the encouragement and approval of the older writer was of great psychological importance to Conrad during the early years of his career. The evidence also leads to the conclusion that both James and Conrad recognized as the most important bond their dedication to the art of fiction and their abiding interest in the methods by which the inner life of characters and the inwardness of situations are best rendered in fiction. These conclusions are the premises on which this study is based.

Chapter 2 compares the two writers' conceptions of the creative process, their ideas about the nature of truth in art, and their understanding of the relation of the writer to his characters and to his readers. Chapter 3, devoted to the narrative methods of James and Conrad, demonstrates the close connection between the ideas each writer expressed in his critical essays and the form and themes of his fiction.

The subjects of the remaining chapters—romance, satire, the grotesque, and tragedy—reflect what is perhaps the most remarkable attribute of both James's and Conrad's fiction: the current "extraordinarily rich and mixed" (to use James's phrase) produced by the mingling of many elements—social realism, romance, comedy, the grotesque, fantasy, and tragedy. The imaginative power which fuses these elements gives James's and Conrad's greatest fiction a kind of complexity and richness that one finds elsewhere in nineteenth-century fiction in English only in the work of Dickens.

I am grateful to the College of William and Mary and its Faculty Research Committee for the award of two summer grants and a semester's leave during 1973–74, which substantially aided me in my work on this study.

For permission to quote from unpublished materials, I am grateful to the following: to the New York Public Library and the Astor, Lenox, and Tilden Foundations for letters of Conrad and the manuscript of *Chance* in the Henry W. and Albert A. Berg Collection; to the British Library for letters of James and Conrad, Ashley Mss. 4792, 492; to Special Collections, Miller Library, Colby College, for letters of James; to the Manuscript Department, Duke University Library, for a letter of James; to Houghton Library, Harvard University, for letters of James and Douglas Goldring; to Barrett Library, University of Virginia, for letters of James, copyright 1976 by Alexander R. James, in the Henry James Collection; to the Beinecke Rare Book and Manuscript Library, Yale Univerity, for letters of James to Edith Wharton and of Conrad to James in the Edith Wharton Papers in the Collection of American Literature, for letters of James to J. B. Pinker in the Collection of American

Literature, and for letters of Conrad and the manuscript of *Under Western Eyes*.

I am grateful to the following copyright holders for permission to reprint material that I originally published in their journals: to the University of Texas Press for "James and Conrad on the Art of Fiction," *Texas Studies in Literature and Language*; to the University of California Press for "The Grotesque in Conrad's Fiction," *Nineteenth-Century Fiction*, 29 (2):144–163, © 1974 by the Regents of the University of California; to *South Atlantic Bulletin* for "*The Portrait of a Lady* and the Gothic Romance"; to *English Literature in Transition* for "Vision and Knowledge in *The Ambassadors* and *Lord Jim*.

JAMES & CONRAD

1

Master and Confrere

During a period of nearly twenty years Henry James and Joseph Conrad maintained a friendly, if not an intimate, relationship. When they first met in the winter of 1897, James was almost fifty-four years of age. He had established himself as one of the foremost novelists of the Anglo-American literary world. He had published *Roderick Hudson*, *The American*, *Washington Square*, *The Portrait of a Lady*, *The Bostonians*, *The Princess Casamassima*, *The Tragic Muse*, and *The Spoils of Poynton*. Conrad, aged thirty-nine, had written two novels, *Almayer's Folly* and *An Outcast of the Islands*; but he was still relatively unknown. The two novelists met at a critical time when each faced a turning point in his life.

James's five years of vain effort to write successful plays for the stage had come to an end in January of 1895 with the failure of *Guy Domville*. He had emerged from the ordeal, sustained by his renewed dedication to the art of fiction but disturbed by the failure of his books to sell. He had experienced the shock of receiving royalties for 1895–96 of only £7.0.5 from the publisher of sixteen of his books.[1] He had suffered rebuffs of magazine editors who had welcomed his early stories and essays. He was convinced that his best work was still to come, but he faced a crisis in his career. In his letter to W. D. Howells of January 22, 1895, he powerfully expressed his sense of exclusion: "I *have* felt, for a long time past, that I have fallen upon evil days—every sign or symbol of one's being in the least *wanted*, anywhere or by anyone, having so utterly failed. A new generation, that I know not and mainly prize not, had taken universal possession and I asked myself what the future would be."[2]

The praise Conrad received for his first two novels encouraged

him to persist, but neither book was a financial success. Doubtful
whether he could support himself by writing, he hesitated to abandon his career as a merchant seaman and invest all his time and
energy in literary work. The manuscript of *Almayer's Folly*, which
he carried with him for six years on voyages to the East Indies and
the Congo, testifies to a continuing powerful urge to write. But the
publication of the novel did not at once determine him to give up
the sea. Conrad had completed what was to be his last voyage in
the merchant marine in January of 1894, but as late as 1898 he was
still making vain efforts to secure a command. The last paragraphs
of *The Nigger of the Narcissus* (1897) can be read as Conrad's val-
edictory to his twenty years of life at sea, but even the writing of
this work did not wholly dispel the feelings of doubt and inner
conflict which oppressed him after *Almayer's Folly* was finished. "I
was a victim of contrary stresses which produced a state of immobility. I gave myself up to indolence. Since it was impossible for me to
face both ways I had elected to face nothing. The discovery of new
values in life is a very chaotic experience; there is a tremendous
amount of jostling and confusion and a momentary feeling of darkness. I let my spirit float supine over that chaos."[3]

When James and Conrad met, Conrad was at the point where
the friendship of a dedicated artist, esteemed and secure in his
eminence, could strengthen the confidence of the younger writer
and confirm him in his choice of the literary vocation. Conrad's
letters in the 1890s show that he was studying the methods of
Flaubert and Maupassant as masters from whom to learn.[4] For his
part James by the 1890s had begun to find deep satisfaction in the
friendship of younger artists and men of letters, such as A. C. Benson, Hendrik Anderson, and Morton Fullerton, whose admiration, affection, and companionship helped to mitigate his feelings
of loneliness and isolation.

The parts that James and Conrad could play in each other's lives
are clear, but the extent to which they actually played these parts
has not been conclusively established. Contradictory answers have
been given to the questions that one naturally asks. Did James
influence Conrad's development, and if so in what ways? How
close was the friendship between the two novelists? Was it of sig-

nificance in James's life? Did James regard Conrad as a genius, the most gifted writer of his acquaintance? We would expect two writers of extraordinary creative energy and exceptional force of character to make a strong impression on each other. Because of the lack of evidence, however, much in the relationship remains obscure. Only three letters of James to Conrad and six letters of Conrad to James have been published in whole or in part. In their correspondence they make reference to other letters to each other which apparently were lost or destroyed. It thus appears that certain parts of the picture are destined to remain blank. But enough evidence exists to enable one to trace the development of the relationship in its main outlines.

I

For several years before they met, Conrad had read and admired James's work. When in 1908 he received from James the first six volumes of the New York Edition, he recalled that he had been introduced to James's fiction when he read *The American* in 1891.[5] By the time he met James he had praised his work in letters to friends. To refute Galsworthy's criticism that James's fiction was cold and heartless in its technical perfection, Conrad cited "The Pupil," "The Middle Years," and "The Altar of the Dead" as examples of James's power to express the most delicate shades of feeling.[6] In the first communication he addressed to James, a letter dated October 16, 1896, which was inscribed on the flyleaf of *An Outcast of the Islands*, Conrad invoked James's books as the cherished companions of his past and present: "Exquisite Shades with live hearts, and clothed in the wonderful garment of your prose, they have stood, consoling, by my side under many skies. They have lived with me, faithful and serene—with the bright serenity of Immortals."[7]

Uncertain whether he should send his book to James, Conrad wrote to Edward Garnett, his literary mentor and friend, on the same day that he penned his tribute to James: "I do hesitate about H. James. Still I think I will send the book. After all it would not be a crime or even an impudence."[8] Nine days later he wrote again to say that he had dispatched his novel "with a pretty dedication; it fills the flyleaf."[9]

The magniloquence of the tribute, which might have amused or embarrassed or displeased another writer, did not offend James. When *The Spoils of Poynton* was published, he sent Conrad a copy with an inscription, dated February 11, 1897: "To Joseph Conrad in dreadfully delayed but very grateful acknowledgment of an offering singularly generous and beautiful."[10] In a letter to Garnett, Conrad gave full expression to his delight in receiving the novel, which he read at once and judged astonishing in its "delicacy and tenuity."[11] Nor did he conceal his pleasure when he wrote again to Garnett a week later: "I had a note from James. Wants me to lunch with him on Thursday next—so there is something to live for—at last!"[12]

One can only imagine the first meeting of the two novelists on February 25, 1897, in London at James's apartment in Kensington, 34 De Vere Gardens. No one else was present, and neither writer recorded his impressions of the day. To Conrad, who had once declared vehemently to Garnett, "I *won't* live in an attic!"[13] the elegance and order of James's rooms with all their signs of the established literary life might well have symbolized the authority of the artist secure in his power and position. In a book in James's library—the first volume of Pepys's *Diary*—Conrad found, in a passage describing the return of Charles II from exile, the epigraph for the recently finished *The Nigger of the Narcissus*: "My lord, in his discourse discovered a great deal of love in this ship."

There may be no connection between the beginning of Conrad's friendship with James and his writing in August of 1897 of his preface to *The Nigger of the Narcissus*, his most famous statement of his artistic aims. Conrad's conception of the artist differs in certain ways from James's, but in his preface Conrad strongly affirms James's fundamental principles: that fiction is an art, that the purpose of the novelist is to create a picture of life, that the moral and aesthetic value of his work lies in its power to produce the illusion of reality. Conrad sent to James a copy of the novel with a letter in French on the flyleaf. Addressing James as *cher maître*, Conrad declares at the beginning and the end of the short letter that he sends the book with James's consent: "Vous m'avez permis de vous envoyer mon livre"—as if to justify the taking of a liberty. The rest of the letter sounds a central theme of Conrad's fiction: the impossibility of conveying to another person the essence of the dreamlike nature of experience: "Rien de si facile comme de raconter un rêve, mais il est impossible de pénétrer l'âme de ceux qui écoutent par la force de son amertume et de sa douceur. On ne communique pas la réalité poignante des illusions."[14]

Conrad had begun his first letter to James: "I address you across a vast space"; in inscribing a second book to James he perhaps again acknowledged his sense of the distance between himself and the master.

From the beginning of his career Conrad enjoyed critical acclaim. Reviewers of *Almayer's Folly* hailed him as a writer of extraordinary gifts; H. G. Wells in the *Saturday Review* praised *An Outcast of the Islands* as the finest novel of 1896.[15] In 1898 *The Academy* judged *Tales of Unrest*, Conrad's first book of short stories, one of the three most promising works of the year and awarded its author a prize of fifty guineas. Nevertheless Conrad, still poor, obscure, and just beginning to make literary friends, had no place in the established literary society where James for nearly twenty years had been at home—a prominent figure in London clubs and drawingrooms, and the friend of such pillars of the establishment as Edmund Gosse, Leslie Stephen, and the archbishop of Canterbury, E. W. Benson.

James and Conrad lived in different worlds and probably would rarely have met had they not become neighbors. In the summer of 1898 James leased Lamb House in Rye; in October of that year the Conrads moved to the Pent, in Aldington, fourteen miles northeast of Rye. Friendly relations between the two writers were stimulated by the presence of other writers living nearby who sought the company of both James and Conrad: H. G. Wells at Sandgate in Kent, nineteen miles from Rye; Stephen Crane at Brede House in Sussex, only three miles from James; Ford Madox Hueffer at Aldington near Conrad, and after 1901 at Winchelsea. Kipling (whose wife, Carolyn Balestier, James had given in marriage to the writer) lived in Rottingdean, near Brighton. In no other part of the country in England at the turn of the century did so many well-known writers live within so small a radius.

Among the writers in Sussex and Kent only one close literary association developed, between Conrad and Ford, who collaborated in writing *The Inheritors* and *Romance* and who maintained a close personal relationship until they quarrelled in 1910 over the publication of Conrad's reminiscences in the *English Review*. James broke with Ford in 1909, at the time of Ford's scandal-ridden efforts to divorce his wife and marry Violet Hunt. By that time James's and Conrad's enthusiasm for Wells had faded as they recognized that Wells, in his indifference to the art of the novel and in his insistence that fiction was but a means to social reform, was irreconcilably opposed to their principles and convictions.[16] In his satire *Boon* (1914), which precipitated his break with James, Wells attacked Conrad and James. In the early years of the century, however, all the writers were on good terms. They corresponded frequently, sent each other their books, and drove or bicycled through the countryside of Sussex and Kent to pay one another visits. Conrad, often accompanied by Ford, was a fairly frequent visitor at Lamb House. "Conrad haunts Winchelsea," James wrote to Wells, "and Winchelsea (in discretion,) haunts Rye."[17] In letters to Ford and Elsie Hueffer, James asks when Conrad will again be with them in Winchelsea and refers to past visits and letters from Conrad, "whom I have, ever, solidly on my mind."[18]

Neither James nor Conrad recorded detailed impressions of their meetings, but the reminiscences of friends and members of their families evoke a picture of the writers together. Jessie Conrad remembered James's unfailing courtesy to her and recalled her small son Borys sitting on James's knee, the child's "instinctive sense of Henry James's personality" holding him still for more than half an hour.[19] James's nephew Billy, William James's second son, observed James with his Winchelsea visitors and recalled how on afternoon walks James and Conrad would go on ahead, leaving Billy to keep Ford company and occasionally to catch a few words, always in French, from the walkers in front.[20] Ford was particularly impressed by the politeness of James and Conrad to each other. "Even if they had been addressing each other from the tribune of the Académie Française their phrases could not have been more elaborate or delivered more *ore rotundo*. James always addressed Conrad as *"Mon cher confrère"*; Conrad almost bleated with the peculiar tone that the Marseillaises get into their compliments *"Mon cher maître."*[21]

Ford's picture suggests a master and his disciples, but the writers who gathered about James did not form a *cénacle* like Flaubert's in the 1870s. According to Ford's friend and biographer Douglas Goldring, the purpose of the *English Review*, which Ford edited in its first year (1909), was "above all, to start a movement and to found in the French sense, a 'school' ";[22] but no group with writers so diametrically opposed as James and Wells or Conrad and Wells could be said to be united by one program or set of principles. Ford, who liked to picture himself as the promoter of a movement which would unite "the Eminent" and "the Young," in later years referred to James, Conrad, Crane, and himself as the leading exponents of the canons of impressionism;[23] but James and Conrad never saw themselves in this way. Conrad's attitude is indicated by his statement about Crane: "He is *the only* impressionist and *only* an impressionist."[24] Both Conrad and James always sought and valued the society of fellow artists; James never repudiated his early statement that "the best things come, as a general thing, from talents that are members of a group; every man works better when he has companions working in the same line, and yielding the stimulus of suggestion, comparison, emulation";[25] but he disliked labels and proscribed doctrines as much as did Conrad, who regarded the appeal to the authority of a school as a "weakness of inferior minds" and often a sign of intellectual cowardice (18:8). Certainly James, Conrad, Crane, and Ford were united by their dedication to the art of fiction, by their abiding concern with style and form, and by their study of Flaubert and Maupassant. But the impulse to transform the writers in England into a cohesive group came only from Ford.

Although James was not the leader of a school, he was nevertheless the preeminent figure, whose mastery and authority Conrad, Wells, Ford, Crane, and Kipling all acknowledged and whose praise they most coveted. Although Wells was later to attack publicly James's fundamental principles, he, no less than Ford and Conrad, valued James as "a shrewd and penetrating critic,"[26] and the very force of his attack on James attests to his sense of James's power and importance in the literary world. Goldring may have exaggerated when he said that Ford and Conrad devoted the editorials of the first issue of the *English Review* to "erecting a pedestal for the master,"[27] but in this issue the editors hailed the publication of James's New York Edition as an historic event, and they ran James's story "The Jolly Corner" first among the works of prose, which included Conrad's "Some Reminiscences" (later entitled *A Personal Record*), the first half of Tolstoy's "The Raid," and the first installment of Wells's *Tono-Bungay*.

James was aware of his position, which he later described to his (and Conrad's) agent, J. B. Pinker, as that "of quasi-paternal delicacy of relation" to several younger writers. Aware of the regard in which his opinion was held, he judged it best to distinguish none of his friends and fellow artists rather than to provoke jealousy by any signs of marked preference, by any "impression of my unfair, my too individual patting of backs."[28] In various ways, however, James distinguished Conrad from the others and showed his regard for him. He permitted Conrad to read a preliminary statement of *The Wings of the Dove*, explaining later to H. G. Wells, who asked for a similar privilege, that he proposed to dictate no more such statements and that Conrad's was the exceptional case.[29] Clearly valuing Conrad far above Ford, he disapproved of their collaboration (as did Wells) and, according to David Garnett, declared the idea "inconceivable," "like a bad dream which one relates at breakfast."[30] (In thanking Ford for the gift of *Romance*, the chief product of the collaboration, he compared the book to a rich bride cake to be kept for "earnest but interspaced degustation."[31]) In November of 1900, when the last installment of *Lord Jim* appeared in *Blackwood's Magazine*, Conrad received what he described as an "absolutely enthusiastic letter" from James about the novel.[32]

The letter has apparently been lost, but James's judgment of Conrad's early work has been preserved in his letter of commendation to Edmund Gosse of June 26, 1902, written to aid Gosse's effort to secure for Conrad a subsidy from the Royal Literary Fund. James's covering letter to Gosse of the same date reads in part: "I lose not an hour in responding to your request about Conrad— whom I had not in the least known to be in the state you mention. . . . *May* my letter, enclosed, and which I've endeavoured to make warm yet discreet, weigh in the scale! It is at least wholly sincere."[33]

In his letter of commendation James describes Conrad as "one of the most interesting and striking of the novelists of the new generation"; his work as "fine, rare and valid," and marked by "disinterested independent nobleness." He gives his highest praise to *The Nigger of the Narcissus*, "the very finest and strongest picture of the sea and sea life that our language possesses—the masterpiece in a whole class; & *Lord Jim* runs it very close." Conrad would have been less pleased by James's holding up the "truth and beauty" of Pierre Loti as the standard by which his own work was judged. Like almost all James's statements about Conrad that have survived, the end of the letter gives the impression of something less than full-hearted tribute. James's reference in the close to Conrad's "charming, conscientious, uncommon work" is favorable, but these are not the words of highest praise.[34]

The difference in the way the two novelists regarded each other can be seen if one compares James's letter to Gosse with Conrad's essay "Henry James: An Appreciation" published in the *North American Review* in January 1905. James's letter is cordial praise of Conrad's works as notable examples of a particular kind—the literature of the sea; Conrad's essay is an eloquent tribute to James as the exemplar of inexhaustible creative power: "In the body of Mr. Henry James's work there is no suggestion of finality, nowhere a hint of surrender, or even of probability of surrender, to his own victorious achievement in that field where he is a master" (18:11). Conrad does not comment on individual works, but in a few paragraphs he expresses a central idea of James's novels: that the personal contests of the characters, although lacking in the excitements of the romantic adventure story, inspire in the protagonists a kind of moral energy which transforms a seeming defeat or an empty triumph into a victory of the spirit. "Nobody has rendered better, perhaps, the tenacity of temper, or known how to drape the robe of spiritual honour about the drooping form of a victor in a barren strife" (18:14). Conrad then goes on to make as emphatic a statement as one is likely to find of James's conviction that in acts of renunciation a character does not withdraw from life but rather most fully manifests his energy of mind and spirit. In Conrad's words "that a sacrifice must be made, that something has to be given up, is the truth engraved in the innermost recesses of the fair temple built for our edification by the masters of fiction. There is no other secret behind the curtain. All adventure, all love, every success is resumed in the supreme energy of an act of renunciation. It is the uttermost limit of our power" (18:15–16).

Presumably James read Conrad's essay, but there is no mention of it in James's letters or elsewhere. It was not Conrad's essay but Percy Lubbock's article on the New York Edition in the *Times Literary Supplement* for July 8, 1909, which James was to praise as "far and away the most appreciative and *fine* tribute I have ever received."[35]

No breach every occurred between James and Conrad such as that between James and Wells, but the evidence indicates that after 1905 James and Conrad for long periods did not see each other. Occasional references to meetings and impressions of each other appear in their letters, however, from which a pattern in the relationship emerges: repeatedly Conrad expresses his regard for James and shows his desire to keep up the friendship; James graciously acknowledges his overtures and apologizes for delays in response. In one letter to Ford and Elsie Hueffer (July 12, 1908), James indicated his wish to see Conrad on his next visit to them and confessed "I am too horribly in his debt."[36] In another letter (October 12, 1909) he reported having just received "a very touching and interesting letter" from Conrad, "to whom I must even now write."[37] In a letter to Pinker on March 31, 1908, Conrad expressed keen regret that he had been unable to attend the opening performance of James's play *The High Bid* in Edinburgh on March 26. He asked Pinker for news of it, and a few days later wrote of his pleasure in the news of James's success, "especially as you say that it was obtained in his own way and by his own method."[38] One should add that James's experience with *The High Bid*, which had several matinee performances in London in 1909, was very similar to Conrad's two ventures in the theater, in 1905, when his play *One Day More* had three performances, and in 1922, when ten performances of *The Secret Agent* were given in London. Both James and Conrad had a persistent desire to write successful plays but scorned the vulgarity of the contemporary theater. Both anxiously oversaw the production of their plays, endured the strain of opening night, received the respectful attention of the critics, and suffered keen disappointment when the play closed after a short run.

The two novelists met at least once during the fall of 1908, for Conrad reported to Pinker in October that he had lunched with James, who was "very lively and interesting."[39] Conrad's great pleasure in receiving from James the first six volumes of the New York Edition is evident in his letter of December 12, 1908, in which he writes of communing all morning with the volumes and reading the preface to *The American*.

This is quite a thrill to be taken thus into your confidence; a strong emotion it is a privilege to be made to feel—*à cinquante ans!* Afterwards I could not resist the temptation of reading the beautiful and touching last ten pages of the story. There is in them a perfection of tone which calmed me, and I sat for a long while with the closed volume in my hand going over the preface in my mind and thinking—that is how it began, that's how it was done![40]

During these years Conrad continued to send James his works accompanied by the kind of depreciatory statement he had inscribed in *The Nigger of the Narcissus*. *The Mirror of the Sea*, which he sent to James in the fall of 1906 had, he assured James, at least the merit of being short. The inscription goes on to express Conrad's belief that James will read the small volume, composed without malice or art, in the understanding spirit of friendship. "Votre oeil ami saura distinguer dans ces pages cette piété du souvenir qui a guidé la phrase tâtonnante et une plume toujours rebelle."[41]

Whether or not James remembered that Conrad had once declared music to be the supreme art, he clearly intended high praise when on November 1, 1906, he wrote in appreciation of Conrad's book: "I read you as I listen to rare music—with deepest depths of surrender, and out of those depths I emerge slowly and reluctantly again to acknowledge that I return to life."[42] There follows as strong a tribute as James ever paid to a fellow writer: "No one has *known*—for intellectual use—the things you know, and you have, as the artist of the whole matter, an authority that no one has approached."

The jaunty figure two sentences later—"You knock about in the wide waters of expression like the raciest and boldest of privateers" —strikes a jarring note, especially in view of Conrad's intense dislike of being classed as a writer of sea stories and his effort to rid himself of his "infernal tail of ships."[43] But James's simile need not be taken as a slighting reference to Conrad. Frequently in letters James indulged in fanciful comparisons without perhaps measuring their effect upon his correspondent. On at least one occasion he was obliged to explain his meaning, when he had to protest to Edmund Gosse that in comparing one of Gosse's books to a densely covered pin cushion he intended not mockery but "the highest possible tribute to your biographic *facture*. What I particularly meant was that probably no such tense satin slope had ever before grown, within the same number of square inches, so dense a little forest of discriminated upright stems!"[44]

In September 1907, a year after *The Mirror of the Sea* was published, Conrad sent *The Secret Agent* to James with a letter asking James to receive the novel "with the indulgence which cannot be refused to a profound and sincere sentiment prompting the act."[45] His references to "your kind inquiries" which Pinker had conveyed to him and to his comfort in knowing that "your thought is sometimes turned towards me and mine" indicate that the two novelists had not been in recent correspondence. Conrad informs James of his move from the Pent and urges James to extend his London visits as far as the Conrads' new house, the Someries, in Luton, "any day when the conjunction of the planets and your inclination point favourably to my request." The tone of the letter suggests one who wishes a relationship to continue but who will not presume upon past favor.

No response has come to light, but James's opinion of *Nostromo*, *The Secret Agent*, and *Under Western Eyes* is recorded elsewhere. To Edith Wharton, James described these works as "impossibilities" and "wastes of desolation, that succeeded the two or three final good things of his earlier time."[46] In the same letter James also implies a not wholly favorable opinion of Conrad himself. His sense of Conrad he describes as "of a rum sort" and "much mixed up with personal impressions" received since their first meeting. Wells in his autobiography recalls that Conrad initially impressed both James and him "as the strangest of creatures,"[47] and many people remarked the extreme tensions of Conrad's high-strung and irritable temperament. In June 1910, when he was recovering from a physical and mental breakdown, Conrad himself confessed to the need to "keep the lid down on the well of my emotions . . . the hot spring boils somewhere deep within."[48] To Bertrand Russell, who met Conrad in 1913 and felt at once a deep sense of kinship with him, Conrad appeared to regard human life "as a dangerous walk on a thin crust of barely cooled lava which at any moment might break and let the unwary sink into fiery depths."[49]

James had his own acute sensibilities, nervous force, and dark visions of irremediable evil. But he rarely hinted at these in his letters, and he did not wish to explore the subterranean depths in his own mind or in the minds of his friends. If he sensed the boiling spring of emotion of which Conrad wrote, it is not surprising that he held himself aloof from it. Nor was James ever moved to write meditations on the absurdity of existence and the futility of action, such as appear in Conrad's letters to intimate friends like Galsworthy and Cunninghame Graham. In this regard James's point of view suggests that of Hawthorne, who deprecated "the morbid state of mind" that he found reflected in Melville's later works and who, after a conversation with his friend on "Providence and futur-

ity, and . . . everything that lies beyond human ken," wondered
that Melville could wander so long in "these deserts, as dismal and
monotonous as the sand hills amid which we were sitting."[50]

The temperaments of James and Conrad account in large part for
the failure of their relationship to develop into a close friendship,
but other circumstances acted to change the basis on which they
had met. Conrad continued to address James as *cher maître*, but
after the publication of *Lord Jim* and *Nostromo* he was hardly in the
position of a disciple or a suppliant. Although none of his books sold
widely until *Chance* became a best seller in 1914, by 1910 Conrad
was widely acclaimed as one of the foremost novelists of the age.
The *Times Literary Supplement* (September 20, 1907) hailed *The
Secret Agent* as a masterpiece destined to enhance Conrad's reputation, "already of the highest." The *Star* (October 5, 1907) praised
Conrad as the only novelist to equal Dickens in capturing the soul
of London. Reviewers of *Under Western Eyes* compared Conrad to
Dostoevsky and Turgenev and acclaimed the novel as "a literary
event of the first importance" (*Manchester Guardian*, October 11,
1911), "a perfectly poised work of art" (*Morning Post*, October 12,
1911), and "a work which must rank with the masterpieces of English fiction" (*Westminster Gazette*, October 14, 1911).[51] His reputation in the ascendant, Conrad by now had himself become the
mentor and sponsor of younger writers, such as Norman Douglas
and Warrington Dawson, who sent Conrad their manuscripts,
sought his acquaintance, and coveted his praise. That Conrad's letters to James continued to be deferential, even obsequious, reflects
Conrad's sense that James did not accept him as an equal. On such
a basis the relationship between the two novelists was bound to be
artificial.

Then in 1910 both novelists suffered prolonged illnesses, and for
some months the normal course of their lives was completely disrupted. Apparently three years elapsed before they corresponded
or met again, but their letters contain occasional references to each
other. James asked Pinker to send him Conrad's address (October
17, 1911); in a letter to John Quinn, the New York lawyer who
bought Conrad's manuscripts, Conrad expressed pleasure when

Oxford awarded James an honorary degree in 1912.[52] Conrad was not one of the nearly three hundred subscribers to James's birthday portrait in 1913, but it seems more likely that he failed to receive a letter from the sponsors than that he declined to contribute.

On June 19, 1913, James dictated in all the elaborate indirection of his late epistolary style an apology for his failure to write to Conrad.[53] To excuse "the absolute *doom* of my silence" which for at least four years had disfigured "the fair face of my general and constitutional good intention" James pleaded the fact of "my dismal and long-drawn recent record." His allusion to a "particular chronic ailment" is the only reference to the nervous depression bringing on anginal attacks, which had forced him in 1913 to abandon Lamb House for most of the year and to take the rooms in Chelsea that he was to occupy during the greater part of the last three years of his life. He promises to inform Conrad of "my achieved installation again at Rye," and after playful reference to the Conrads' new car—"the most dazzling element for me in the whole of your rosy legend"—he urged Conrad to call on him in July.

Four months later, on October 13, 1913, James wrote in even more extravagant terms of apology: "Will you conceive of me as approaching you as the most abject of worms, most contrite of penitents, most misrepresented—by hideous appearances—of all the baffled well-meaning and all the frustrated fond?"[54] James's allusion to "your afternoon call of some weeks, horribly many weeks ago" explains the "hideous appearances" as James's failure to see or receive Conrad when he came. The note of a genuine desire to see his fellow writer sounds in James's offer to come to Conrad if he cannot accept an invitation to Lamb House to lunch. "I do want to see you, and to tell you, and to convince you, and to harrow you up." In the postscript James invites Conrad to come any day of the following week; on Thursday, October 16, James wrote to Pinker of a visit from Conrad two days before: "The first sight of him I have had for a long time and a very good and happy impression—one of the best he has ever given me."[55]

Whether Conrad sent James any more of his novels after *The*

Secret Agent we do not know, but James's interest in Conrad's work did not lapse. In a letter to Pinker, February 5, 1914, James wrote in a postscript, "I have just finished Conrad's very remarkable *Chance*—in which he affects me as having picked himself up extraordinarily from some comparative recent lapses. It's a very great pleasure to recognize that power in him (after doubting it a little)." Although the narrative method of *Chance* struck him as " 'rum' beyond words" the novel had for him "great fineness and beauty and individuality (to J. C.)."[56] Apparently Pinker was the means of communication, for on February 11 Conrad wrote to his agent: "I am glad to hear that Henry James likes the novel."[57] This time there seems to have been no "absolutely enthusiastic letter" from James himself, such as Conrad had received fourteen years earlier.

Six weeks later, in the second of two articles that James wrote for the *Times Literary Supplement*, his one published criticism of Conrad's work appeared. Under the title "The Younger Generation," James in the first article (March 19, 1914) dealt chiefly with H. G. Wells and Arnold Bennett; in the second article (April 2), with Hugh Walpole, Conrad, Edith Wharton, and Compton Mackenzie.

The tone of the articles is that of the critic who views his subject with benevolent interest from an unassailable height. Rather than attacking directly, he often implies the defects of a novel by praising its virtues. When he criticizes directly, he often delivers the thrust in a witty metaphor. The thesis of the articles can be put simply: the novelists of the younger generation divide themselves into two groups: those who concern themselves with the treatment of their subject—with selection and form and method, and those who do not. If half the novelist's authority derives from his knowledge or possession of his subject and the other half from his treatment of it, then the majority of contemporary novelists belong to the group represented by Wells and Bennett, whose authority resides wholly in the power to create value "by *saturation*."[58] Such novels as *Tono-Bungay*, *Ann Veronica*, *Clayhanger*, and *The Old Wives' Tale* are admirable in their density and detail and precise delineation of conditions, James observed; but they lack a center of interest and a ruling idea. If these authors' knowledge is compared to a large juicy orange, then the act of squeezing the orange constitutes their only "treatment" of the subject.

James seems to praise Conrad when he declares Conrad to be at the opposite extreme from Wells and Bennett, but his approval is persistently qualified. In stating that Conrad is "absolutely alone as a votary of the way to do a thing that shall make it undergo most doing,"[59] James implies that Conrad is preoccupied with technique for its own sake. In particular James objected to the succession of narrators by whom the substance of *Chance* is relayed to the reader "in the manner of the buckets of water for the improvised extinction of a fire."[60] In his letter about Conrad to Edith Wharton, James had described *Chance* as "*yieldingly* difficult and charming," but here he wonders that Conrad should deliberately have embarked on "so special, eccentric and desperate a course," by which the most precious value, objectivity, is "not only menaced but definitely compromised."[61] What *Chance* achieves, James concludes, is not the fully realized picture of a situation but the impression of a mind "beautiful and generous" hovering and circling over the ground, expending itself in "conditions comparatively thankless."[62]

In the last part of the essay James returns briefly to *Chance* but only as a standard by which to judge Edith Wharton's art more successful than Conrad's. Not only does James prefer the "satiric light" of *The Custom of the Country* to the "circumvallations" of *Chance*; he names her, not Conrad, as the one novelist who commands the power of metaphor and analogy—as if *The Nigger of the Narcissus* and *Lord Jim* had not been written. Of the dozen novelists in English discussed in the essay, only Edith Wharton is praised without qualification. One would scarcely guess from what James says that Conrad was a highly regarded writer, whom reviewers ranked with Hardy and James as one of the greatest living novelists.

James's leading articles in the *Times Literary Supplement* created a stir both before and after their publication. Frank Swinnerton recalls that weeks before the articles appeared James was "pelted" with novels of young writers who hoped for a favorable notice of their work.[63] "The Younger Generation" provoked Wells to retaliate by satirizing James in *Boon*, and Conrad was hurt by James's criticism. In a letter to John Quinn several months after James's death Conrad confessed that "this was the *only time* a criticism affected me painfully."[64] He observed that James had restricted himself to an analysis of Conrad's method, which he "rather airily condemned in relation to the methods of two young writers." Not only had James compared Conrad unfavorably with Edith Wharton; but he had mentioned none of Conrad's works except *Chance*, and in designating Conrad one of the "younger generation" he had appeared to place Conrad, aged fifty-six, the author of seven novels and four volumes of stories, with novices like Hugh Walpole and Compton Mackenzie.

No sense of injury, however, appears in Conrad's letter to James of July 24, 1915, the last of the six extant letters to James. When James at Edith Wharton's request asked Conrad, among others, for a contribution to *The Book of the Homeless*, published by Scribners in 1916 to raise funds for war relief, Conrad replied at once with his customary salutation "Très cher maître"; he agreed to make a contribution (he wrote "Poland Revisited" for the volume), concluding: "I commend myself to your indulgent thoughts and am always yours de tout mon coeur."[65]

Frederick Karl, the editor of Conrad's letters, has noted that in a letter to Lady Sidney Colvin, Conrad wrote that his wife on that same day (July 24) underwent an operation on her knee, a fact he did not mention in his letter to James.[66] All the published letters of James and Conrad to each other confirm the implication of Karl's observation—that theirs was not a friendship in which the day-to-day facts of private life were communicated. Indeed Conrad's reference in his letter of September, 1907, to Borys's illnesses in France and his recent departure for school is the only mention in the whole correspondence of family or domestic matters. Clearly Conrad valued his friendship with James but never wrote to him with the freedom and unrestrained confidence that mark his letters to Galsworthy and Cunninghame Graham. It is evident that James esteemed Conrad's work—several scholars have noted that James in the *TLS* articles reserved the word *genius* for Conrad alone—

and that he wished not to lose touch with Conrad, but he was never to feel for Conrad the deep affection that he felt for close friends like Hugh Walpole, Jocelyn Persse, and Arthur Benson. As Ian Watt suggests, if the two novelists sensed that one's devotion exceeded the other's, their awareness may help account for the elaborate formality of their letters. James's abstractions and circumlocutions and Conrad's ceremonious disclaimers and expressions of regard may have served to protect the feelings of both the writer of the letter and the recipient.[67]

Whatever Conrad's private feelings might have been, he always wrote and spoke publicly of James in terms of constant affection and admiration. In a letter to Henry Arthur Jones (November 3, 1922) he recalled the day when "dear Henry James" presented Conrad to the dramatist at the Reform Club.[68] Christopher Morley, who wrote a series of articles on Conrad's visit to the United States in 1923, reported that Conrad spoke with "great affection" of James.[69] The complexity of Conrad's feelings, from which he could not banish a residue of doubt, is most clearly revealed in the letter of May 24, 1916, to Quinn. After admitting the painful effect of James's criticism, Conrad continued: "But in our private relations he has been always warmly appreciative and full of invariable kindness. I had a profound affection for him. He knew of it and he accepted it as if it were something worth having. At any rate that is the impression I have. And he wasn't a man who would pretend. What need had he?—even if he had been capable of it."[70]

II

Conrad's reverence for James's work, coupled with his opportunities to meet and correspond with James, naturally raises the question of influence. To what extent was Conrad affected by James? Would the development of Conrad's art have been different had he not known James or read James's novels? Granted that such literary questions are among the most difficult to answer, that so many forces act upon and within the artist that analysis in terms of influences is usually possible only in tentative and general terms, does the evidence enable one to reach any conclusions about the importance of James in Conrad's career?

Conrad never spoke of himself as the disciple of James or of anyone else. His first advice to young writers was *"imitate no one!"*[71] He insisted upon the original nature of his own work, observing to Pinker, "One may read everybody and yet want to read me—for a change if for nothing else. For I don't resemble anybody."[72] He regarded at least three of his novels—*Nostromo*, *The Secret Agent*, and *Under Western Eyes* as without parallel in English fiction. Moreover in none of the published letters does Conrad make reference to particular aspects of James's method; his praise is always in terms of general qualities of delicacy, feeling, and inexhaustible vigor. Nor did Conrad ever say of James, as he said of Maupassant, that he was "saturated" with his work.

On the other hand James was probably to Conrad the most powerful example of the dedicated artist that he had personally known. As Conrad's essay suggests, James's intelligence, integrity, and energy made him to Conrad a supreme figure, all the more compelling in that he extended his friendship to Conrad when the younger writer was just confirming his dedication to the craft of fiction. The fact most suggestive of influence is that Conrad in the story "Youth" (1898) introduced his narrator Marlow and for the first time adopted James's practice of making the consciousness of the protagonist the register of the action.[73] Leon Edel has shown how the second Marlow story, *Heart of Darkness*, resembles James's *The Turn of the Screw* in the use of the first-person narrator to create a mounting sense of mystery and fear and hidden unnameable evil.[74] How much *Heart of Darkness* owes to *The Turn of the Screw*, which Conrad read and praised when it was published in 1898, we do not know, but the impression which James's tale made upon Conrad—it "evades one, but leaves a kind of phosphorescent trail in one's mind"[75]—might well be a reader's impression of *Heart of Darkness*.

With the publication of *Lord Jim* reviewers began to compare Conrad with James. A favorable review of Conrad's novel in the *Bookman* begins: "If Mr. Henry James had a consummate knowledge of life at sea and in the Pacific Coast towns and settlements, he could write a novel very like *Lord Jim*.[76] Less favorable to Conrad, the reviewer in the *Pall Mall Gazette* found in the method and style of *Lord Jim* "a strange commingling of Mr. Henry James and the late Mr. Stephen Crane."[77] Of all Conrad's novels *Chance* has prompted the most frequent comparison with James.[78] C. C. Montague of the *Manchester Guardian*, in one of the most intelligent and well-informed reviews of *Chance*, presented the novel as a successful illustration of what James called the "fine little law," by which a situation is "enriched by the way" when it is presented not directly by the author but indirectly through the perceptions of the characters.[79] James's criticism of *Chance* indicates that he saw Conrad's method in that novel as alien to his own.

Conrad's close friends who wrote essays about him—Ford, Galsworthy, and Richard Curle—all testify to his abiding admiration of James's art; but they differ on the question of influence. None describes Conrad as James's disciple, and Galsworthy denies even any significant resemblance between Conrad and James. "He was as different from Henry James as East from West. Both had a certain natural intricacy and a super psychological bent but there the likeness stops."[80] Curle in his *Joseph Conrad: A Study* devotes several pages to comparing the fiction of Conrad and James, emphasizing as the most important resemblance their "passion for their theme."[81] He concludes that among the modern writers James, Flaubert, Maupassant, France, and Turgenev were of most "immediate importance" to Conrad, but he does not explain the nature of the importance. Although many of Ford's impressions have been proved false to facts, he probably comes as close to the truth as the others do when he recalls that James "sowed around him, like the mistletoe-spreading birds, an infinite number of literary Impressionist germs. And if Conrad, as is literally true, learned nothing directly of James, yet he found prepared for him a medium in which . . . his work could spread."[82]

From recent critics and scholars come diverse judgments. F. W. Dupee and Leon Edel refer to Conrad as a disciple of James,[83] and others too have assigned to James a place of the first importance in Conrad's development. According to Irving Howe, James was the "model of the literary man" to Conrad and, with Dostoevsky, was one of the two writers who "mattered most in Conrad's life."[84] Ian Watt notes that after *The Nigger of the Narcissus* Conrad turned away from the influence of Flaubert and Maupassant and concludes that "it was probably James's example which, more than anything else, helped Conrad to evolve his mature technique at a crucial stage in his development."[85] Jocelyn Baines in his biography of Conrad, however, makes only passing references to James and declares that Flaubert and Maupassant were Conrad's masters.[86] On the other hand Zdzislaw Najder, the editor of Conrad's Polish letters, after citing twenty-three English and European contemporaries of Conrad, asserts that "with the sole exception of Henry James, another expatriate and spiritual solitary, there is not another name on this list which one could link with Conrad's to form a distinct 'micro-group.' "[87] Few critics have denied that the novels of James and Conrad resemble each other in important ways, but few have flatly declared these resemblances to be the result of direct influence.

In the past forty years, marked by the publication of more than a hundred books on James and more than sixty books on Conrad, only a few comparative studies of their novels have appeared. E. K. Brown, whose article in the *Yale Review* (1946) is the first long essay on the two novelists, compares *The Wings of the Dove* and *Lord Jim* in their use of characters as "lenses" through which the protagonist is seen. Walter O'Grady, in an essay on Hardy, James, and Conrad (1965), compares the relation of character and incident in *The Ambassadors* and *The Secret Agent*. Ian Watt concludes his biographical study of the relationship with an analysis of *Chance* as the best example of Conrad's application of James's methods. Jessie Kocmanova emphasizes Gissing in her "The Revolt of the Workers in the Novels of Gissing, James and Conrad" (1959), but briefly contrasts the terrorist plots and their victims in *The Princess Casamassima* and *The Secret Agent*. Ivo Vidan, in an article on Balzac, James, and Conrad (1966), supports his claim that "the presence of *The Princess Casamassima* in *The Secret Agent* cannot be denied" by pointing out a number of similarities between the two novels. In the most recent article (1971) Roger Ramsay compares the narrative methods of *The Turn of the Screw* and *Heart of Darkness*.[88]

The list is short, but other critics have remarked many points of resemblance in the fiction of James and Conrad: they present action from different perspectives, gradually disclosing facts initially concealed; they define the novel as a picture, and compare scenes to paintings, and characters to portraits and works of sculpture; they strive to represent states of mind, as well as physical action, in visual images. They conceive of the action as a drama and present situations in the form of dramatic scenes. They create irony by portraying characters blind to the truth about themselves and others; they concern themselves with the themes of guilt and betrayal, always centering the narrative on the response of characters to the situation. They value seeing—observation and insight—as the only way to truth and enlightened conduct but they often depict states of anxiety and doubt which the action of the novel never wholly dispels.[89]

The reader of James's and Conrad's letters sees that the two novelists also had certain personal traits and attitudes in common: their sense of honor and their probity in business matters, their care for their position in the literary world, their moral rectitude and their dislike of the Bohemian life, their capacity for tender and faithful devotion to close friends, and their power to inspire devotion in others. According to Hugh Walpole, who knew both James and Conrad, the two novelists were "singularly alike" in that "they placed loyalty and fidelity above all other virtues."[90] Both James and Conrad disliked reformers and in England remained aloof from political parties and causes. They accepted society's hierarchies but valued individual liberty above class privileges and actively opposed forces like censorship that threatened intellectual and artistic freedom.

James was an expatriate citizen of a new and growing nation; Conrad lived in exile from a people struggling to regain national independence. Both novelists were preoccupied in their fiction with the subject of personal identity and in novel after novel portrayed the contrast and conflict of characters of different nations and cultures. James, the creator of American characters seeking to form themselves and to achieve their destinies in the established societies of Europe, may be compared with Conrad, the creator of European characters who struggle to advance themselves in the outposts of Africa, Malaysia, and South America. Conrad wrote only one story about Poland, the land of his birth; whereas James set *The Europeans*, *Washington Square*, *The Bostonians* and *The Ivory Tower* in America and created American protagonists for seven other novels. Conrad, no less than James, however, felt himself rooted in his native literary tradition: what Emerson and Hawthorne were to James, the nineteenth-century Polish romantic writers Mickiewicz and Słowacki were to Conrad.

James's and Conrad's attitudes toward the literary profession were virtually identical. Both scorned the trivial best-selling novels that poured forth, sometimes as many as thirty in a month; but both longed for popular success on their own terms. They wished to reach a wide audience but they refused to debase their art for the sake of the idle-minded. James recognized an artist like himself when, in his letter to Gosse, he described Conrad's work as "of the sort greeted more by the expert & the critic than (as people say,) by the man in the street."

Without question their dedication to the art of fiction, more than anything else, drew the two novelists together and sustained James's interest in Conrad and his reverence for James during the years of their relationship. Their ideas of the nature of fiction and the creative imagination thus make an appropriate point at which a comparative study may begin.

2

The Art of Fiction

In letters, critical essays, and prefaces James and Conrad sought to define the effects or the ends of fiction and to analyze the means by which these ends are achieved. Tracing the growth of his novels from their origins in impressions, ideas, and anecdotes, James gave, in his prefaces, the fullest analysis ever made by a novelist of the methods of his art. Conrad often disclaimed his powers as a critic,[1] wrote no essay on the nature of criticism as did James, and did not set forth his critical principles and methods in a long essay. Nevertheless, his letters, which illuminate his literary development over a period of some thirty-five years, his preface to *The Nigger of the Narcissus*, and his essays, especially those on James and Maupassant and books, provide the basis for comparison of his ideas and purposes with those of James.

Their letters and essays show that James and Conrad saw fiction as an art that required of the artist unremitting patience, discipline, and sacrifice. With James's insistence that "a coherent picture of anything is producible [only] by a complex of fine measurements"[2] one may compare Conrad's emphasis upon "that exact knowledge of the means and that absolute devotion to the aim of creating a true effect—which is art" (18:31). Both James and Conrad acknowledged the spontaneous or unconscious nature of art; at the same time they repeatedly described their novels as the result not merely of conscious decisions but of a "system" or a "method." As often as James compared the novel to an organism—to a tree or a plant that seemingly forms itself—he figured the novel as a building or a tapestry which the novelist creates, knowing that he has "to *build*, is committed to architecture, to construction at any cost" (9:xvi). Although Conrad often declared that his work was produced unconsciously, he also, in a letter of May 31, 1902, to William Blackwood, attributed the value of his work to "my method based on deliberate conviction," and declared that "all my endeavors shall be directed to understand it better, to develop its great possibilities."[3] Ford emphasized the importance of this method as it evolved in the collaboration of Conrad and himself and showed that in their effort to break with conventional narrative patterns they placed paramount importance upon technique, upon the creation of a "planned novel," in which every word advances the story and every part illuminates what precedes and follows it.[4]

Because James and Conrad saw form and substance as inseparable and because they regarded the achievement of formal perfection as a moral as well as an artistic obligation, they rejected sharp distinctions between moral and aesthetic values in fiction. Their idea of the novel was neither didactic nor narrowly technical. Both frequently describe the novel as "picture" and use the terms of the painter, but their pictorial conception of fiction is constantly informed by their conviction that essential value lies in the apprehension of the inwardness of experience. For both James and Conrad the air of reality in a work of fiction depends not merely on the accurate rendering of surfaces but upon the power of the artist's particular vision of the world—in Conrad's words upon his "expression of the inner character of things which demands interpretation, and is, so to speak, personal to the interpreter."[5] Both writers, therefore, valued the work of fiction as James defined it in "The Art of Fiction," as "a personal, a direct impression of life,"[6] to be analyzed as the expression of the writer's mind and history. James's conviction that "the deepest quality of the work of art will always be the quality of the mind of the producer"[7] was shared by Conrad, who asserted that "the novelist stands confessed in his works" (9:95) because "the creator can only express himself in his creation" (11:xx).

Given the agreement of James and Conrad on essential matters, it is striking that the two writers consistently use different terms to describe the purpose or the object of the novelist. James habitually defines the novelist's art as the art of representation; Conrad defines it as the art of self-expression. "The most fundamental and general sign of the novel," James declared in "The Lesson of Balzac," "is its being everywhere an effort at *representation*—this is the beginning and the end of it."[8] Of course James, in extolling the art of representation, "my irrepressible ideal" (23:vi) was not urging the novelist to attempt a literal copy or a photographic reproduction of what he sees, any more than Flaubert was when he declared: "L'art est une représentation, nous ne devons penser qu'à représenter."[9] James's favorite images of the imagination, as a crucible or a cauldron into which the artist pours his material for reduction to "savoury fusion" (15:vii), prove that for him representation is above all a transformation effected by the imagination of the artist of the substance of consciousness into new forms. In James's words, art is a "chemical transmutation for the aesthetic, the representational, end."[10] What the process of transformation requires of the artist is suggested when James distinguishes between "statement," which merely informs the reader of facts, and "representation," which renders the reality of an experience (7:xix, 9:xv). At the beginning of his first preface (to *Roderick Hudson*) he sees the artist as a "rash adventurer," who embarks "under the star of 'representation,'" knowing that "the art of interesting us in things . . . can *only* be the art of representing them" (1:x).

Conrad is no less explicit in his critical essays. The artist that he describes in his prefaces and author's notes is one "for whom self-expression must, by definition, be the principal object, if not the only *raison d'être*, of his existence" (22:140–141). By this statement Conrad does not mean that the novelist's subject is necessarily himself or that the novel exists to enable the writer to expatiate on his feelings; when Conrad refers to a popular notion which holds the novel to be "an instinctive, often unreasoned outpouring of [the artist's] own emotions" (22:132), it is clear that he does not see his own fiction in this way. Nor is the novel a form of confession or a literal rendering of the writer's past. The object of *The Shadow Line*, which Conrad described as "exact biography" and entitled "A Confession," was not, he insisted, "the usual one of self-revelation. My object was to show all the others and the situation through the medium of my own emotions."[11] Indeed, for Conrad, art is self-expression only insofar as the artist creates "for himself a world, great or little, in which he can honestly believe" (18:6). If art issues "straight from our organic vitality" (18:73), then art is self-expression in the sense that the work, in a mysterious unanalyzable way, expresses in its cadences and rhythms the pulse of the artist's vital force. Also important in Conrad's idea of art as self-expression is his belief that the gestation of a work of art in the writer's mind causes him to accept what he creates as "necessity" and "truth," prepared as he is for his emerging work by the "processes of [his] imagination and of [his] intelligence."[12]

What Conrad says of the self-expressive nature of art is applicable to James's art as well as to Conrad's, and it is compatible with James's own critical statements. The processes and the effects which James defines as "representation" are Conrad's ideal no less than James's. The two writers, however, emphasize different aspects of the artistic experience; they use different images to describe the processes of creation or they use the same image in different ways. These differences are reflected in their statements about the creation of truth in art, in their conception of the writer's relation to his characters, and in their definition of the powers most to be valued in the artist.

In "The Art of Fiction" James sets forth one of the ruling ideas of his criticism when he defines experience as "an immense sensibility, a kind of huge spider-web of the finest silken threads suspended in the chamber of consciousness, and catching every airborne particle in its tissue."[13] Repeatedly, James sees the artist as one who immerses himself in life, who reaches out and draws into himself the substance he transforms into art. In his notebooks James pictures himself as nourished by "the big suggestive, swarming world around me, with all its life and motion—in which I only need to dip my ladle."[14] The process of creation begins when the artist recognizes in what he sees or hears or remembers latent possibilities of development, the germinal stirrings of a subject. If the artist is, in James's words, a "man of genius," his mind "takes to itself the faintest hints of life, it converts the very pulses of the air into revelations."[15] To live in "the world of art" is to engage in "that whole intimate restlessness of projection and perception."[16]

Underlying James's statements is the distinction that he made on several occasions between the poet who in expressing his inward states expresses "life itself, in its sources" and the novelist who in representing his world creates "the *image* of life." Whereas the poet, whose world is the "world of Expression," portrays his "own intimate, essential states and feelings," the novelist strives to represent what is apart from himself.[17] The "constant effort" of the novelist, James states, is "to convey the impression of something that is not one's self."[18] Consequently most of James's images of the artist picture the pursuit or the observation of what is outside the self: the artist is the "embroiderer of the canvas of life" (1:vii); he guards his characters as a pawnbroker holds a rare treasure deposited by a mysterious customer (3:xii); he pursues his subject as the hunter pursues his quarry (21:ix); most memorably, the artist is a watcher, a "posted presence," in the House of Fiction, standing at the window through which he views "the spreading field, the human scene" and receives an impression "distinct from every other" (3:xi).

No less emphatically than James, Conrad stresses the importance of the artist's rendering of what is not himself. His definition of art as "a single-minded attempt to render the highest kind of justice to the visible universe" (3:xi) springs from his conviction that the earth, and not the "cold and immutable heaven" (11:95), is the source of the novelist's inspiration; thus the aspiring artist should "mature the strength of his imagination amongst the things of this earth" (18:10). Nevertheless the picture of the artist which emerges from Conrad's letters and critical essays is not identical with James's picture. Whereas James defines the experience of artistic creation as a "luxurious immersion" enabling the artist to enjoy "the great extension, great beyond all others, of experience and of consciousness" (2:xiii–xiv), Conrad defines creation as the pressing out of oneself the substance of one's work. He advised an aspiring writer, Edward Noble: "You must squeeze out of yourself every sensation, every thought, every image . . . so that at the end of your day's work you should feel exhausted, emptied of every sensation and every thought."[19] In letters he frequently speaks of "tearing" or "spinning" or "squeezing" or "dragging" or "hammering" the sentence or the tale or the novel out of himself. In contrast to James, whose images suggest the artist's discovery and possession of what is outside himself—James sees Balzac as a rider "astride of his imagination" charging "at every object that sprang up in his path,"[20] Conrad emphasizes the mind's introspective power in images that represent creation as the exploration of one's inward darkness. The "artist descends within himself, and in that lonely region of stress and strife, if he be deserving and fortunate, he finds the terms of his appeal" (3:xii).[21] Whereas James sees the artist as a watcher in the window in the House of Fiction, Conrad sees himself as a miner who descends into the dark pit of himself to extract his material. In replying to Garnett's criticism of *Lord Jim* Conrad accused himself of failure to breathe life into "my lump of clay I had been lugging up from the bottom of the pit."[22] Years later he described himself as working "like a coal miner in his pit quarrying all my English sentences out of a black night."[23]

James, too, on occasion defines artistic creation by using images of mining, as in his preface to *The Spoils of Poynton*, where he describes, with adroit use of the pun that recalls Thoreau, how the artist "lays together the blocks quarried in the deeps of his imagination and on his personal premises" (10:viii). Almost always, however, James uses the image of the mine to suggest not the mind of the artist but the world outside to which the imagination of the artist responds: the neglected subject of the early nineteenth-century Americans' response to Europe is a "gold-mine overgrown and smothered, dislocated, and no longer workable" (11:xvii); a subject comes to his hand as a "tiny nugget" in which "hard latent *value*" is discovered when the nugget is "washed free of awkward accretions and hammered into a sacred hardness" (10:v–vi).

In this image James suggests what he means by "expression," which he, no less than Conrad, sees as an essential part of the creative process. "All art is *expression*" (21:xxi), he asserts in the preface to *The Ambassadors*; once the artist has gathered his material "in the garden of life" he must devote himself to the "process . . . of expression, the literal squeezing-out of value" (21:x). Whereas Conrad emphasizes the artist's pressing the work out of himself, James reserves the term *expression* for the artist's pressing of value from his subject. The difference is reflected in the writers' use of organic metaphors. For Conrad it is the artist's individuality that like a "seed in the ground expresses itself, manifests itself, in plant and flower";[24] for James it is the *donnée* or the subject that is like the germ or the seed which possesses "lurking forces of expansion" (3:vii) and which the artist must nourish and cultivate, as a gardener tends plants, thereby insuring the expression of what is latent in the subject.

These observations might suggest that James's art owes more than Conrad's to impressions and memories of the external world, but if anything the opposite is true. James rejoices in the power of the artist's imagination to draw from the germ or nugget in an anecdote the form and substance of a novel. He recalls occasions when, having felt the "prick of inoculation," he longed to suppress further report of facts, knowing that "life has no direct sense whatever for the subject and is capable . . . of nothing but splendid waste" (10:vi). Like James's novels certain of Conrad's works, such as *Lord Jim* and *Nostromo*, sprang from the germ of remembered facts and impressions to become highly complex creations of the artist's imagination. All the evidence suggests, however, that Conrad, to a far greater extent than James, drew upon memory in creating the characters and situations of fiction. Norman Sherry has pointed out that Conrad, in disclaiming the possession of an inventive gift, stressed the importance of accuracy with respect to names, numbers, places, and historical events. According to Sherry, Conrad often created a character by joining to certain traits observed in one person the features of other persons remembered from the past.[25] Conrad himself describes the process in the second author's note to *Victory*, where he recalls the persons on whom he based the characters of Mr. Jones, Ricardo, Pedro, and Heyst, on whom "I have fastened . . . many words heard on other men's lips" (15:xi). For James "representation" means above all the rendering of what the imagination has brought into being; for Conrad "self expression" usually involves the drawing from oneself, from one's memories, the substance of one's work.

The differences observed thus far are reflected in differences in the two novelists' ideas of truth in art. Both writers make the essen-

tial distinctions between statement and the rendering of experience, and between "fact" and "truth," which the artist creates in
creating an illusion accepted as reality by the reader. In going beyond these distinctions, however, James and Conrad emphasize
different acts of the imagination and analyze different means by
which truth in art is achieved.

Several times in the prefaces James recalls his concern for verisimilitude in a particular novel or tale, but what most fully absorbs
him—indeed in general terms the subject of the prefaces—is the
creation of the truth he defines as "intensity," upon which the
value of the impression depends and to which the artist will sacrifice if need be all other qualities (21:xv). This truth or intensity,
attained when the artist fully expresses his subject, is achieved not
primarily through style but through form, through roundness and
tightness of structure. "The sense of fluidity is fundamentally fatal
to the sense of particular truth," James notes in explaining why
George Sand's novels lacked "plastic intensity."[26] To create "the
sense of particular truth" the novelist must master the principles of
economy, for "working out economically almost anything is the
very life of the art of representation" (15:xii). In particular, two
processes are essential to the creating of intensity in art. One is
foreshortening, "the most interesting question the artist has to consider" (1:xv); the other is creating the point of view, equally important because "there is no economy of treatment without an
adopted, a related point of view" (19:xvi). By foreshortening the
novelist contrives to convey the essence of thoughts and actions
without fully dramatizing them, "to give all the sense . . . without
all the substance or all the surface" (1:xv). By establishing the point
of view in the consciousness "subject to fine intensification and
wide enlargement" (5:xii), the novelist expresses the fullest value of
the subject within the limits of the form and enables the reader to
feel the character's situation more completely than would otherwise be possible. To restict the field of the novel to one consciousness was for James the means of getting "*most* picture and *most*
impressionistic truth . . . as well as most intensity and unity."[27]
The creation of the central consciousness was thus James's principal means of securing for his novel the center which he deemed

indispensable in the creation of a firm structure. Although James's main characters, such as Strether, Hyacinth Robinson, and Maggie Verver, see themselves moving inward from the surface of a situation to meaning hidden at the center, James usually saw the creating of a novel as the working out from a center, usually the consciousness of one character. By providing a center for his subject, the novelist "most economise[s] its value" (2:xxi).

In contrast to James, who is chiefly concerned with the truth or intensity of illusion achieved through composition, Conrad frequently refers to truth that exists apart from the work, which it is the artist's task to reveal. According to the preface to *The Nigger of the Narcissus*, the artist "seeks the truth" which like a residuum below the surface of things is "manifold and one, underlying . . . every aspect" of the "visible universe" (3:xi). One of Conrad's favorite images, of the mist or veil through which the novelist or his characters attempt to look, also suggests that beyond visible surfaces some essence or reality lies hidden. Exactly what is the nature of the truth "underlying every aspect" of the universe Conrad does not say; he makes clear in the preface that the truth to be unveiled is not one of the laws of nature; nor, it seems apparent, is the underlying truth a kind of transcendent reality of which the surface or object is a symbol or an emanation. The problem is complicated by the fact that Conrad elsewhere denies the existence of any kind of unchanging absolute truth and insists that all truth is relative because men's conceptions of the world change and what is truth to one generation is not truth to another. Nor are the artist's powers unlimited: in a letter to Warrington Dawson, Conrad states emphatically that "form is the artist's (and the scientist's) province, that is all we can understand (and interpret or represent) and that we can't tell what is behind."[28] Moreover, as Edward Said has pointed out, much in Conrad's fiction expresses a conception of truth as a "dark, sinister and fugitive shadow with no image" by which Conrad implies that the "underlying truth" is but a void, a primal darkness without form.[29] It is notable that in the first draft of the preface to *The Nigger of the Narcissus* Conrad sees the artist disclosing not the "inspiring secret" of the "rescued fragment of life" but its "convincing silence."[30]

Conrad's statements suggest that the underlying truth to which he refers in his most famous preface may be either ungraspable or nonexistent. What does exist, to be expressed in the work of fiction, is the writer's own consciousness of "the visible world" whose inmost reality he seeks to capture. The truth to which the writer must be faithful, then, is the truth of his own feelings. As binding to Conrad as any principle of conduct is the obligation of "scrupulous fidelity to the truth of my own sensations" (14:viii). In 1896 Conrad declared to Edward Garnett that "fidelity to passing emotions" one might well find to be "a nearer approach to truth than any other philosophy of life."[31] Conrad's assertion of the importance of "absolute loyalty" or "fidelity" to the truth of one's sensations is the leading idea of his author's notes.

In the expression of truth nothing to Conrad is more important than the structure of a work of fiction—the placement of narrators, the organization of images, the sequence of scenes which break the conventional framework of chronological time—all that Conrad implied by his reference, in a letter to Richard Curle, to "my unconventional grouping and perspective, which are purely temperamental and wherein almost all my 'art' consists."[32] No less strongly than James, Conrad insisted that details are parts of a whole, important only in terms of the ruling idea of the entire work: "The value of creative work of any kind is in the *whole* of it . . . phrasing, expression—*technique* in short has importance only when the conception of the whole has a significance of its own apart from the details that go to make it up—if it (the conception) is imaginative, distinct and has an independent life of its own—as apart from the 'life' of the style."[33]

Given these statements, it is surprising that Conrad says practically nothing about his methods of constructing novels, methods he clearly regarded as essential in producing the illusion of life. In contrast to James, who emphasizes the kind of truth or intensity created through form, Conrad dwells upon the kind of truth achieved through precision in style. Conrad repeatedly asserts that the novelist's first task is to discover the words which will express without distortion the emotions evoked for him by the events and persons he portrays. To Hugh Clifford, Conrad counselled the utmost care in the use of words lest "the picture, the image of truth abiding in facts, should become distorted—or blurred."[34] Whereas James suggests that the truth he defines as intensity is a quality brought into being when the values of the subject are fully expressed, Conrad suggests here and elsewhere that the truth the artist seeks is a quality within the core of an experience, to which truth the artist must penetrate and which he must disclose through the resources of language. The revelation of truth requires above all the search for the precise figure and the exact word: illusion is sustained not by explicitness ("fatal to the glamour of all artistic work"[35]) but by suggestiveness, which "must be obtained by precise expression."[36]

In contrast to James, who warned against fluidity or looseness of structure, Conrad saw the greatest threat to the precise or truthful rendering of one's feelings in the temptation to inflate one's emotions and to allow eloquence to falsify the truth. The writer's integrity depends upon his maintaining "that asceticism of sentiment in which alone the naked form of truth . . . can be rendered without shame" (9:111–112). Conrad's statement reflects the awareness of a powerful impulse within himself—not always resisted—to indulge in high-colored rhetoric. He dramatizes the dangers in *Heart of Darkness*, in the portrayal of Kurtz, whose rhetoric seduces himself and others when he is released from the restraints of conventional society. In the darkness of the writer's inner world where "there are no policemen, no law, no pressure of or dread of opinion to keep him within bounds" (11:xxii), the writer no less than Marlow in the jungle is beset by temptations or "fascinations" and must exercise restraint, even as "the austere anchorite" withholds himself from the "glittering cortège of deadly sins" (18:26–27).

Underlying James's and Conrad's statements about artistic truth and the ways it is rendered are their conceptions of the relation of the artist to his characters and of the characters to the reader. In James's view the novelist succeeds to the degree that his work produces for his readers the illusion that makes them feel that they have "lived another life," that they have had a "miraculous enlargement of experience."[37] In producing this illusion for others the novelist himself enjoys vicariously the experience of the characters he creates; he enters into states of consciousness separate from his own; he enjoys "the sense of another explored, assumed, assimilated identity."[38] No less than the critic, whose prime office is to enter into the experience of his subject, "to lend himself, to project himself and steep himself,"[39] the novelist lives a life "immensely vicarious" in his enjoyment of the "act of personal possession of one being by another at its completest" (2:xxi).

The artist's sense of living in another's self of course reinforces James's idea of creation as "luxurious immersion" and his idea of the novel as a rendering of what is not oneself. Such "multiplications of the candid consciousness" (14:xx) are to James essential to the process of representing life. It is true that a number of James's characters are fashioned in the image of their creator and that in entering the minds of such protagonists as Strether or Isabel Archer or Hyacinth Robinson, James enters minds whose mental processes are similar to his own. Such resemblances, however, do not prevent the novelist from regarding all his characters, like and unlike himself, as independent beings, separate from himself, possessed of their own vital principle of development which the novelist must respect. The artist's delight in the independent vitality of his characters, his "love of each seized identity," enables him to possess them and to live as from their consciousness. "It was by loving them . . . that he knew them," James said of Balzac and his characters; "it was not by knowing them that he loved."[40] To James the novelist's respect for the freedom of his characters was *the great sign of the painter of the first order.*"[41]

In the writing of his novels, Conrad entered as fully into the experience of his characters as did James into that of his. On finishing *Almayer's Folly* Conrad wrote to Marguerite Poradowska that he felt as if part of himself were buried within the pages just completed.[42] (Conrad characteristically expresses the relation in terms of a depletion, a loss from himself.) Marlow comes as close to being an alter ego of his creator as any character in fiction. Conrad does not, however, describe the relation of the author to the characters or of the characters to each other in James's terms of "intimacy," "personal possession," "saturation," and "assimilation" of another's identity. Instead the emphasis in Conrad's letters and novels is on the impossibility of knowing another or of entering into another's consciousness. Marlow, in encountering the main characters of *Heart of Darkness* and *Lord Jim*, acknowledges his uncertainties, his feeling that he sees only the surfaces, beyond which he occasionally glimpses, as through a veil or a mist, a reality he can never fully know. One of the themes of *Lord Jim* is expressed in Marlow's realization of "how incomprehensible, wavering, and misty are the beings that share with us the sight of the stars and the warmth of the sun" (4:180).

Despite his belief that what is not oneself is unknowable, Conrad sees the artist's ultimate task as the awakening in his readers of the consciousness of their kinship with others, of the "subtle but invincible conviction of solidarity that knits together the loneliness of innumerable hearts" (3:xii). By rendering truthfully his own emotions the artist seeks to penetrate to the source of the reader's emotions, to "the very fount of laughter and tears" (11:xxiii). If the writer succeeds he creates in the reader the emotions that he has felt; and thus he forges the bond between himself and his reader. Edward Said is right in seeing in many of Conrad's declarations of purpose an effort to create a public self that would mask his inward conflicts and uncertainties.[43] Nevertheless there is a solid artistic basis for Conrad's statements about fellowship and solidarity, despite the flourishes of sentiment in some of them. As R. G. Collingwood points out in his discussion of art as expression, unless a writer shares the emotions of others, unless he expresses emotions which others are capable of experiencing, he can communicate nothing.[44] Therefore Conrad insists that the novelist cannot regard himself as different from other men, that "a novelist who would think himself of a superior essence to other men would miss the first condition of his calling" (18:9). Thus Conrad is concerned to show that the exotic world in a novel like *Almayer's Folly* is not divorced from the realities that we know, that "there is a bond between us and that humanity so far away" (1:x)—a bond created by the recognition that all men are subject to the same fate—to the vicissitudes of fortune and the realities of suffering and death

(18:194). With one's characters and the persons who inspired them, the novelist thus feels a sense of kinship which is the spring of his desire to portray them in a work of art. The ground on which the persons of *Almayer's Folly* first made their appeal to Conrad was "that mysterious fellowship which unites in a community of hopes and fears all the dwellers on this earth" (11:9).

James's stress on vicarious experience and Conrad's stress on solidarity and fellowship are reflected in their judgments of other writers. Emphasizing the novelist's power to explore and assimilate what is outside himself, James valued above all the "penetrating" or "grasping" imagination which enables the writer to enter into and to possess what is "not one's self." Balzac's most remarkable power was the "wealth of his vicarious experience,"[45] just as Zola's was "the scale and energy of [his] assimilations."[46] What testified most vividly to George Eliot's genius was her power to "enter into the life of other generations" and "reconstitute conditions utterly different from her own."[47] James's fascination with what was "other" is expressed also in his particular interest in writers who had mastered experience remote from his own. James emphasized Conrad's possession of rare knowledge in his tribute to *The Mirror of the Sea*. "The book itself is a wonder to me" he wrote to Conrad, "for its so bringing home the prodigy of your past experience . . . the immense treasure and the inexhaustible adventure. . . . I thank the powers who so mysteriously let you loose, with such sensibilities, into such an undiscovered country—*for* sensibility."[48]

What Conrad most valued in the writer is a vision of the universe which inspires an attitude toward humanity at once ironic and compassionate. If men are bound in a "mysterious fellowship" by their common subjection to unfathomable forces, then the writer's proper attitude is one of sympathy, pity, and respect. He does not wring pathos from his characters' plights by forced eloquence; nor does he deride their pettiness and weakness. Conrad defined the ideal combination of powers in praising in Anatole France a mind "marvellously incisive in its scepticism" and a heart capable of "profound and unalterable compassion" (18:33). Likewise, in his essays on Maupassant, Turgenev, Daudet, and Galsworthy, Conrad emphasized the writer's compassion and sympathy informed by insight as his most important qualities. To manifest his respect and his compassion for his characters, the novelist writes of them in a spirit of dignity and restraint which Conrad described as "a sentiment akin to piety" (11:10). The "spirit of piety" to which Conrad frequently refers in his letters might be compared to the "respect unconditioned"[49] by which the artist, according to James, demonstrates his acceptance of and love for the freedom of his characters. James's statement, however, emphasizes the artist's respect for the separateness of author and character—just as in his fiction the characters whom James most values are those capable at once of sympathetic imagination of others' lives and respect for their independence and freedom to develop according to their own vital principles. Piety for Conrad arises from and reinforces the writer's sense of solidarity and fellowship with characters and readers and so finds its parallel, in the novels, in the idea of fidelity and of keeping one's place in the ranks and in the conviction of Marlow that "we exist only in so far as we hang together" (4:223).

The differences in emphasis are mainly owing not to differences in aesthetic theory but to temperament and personal history, which are strikingly illustrated by the kinds of experience and feeling that James and Conrad associated with artistic creation. As Leon Edel has shown, James suffered periods of disillusionment, depression, and ill health; in the 1890s particularly he endured personal loss, the destruction of long-nourished hopes and a powerful sense of being unwanted as a writer—all of which found expression in more or less disguised form, in his fiction. In his prefaces, however, James dwells not upon the hardships and frustrations of art but upon its rewards and privileges, upon problems solved and difficulties mastered. James's metaphors vary, but whether the novelist is the builder piling brick upon brick, or the packer filling a ship with valuable cargo, or the embroiderer of tapestry surveying the multitude of spaces his thread will color, the image is of the artist possessed of a rich abundance, which he must strive to fit into place.

Conrad's creative life was not unblessed by feelings of confidence and joy in the exercise of his powers. In his letters and reminiscences, however, it is upon the other side of the picture that he dwells. No writer has expressed more graphically than Conrad feelings of anguish, frustration, and exhaustion and the terrible dread of being unable to write. From Conrad's letters to Edward Garnett, Galsworthy, E. L. Sanderson, and others, there emerges a powerful image of the writer engaged in perilous or exhausting labor—whether he is straining to lift an enormous weight, or is balancing on a tightrope, or is struggling at the bottom of a steep, smooth-walled chasm looking up helplessly at his would-be rescuer at the top.[51] James generally uses metaphors to illustrate ideas, but Conrad uses them to express the emotions that accompanied the composing of novels. Writing *Nostromo* was to wrestle " 'with the Lord' for my creation" and to engage on a "cruel battlefield" in a "long, long and desperate fray" (11:96, 100). The writing of *Chance* required him to "go on spinning out of myself like a disillusioned spider his web in a gale."[52] When James compares the artist in quest of his subject to the explorer sailing to unknown lands, his image suggests a calm sea and a prosperous voyage (1:vi). When Conrad seeks the material equivalent of the artist's struggle he finds it only in "the everlasting sombre stress of the westward winter passage round Cape Horn" (11:99).

James extolled "the luminous paradise of art" and saw his artist's workroom as a blessed sanctuary, his effort to create perfect works as "the refuge, the asylum."[53] Conrad continually stressed the feeling of isolation and unreality which overwhelms the writer in his private world, to be likened to a desert or a "cave without echoes" where, in utter solitude, the artist comes to doubt even the reality of his own existence.[54] When James writes of the novelist's being "terribly at the mercy of his mind," he seems to rejoice in the fecundity of the imagination, which has "only to exhale . . . a fostering tropic air in order to produce complications almost beyond reckoning" (9:viii). When Conrad describes himself at the mercy of uncontrollable forces, he is nearly always expressing the anguish of being unable to write, even as sentences and scenes unwind themselves remorselessly in his mind. As the "agent of an unreliable master,"[55] as he described himself to David Meldrum, he was powerless.

Such differences, notable though they are, should not obscure the fact that James and Conrad are as one in their dedication to the artist's craft and in their sense of the all-absorbing and fulfilling nature of the artist's life. At the same time, both writers judged the writer of fiction by his moral vision, by his understanding of "the whole deep mystery of man's soul and conscience."[56] It is this union of the aesthetic and the moral concerns which distinguishes James and Conrad from the contemporaries with whom they have most in common. Both novelists, for instance, shared Flaubert's conviction that the true artist "works for himself alone,"[57] and that the creation of a perfect work is itself the goal and justification of the artist's effort. But James, in stressing artistic creation as "luxurious immersion," and Conrad, in stressing the solidarity of mankind furthered through art, reject the idea which emerges in Flaubert's letters of the artist who in disgust of the world holds himself aloof, isolated in the ivory tower of art, where "one must live alone and seal one's windows lest the air of the world seep in."[58]

In the 1880s and 1890s, when James and Conrad published their most famous essays on the art of fiction, a number of their ideas were expressed in both English and French literature.[59] Pater and Ruskin, as well as Flaubert and his followers, affirmed that the creation and appreciation of beauty are in themselves moral acts, that form and matter should be inseparable, that the artist renders not the "mere fact" of the world but his sense of the world and that his art is great "in proportion to the truth of his presentment of that sense."[60] In particular a number of statements in the conclusion to *The Renaissance* (1873) remind one of James or Conrad. In equating "experience" with the "impressions of the individual mind,"[61] Pater anticipates James's definition of experience in "The Art of Fiction" as "the very atmosphere of the mind."[62] In affirming that success is measured by the intensity with which one sees and feels, that the greatest good is the "fruit of a quickened, multiplied consciousness,"[63] Pater expresses the leading idea of James's fiction and criticism. When Pater argues that the greatest service of philosophy and culture is to rouse the human spirit to "constant and eager observation,"[64] when he inveighs against theories or systems which discourage observation or discount its fruits, he expresses convictions of both James and Conrad. Pater's idea of experience as a flux, as a stream of impressions, "unstable, flickering, inconsistent,"[65] suggests Conrad's definition of the artist's task: "To snatch in a moment of courage, from the remorseless rush of time, a passing phase of life" (3:xiv).[66] Conrad repeatedly embraces Pater's view of the separateness of persons, isolated by "that thick wall of personality through which no real voice has ever pierced on its way to us . . . each mind keeping as a solitary prisoner its own dream of a world."[67]

Probably no other essay anticipates James and Conrad at more points than does Pater's conclusion to *The Renaissance*, but his emphasis is different from that of the two novelists in their criticism. Whereas Pater celebrates the art of life, James and Conrad affirm the active nature of the life of art. In Conrad's words "a book is a deed . . . the writing of it an enterprise as much as the conquest of a colony (22:132). James in defining the artist's work in terms of many activities—hunting, mining, fishing, building, cultivating, navigating, and exploring—implies that the artist's life is self-sustaining and all-embracing. To both writers the creation of a novel not only was action but was, in James's words, "an act of life."[68] "The artist in his calling of interpreter creates . . . because he must," Conrad wrote in his essay on James. "He is so much a voice that, for him, silence is like death" (18:14). To James the artist was the "modern alchemist" who in the full possession of his powers knows "something like the old dream of the secret of life" (10:ix).

Statements like these show most clearly what sets the criticism of James and Conrad apart from that of other novelists in England in the nineteenth century. As Richard Stang has pointed out in *The Theory of the Novel in England*, Victorian novelists and critics set forth many of the critical precepts that figure importantly in the essays of James (and of Conrad, too, one may add).[69] That the principles of economy and selection must be observed in the writing of fiction, that the ultimate value of a book depends upon the quality of the mind of the author, that the novel is a picture of life which binds readers together by enlarging their sympathies and enabling them to experience the emotions of others—these ideas are fully elaborated by George Eliot in her essays in the *Westminster Review*. But one does not find in them, or in the criticism of Dickens or Scott or Thackeray or Trollope, the kind of passionate affirmation of the validity and importance of the aesthetic consciousness and its power which James and Conrad express. James defines the artist's power as a going outward, to sources of being beyond himself, while Conrad expresses the power in terms of a rescue of moments of experience from the obliterating flow of time. In James's words the artist "in his commonest processes [carries] the field of consciousness further and further, making it lose itself in the ineffable. . . . It is . . . the artistic consciousness and privilege in itself that thus shines as from immersion in the fountain of being."[70] In Conrad's words "it is rescue work, this snatching of vanishing phases of turbulence, disguised in fair words, out of the native obscurity into a light where the struggling forms may be seen, seized upon and endowed with the only possible form of permanence in this world of relative values—the permanence of memory" (18:13).

3

The Drama of Perception

Underlying the artistic principles and methods of both James and Conrad is their conviction that the novelist's chief concern is the inner life of character. James's belief that "what a man thinks and what he feels are the history and the character of what he does" (5:xi) was shared by Conrad, who affirmed in the preface to *Typhoon*: "As in most of my writings I insist not on the events but on their effect upon the persons in the tale" (3:ix). The criticism of James and Conrad defines, and their fiction illustrates, two ways of revealing the inner life of characters in fiction. In one case the novelist, intent on the moral and psychological aspects of his subject, renders the external actions of a character as reflections of an inward state. Conrad counseled a young writer to "treat events only as illustrative of human sensation—as the outward sign of inward feelings."[1] The novelist also reveals the thoughts and feelings of a character by representing what passes in the mind of the character. Of *Roderick Hudson* James observed: "The centre of interest . . . is in Rowland Mallet's consciousness, and the drama is the very drama of that consciousness" (1:xvii).

In his prefaces James repeatedly locates the center of a work and its source of interest in the consciousness of the central character, defining experience not as "what happens" but as "our apprehension and our measure of what happens to us as social creatures" (5:x). James not only insists that the "doing" and the "feeling" of a character are not to be separated; he also argues that thinking and feeling are forms of action: as the narrator of an early story declares to his friend: "All this passionate consciousness of your situation is a very ardent life."[2]

Conrad would not have denied that Marlow's brooding meditation upon Kurtz is action and is life as "ardent" as his struggle with Kurtz in the jungle. But Conrad, in defining the novelist's aims, emphasizes—not the consciousness of characters—but the inward nature of the situation in which characters are engaged: he seeks to capture the "psychological moment" of a situation (13:426), to disclose "the stress and passion within the core of each convincing moment"(3:xiv).[3] James's emphasis on consciousness and Conrad's emphasis on the inwardness of situations reflect important differences in the fiction of the two writers. But equally prominent is the bond between them: their repudiation of what James described as "the everlasting vulgar chapters of accidents, the dead rattle and rumble, which rises from the mere surface of things";[4] and their determination to penetrate beyond surfaces, whether the focus is the "psychological moment" of a situation or the movements of the consciousness that reflects the situation.

In defining the novelist's subject, both writers affirmed the uniqueness of each person's vision of the world. James's defense of the artist's freedom in "The Art of Fiction" shows him fully in sympathy with Conrad's belief that "everyone must walk in the light of his own heart's gospel. . . . That's my creed from beginning to end. That's my view of life,—a view that rejects all formulas, dogmas and principles of other people's making."[5] Neither writer ever asserted that the reality of an object resides only in one's consciousness of that object; but as novelists they saw the external world in terms of the personal impressions of characters, each with his own sense of reality, like the observers in James's House of Fiction, each of whom receives "an impression distinct from every other" (3:xi). No less than novelists, characters within novels prove that "humanity is immense, and reality has a myriad forms."[6]

Preoccupation with the way characters see their world and, in James's words, "feel their respective situations" (5:vii) led both novelists to create characters who serve as centers of consciousness and whose point of view provides a unifying frame for the work. Conrad never insisted, as James did, that the intensity of the work depends upon the richness of the reflecting consciousness, upon the extent to which it is "subject to fine intensification and wide enlargement" (5:xii). A number of Conrad's characters, however, exhibit powers of feeling, observation, and analysis that distinguish them from those around them and make them, like James's characters, "intense *perceivers* . . . of their respective predicaments" (5:xvi).

Because James believed that his method was best exemplified in his third-person narratives, one might think that the characters of Conrad who most nearly resemble those of James would appear in Conrad's novels which are narrated mainly in the third person. But, as some critics have noted, when Conrad speaks through first-person narrators, he penetrates more deeply into character and creates a greater sense of reality than when he casts his narrative in the third person.[7] Ian Watt is right in saying that "it was through Marlow that Conrad achieved his version of James's registering consciousness."[8] Conrad's first-person narrator who seems to be most like a Jamesian central character is not the Marlow of *Chance* (the work which Watt analyzes) but the Marlow of *Lord Jim*—the novel in which Conrad seems to share most fully the central concerns of James. In its portrayal of Marlow's efforts to understand Jim and the meaning of his life, *Lord Jim* is akin to the works of James which reveal how a character comes to know the motives and feelings of others. As fully as any of James's novels *The Ambassadors* pictures the efforts of an observer (who is not a first-person narrator) to interpret appearances and to distinguish between the realities that they express and conceal. Comparison of *The Ambassadors* and *Lord Jim*, both written during 1900, should, then, reveal as clearly as any two novels the likenesses and differences between the dramas of perception of James and Conrad.

One cannot help wondering whether James or Conrad noticed the resemblances between the novels that they wrote in the last year of the century. Both *The Ambassadors* and *Lord Jim* portray the bond between a man of middle-age and a young man at the start of his career, a bond created by the older man's feeling of responsibility and concern for the younger. Both Strether and Marlow initially see their protégés as persons who must be rescued— Chad Newsome from what Strether and his patroness Mrs. Newsome believe to be a sordid affair with a base woman; and Jim from the dangers of the derelict's life to which his disgrace, his desertion of the *Patna*, threatens to condemn him. Both Strether and Marlow see the young men whom they propose to rescue as mysterious figues not easily fathomed. Also mysterious or inscrutable to the observer is the woman who loves the young man and fears losing him. Madame de Vionnet expresses her deep-seated anxiety when she pleads with Strether to "save" her (i.e., assure Chad's continued presence in Paris); Jewel more openly betrays her obsessive doubts when she begs and disallows Marlow's assurances that Jim will never leave Patusan.

In their effort to understand and help the persons to whom they feel committed, both Strether and Marlow seek the advice of a friend whose wisdom they believe to surpass their own. It may be forcing the comparison to link Maria Gostrey and Stein, but both are confidants and connoisseurs whose collections—whether of works of art or of butterflies and beetles—suggest their mastery, in James's words, of "a hundred cases or categories" (21:11) in terms of which human experience may be understood. Finally one notes in each novel the elder man's awareness that his nature is essentially different from that of the young man. Strether sees in Chad and Marlow sees in Jim a kind of glamor or power that the older man feels wanting in himself. At the same time both Strether and Marlow exhibit a generosity of spirit and a disinterested care for others' well-being that distinguish them from the egoistic subjects of their concern, although Jim, a "simple and sensitive character" (4:viii), is clearly superior morally to Chad.

The compassion and patience which distinguish both Strether and Marlow suggest the essential resemblances between the two novels: their preoccupation with the way the truth of a situation is revealed, and their stress on the insufficiency of one kind of knowledge as compared with another. Both novels dramatize the difference between bald statements of fact—that Jim deserted the *Patna*, that Chad is the lover of Madame de Vionnet—and the emotional realities of the situations. Both novels demonstrate the inadequacy of certain kinds of inquiry; both dramatize the determination of the observer to go beyond the surface aspects to the underlying truths of a case.

In their quest for truth both Strether and Marlow show themselves keenly sensitive to the significance of seemingly trivial impressions. *The Ambassadors* and *Lord Jim* perfectly illustrate the practice of both novelists of investing with meaning the slightest acts—a glance, a shrug of the shoulders, the presence of a character motionless at a window. Chad's entrance into the box in the theater, his gesture in the cafe pushing back his hat, the appearance of Mamie Pocock standing alone on the balcony—such small occurrences illuminate for Strether the characters' situations, just as Marlow owes his knowledge of Jim and others to his impressions of acts as little momentous: Jim's unexpected composure after the incident of the yellow dog, the "commonplace" remark of the French lieutenant which presses the spring of "a moment of vision" (4:143), the sight of Jim alone on the balcony facing into the night. In each instance the observer's impression has the impact and the importance of a dramatic event.

To perceive the similar concerns and methods of the novels, however, is to become aware at once of fundamental differences between them. One of the most obvious is the difference (reflected in their criticism) between James's and Conrad's view of the extent to which one person can know another or enter into another's experience. Strether does not subject Chad to rigorous analysis, but by the end of the novel he sees Chad clearly. The "prime-producing cause" (21:161) of Chad's seemingly miraculous transformation has been identified in the person of Madame de Vionnet; the superficial nature of the change in Chad has been revealed, and the essential mediocrity of Chad's character, in all its carefully controlled callousness and selfishness, is made manifest. Likewise Madame de Vionnet, at first to Strether a baffling figure, whose charm for him is even enhanced by his sense of the "vastness and mystery of the domain" of which she is mistress, is by the end revealed to him as the tragic victim of a passion to be clearly defined as "mature, abysmal, pitiful" (22:9, 286).

In contrast to Strether, whose mission is to "find out all" (21:189), Marlow never feels himself in possession of Jim's character. He emphasizes the impossibility of knowing Jim fully, of pronouncing conclusive judgment. "I don't pretend I understood him"; "He was not . . . clear to me"; "I cannot say I had ever seen him distinctly—not even to this day" (4:76, 177, 221)—such statements are a ground, a recurring theme, in the novel. Chad carefully with-holds from Strether certain essential facts about his life; Jim opens himself fully to Marlow—"he confessed himself before me as though I had the power to bind and to loose." Yet, just as Jewel, who also tells her story to Marlow, seems "more inscrutable in her childish ignorance than the Sphinx propounding childish riddles to wayfarers," so Jim remains obscure, a point of light "at the heart of a vast enigma" (4:97, 307, 336).

Strether, too, is a limited observer, who at many points fails to see clearly. The limitations of Strether and Marlow, are, however, basically different. Strether's imperfect vision initially reflects the circumscribed character of his own life and the provincial attitudes of the world from which he comes. His failure to recognize or to admit to himself the nature of Chad's and Madame de Vionnet's relation is also owing in part to a deep-rooted impulse to draw back from the ugly or disturbing—an impulse reinforced by his longing to take a part in the lives of Chad and Madame de Vionnet, a part that he can feel morally justified in playing. Therefore he is ready to believe in the "virtuous attachment" which presumably binds them and sanctions his role as the "saviour" of Madame de Vion-net. Marlow, however, who appears to have the knowledge of men and the world which Strether feels woefully lacking in himself, is not burdened by the inhibitions that at times distort Strether's vi-sion. It is true that Marlow, no less than Strether, is moved by private considerations—that his view of Jim is affected by his own needs, anxieties and doubts, in particular by the doubt that Jim casts upon Marlow's faith in his own powers of judgment and upon his faith in the "sovereign power" (4:50) of a fixed standard of con-duct to sustain anyone (including himself) in time of crisis. While Strether at the time cannot measure the effect of his naiveté upon his judgment, Marlow, in retrospect, and even during the time of Jim's recital, is acutely conscious of the effect of his own feelings upon his judgment of Jim. Awareness of his feelings sharpens

rather than obscures his vision and makes him more than ever re-
luctant to pronounce conclusively on Jim's case.

Like Strether, Marlow makes statements which later events
prove to be false, as for instance when he assures Jewel that the
world beyond Patusan will never seek Jim, that she shall "never be
troubled by a voice from there again" (4:317). But Marlow errs
simply because he is unable to read the future and foretell the
arrival of Gentleman Brown. When Marlow narrates Jim's story to
the group of dinner guests, the last days of Jim's life in Patusan are
still to come.

This alone, however, does not explain why Jim is such a perplex-
ing figure to Marlow. As Albert Guerard has observed, Jim's is not
a complicated nature; it is only Marlow's repeated insistence on the
enigmatic quality of Jim that makes him seem complex.[9] Marlow's
vision of Jim reflects primarily the complexity in Marlow, and he
seems to be perfectly capable of penetrating to the root of Jim's
personality. When Marlow perceives that Jim after his disgrace is
more distressed by what he has failed to gain than by what he has
lost, when he can see in Jim's glance "all his inner being carried on,
projected headlong into the fanciful realm of recklessly heroic aspirations" (4:83), one feels that Marlow has gone as deep into Jim's
character as it is necessary to go. Ultimately, for Marlow, the tormenting question is not what kind of person is Jim? but how is one
to regard him? How is one to judge his actions? If on the *Patna* he
exhibits the weakness of a passive dreamer and in Patusan the
strength of a legendary hero, which side—the strong or the
weak—weighs more heavily in the balances? In the end what
makes it impossible for Marlow to render a verdict in his private
inquiry into Jim's case is his awareness that the line between courage and cowardice, between egotism and selflessness, may be so
fine—"as with the complexion of all our actions, the shade of difference was so delicate" (4:197)—that certainty is impossible.

The Ambassadors, of course, presents conduct in which "the
shade of difference" between selflessness and self-interest is just as
delicate and difficult to fix. No less than *Lord Jim* James's novel
raises questions to which readers have given widely divergent answers. To what extent is Strether really transformed by his experi-

ence? Do his renunciations at the end represent a transcendence of private interests or a submission to the initial fear of passional experience? These questions are not posed by characters within the novel, however; and the questions which Strether asks himself, unlike Marlow's questions, are eventually answered. By the end of the novel Strether has judged the situation, has determined where Chad's first obligations lie, and has decided what must be his own course of action; by the end he feels himself "well in port, the outer sea behind him . . . it was only a matter of getting ashore" (22:294). But Marlow's journey has no end; as far as his knowledge of Jim is concerned, he is never "well in port." The questions that he asks years after the events of the novel take place continue to preoccupy him. Was Jim in his actions after the *Patna* disgrace "shirking his ghost" or "facing him out"? (4:197). In Patusan did he realize his heroic dream of self or merely repeat his failure? Marlow will not answer the questions, even for himself, concluding only that he can "affirm nothing. . . . It is impossible to see him clearly" (4:339).

One may object: aren't these differences simply the result of the difference between the role of Strether, who is the protagonist of the novel as well as the observer of Chad, and the role of Marlow, who is the principal narrator but not the central character of *Lord Jim*? Naturally Strether, whose transformation is the subject of the novel, does not raise the kind of questions about himself that Marlow, whose main function is to present another character, asks about Jim. This is true, of course; and yet the source of difference lies deeper than this. The difference is itself the result of the fact that in *The Ambassadors* and *Lord Jim* James and Conrad are concerned with basically distinct kinds of action and mental experience—a distinction readily apparent if one compares in the two novels the images which mark moments of awareness of what was hitherto concealed.

In *The Ambassadors* several kinds of images marking Strether's gradual progress from ignorance to understanding in themselves imply the possibility of attaining complete knowledge. For instance the frequent expression of Strether's insights in terms of debts, prices, and sums attests not only to the importance of the principle of compensation in James's and Strether's concept of morality—the acknowledgement of one's debts, spiritual as well as financial; the metaphors of debts and prices imply the existence of that which can be measured, of problems which can be solved. Not only does Strether recognize in Chad's transformation the magnitude of the "sum he was setting you" (21:137); Strether's own mental state requires analysis into items, which, when added, "sufficiently accounted for the sum" (21:81). If the transformation of Chad has cost a price, placing Madame de Vionnet in a "position to have sent in her bill for expenses incurred in reconstruction" (21:236), Strether's own experience likewise has its price, requiring him to hold "himself ready to pay in instalments" (22:53).

Likewise suggestive of the mystery which has a solution is Strether's impression that the acts of characters who hide their motives are moves in a game: Chad has "his game, his plan, his deep diplomacy" (21:193); Sarah, in refusing to acknowledge the improvement in Chad, plays "a deep game"; the announcement that Jeanne de Vionnet is to be married "affected [Strether] on the spot as a move in a game" (22 : 111, 126). Consistent with these impressions are Strether's sense of the transformation of Chad as a mystery to which he lacks "clues" and "clues to clues" and his sense of the situation as a labyrinth, a "maze of mystic closed allusions" (21 : 161, 279) in which he struggles to keep hold of his thread. As it is the nature of clues to lead to discovery, so it is in the nature of a maze to offer an exit to the person who keeps the thread. Moreover the existence of "closed allusions" suggests not only hidden meanings but a system in which parts connect, a closed world which contains the key to the unlocking of its mysteries.

This is not to imply that the drama of *The Ambassadors* is reducible to a simple puzzle or that the serious issues raised by the novel are resolved when Madame de Vionnet is identified as the "prime-producing" cause. No one could be more sensitive than James to the mysteriousness of human character or less disposed to fix characters by labels. Nothing in the novel suggests that a formula exists by which the values of Strether's experience and the essential nature of his transformation can be easily calculated. Nevertheless in a number of ways the novel creates the picture of a gradual but steady movement from the darkness of ignorance to the light of knowledge. Although observation reveals to Strether a situation increasingly more complex and ambiguous than he had at first imagined, although doubts and questions thicken about him, Strether repeatedly experiences moments of insight which seem to flood the scene with light. Successively he feels "in presence . . . of truth spreading like a flood" (21:225); he feels "his sense of things cleared up and settled" (22:45); he jumps "to supreme lucidity" (22:197). The comic exaggeration of statement underscores the fact that what appears "supreme lucidity" may be but the prelude to a sense of deeper uncertainty, but James's references to the "march of my action" and the "demonstration of [Strether's] process of vision" (21:vi) imply an unfolding, a movement forward to a conclusion; and throughout the novel Strether has the sense of going forward, able to measure the distance he has come. Combining in one image two controlling metaphors—the light of knowledge and the current of life, Strether expresses the central action of the novel when he declares to Sarah Pocock that "from our queer ignorance . . . an inexorable tide of light seems to have floated us into our perhaps still queerer knowledge" (22:201).

What Marlow experiences in *Lord Jim* is not a "process of vision" such as James dramatizes but a succession of moments of insight, isolated, without causal or logical connection. To Marlow these moments are like glimpses of a landscape through a fog or a mist which may yield "bits of vivid and vanishing detail" but give "no connected idea of the general aspect of a country" (4:76). The most Marlow can hope for is "another glimpse through a rent in the mist in which [Jim] moved and had his being" (4:128). His knowledge of Jim comes in flashes, sudden and short-lived, often represented by images of flickering light in darkness. Whereas the illumination of Chad's face creates for Strether "a link in the chain" (21:156), an expression of Jim's face is "violent, short-lived, and illuminating like a twist of lightning that admits the eye for an instant into the secret convolutions of a cloud" (4:118–119). *The Ambassadors* creates a closed and complete world, containing the answers to its mysteries; the imagery of *Lord Jim* evokes a world bound on one side by the land, elsewhere opening out to shoreless darkness. Repeatedly Marlow sees Jim as a figure poised at the edge of a vast sea

(4:128, 173, 177); his last view of Jim is as a point of light in darkness (4:336). At the end of *The Ambassadors* Strether can say of Mrs. Newsome, once the most important person in his life: "I *see* her" (22:323). At the end of *Lord Jim* Marlow declares that Jim "passes away under a cloud," implying not the past disgrace but the ultimate obscurity of the figure who remains "inscrutable at heart" (4:416).

As is evident in *The Ambassadors* and *Lord Jim*, both James and Conrad portray characters involved in the action but able to view their impressions as if from a distance. So, likewise, the novelist must be at once engaged in and detached from the inward experience that he represents. We now see that James and Conrad achieve the necessary closeness and distance in different ways. Through the creation of the central consciousness like Strether, James sought to assume the identity of his character, to achieve "the act of personal possession of one being by another at its completest" (2:xxi). At the same time by narrating in the third person he maintains the necessary detachment: he makes objective the mind of the character, presenting it as a picture or a stage, to be watched as a spectator watches a performance in a theater.

Conrad in his first-person narratives ostensibly takes upon himself the identity of the first-person narrator. Simultaneously he bars himself entrance to the mind of any other character and thus, like the narrator, remains at a distance from the other characters to be observed. James too, of course, in such novels as *Roderick Hudson*, *The American*, *What Maisie Knew*, and *The Ambassadors* enters the mind of only one character. By limiting the point of view, he expresses through the method itself the isolation of the central figure. But, as we have seen, a character like Strether comes to command considerable insight into the minds of others, and by narrating in the third person James can affirm the validity of the character's perceptions. Marlow in *Heart of Darkness* and *Lord Jim* is a sensitive and intelligent observer of other characters, but in a first-person narrative the novelist cannot give the narrator's statements the support of statements in his own voice. Whether Kurtz did in fact win a "moral victory" or whether Jim at the end is "satisfied" cannot be known, and when the narrator is himself beset by doubts, the impossibility of certain knowledge becomes even more apparent; the separateness of persons, inescapably confirmed.

II

The Ambassadors and *Lord Jim* illustrate the important differences evident in James's and Conrad's work as a whole. Differences in the structure of their novels, in the function of images, and in the nature of the bond between characters are all traceable to the kinds of mental experience with which the two novelists are concerned.

What James dramatizes in his novels—notably in *What Maisie Knew*, *The Ambassadors*, and *The Golden Bowl*—is a highly complex process in which powers of observation, intuition, and imagination act in conjunction with the logical faculties of the mind to lead the protagonist from ignorance to the understanding of his situation. That the process requires the exercise of the nonrational powers is indicated in *The Ambassadors* by frequent images of flight and growth: the mind raises its wings and takes flight (21:51, 87, 112); ideas germinate like seeds buried in the earth (21:86); the mind is floated on a "current of association" (21:90). That the process of vision employs the logical faculties is evident in James's repeated use of logical terms to define his characters' mental acts. Strether posits the existence of someone like Madame de Vionnet, accepting as his premise "the general law that strong cases were liable to control from without" (21:137); seeking "links" and "connexions" (22:181) he turns repeatedly to Maria Gostrey to put into situations and decisions the "logic" which other characters have failed to supply (21:181). The range of faculties exercised in the process of Strether's vision is suggested by James's references in the preface to Strether's "blest imagination," "his lifelong trick of intense reflexion," and his "whole analytic faculty" (21:xiii, xiv).

Strether's primary mode of knowing is intuition, in which feeling, and not analysis, operates; but each moment of insight becomes a connecting part of a series: Strether's impression of Chad as a man "marked out by women" at once falls "into its relation" (21:154) and becomes "such a link in the chain as might practically amount to a kind of demonstration" (21:156). Feelings, facts, perceptions, and impressions are "pieces" that "had to fit themselves"; in Strether's mind they fall into a "close rapid order" (22:188). Strether owes his knowledge of Chad and Madame de Vionnet to his intuitive, not his analytical, faculties; but situations once experienced must be explored; impressions must be analyzed, and the mind must establish connection between one perception and another. The result is a linked chain which has the tightness and inner coherence of a syllogism.

The nature of Strether's mental experience is further illuminated when one observes the close correspondence between the process of vision dramatized in the novel and the creative process as James analyzes it in the preface to the novel. In telling "the story of one's story itself" (21:x) James uses the same images by which he represents Strether's process of vision, thus implying that the interplay of intuitive and analytical powers dramatized in the novel is comparable to that which brought the novel itself into being. James's "demonstration" of the process of vision, no less than Strether's accomplishment of his mission, suggests the logician's task. The donnée of the novel was a "frank proposition"; proceeding from "the whole bunch of data, installed on my premises," the novelist rejoiced to "feel my postulate firm." As the "pieces" in Strether's mind fall into a "close rapid order," so for James, the "*steps*, for my fable, placed themselves with a prompt and, as it were, functional assurance . . . these things continued to fall together, as by the neat action of their own weight and form." Advancing by "inductive steps" which "could only be as rapid as they were distinct," the novelist moved toward his "finely calculated" goal, determined that he would account "for everything" (21:vii–xiii passim).

The work of art is of course the result of unconscious growth as well as of calculated conscious effort: germs or seeds of suggestion take root and flower in the soil of the artist's mind, just as Strether's long buried hopes "sprouted again under forty-eight hours of Paris" (21:86). The artist's sudden flash of insight, however, is often the reward of patient search: like Strether, the novelist himself plays a "game of difficulty" as he looks "for the unseen and the occult, in a scheme half-grasped, by the light or . . . by the clinging scent, of the gage already in hand" (21:ix). Here and elswehere in the preface James implies what he demonstrates in *The Ambassadors*— that something initially concealed is to be fully revealed. Strether's situation is like a tissue which "one had really but to keep under the lens for an hour to see it give up its secrets" (21:xi). In the donnée of the novel were "sealed up values infinitely precious," but the novelist could break the seal and count over "each item of the packet" (21:vii).

The principles of composition to which James's subject, the process of a character's vision, committed him are set forth in the prefaces and fully realized in *The Spoils of Poynton*, *What Maisie Knew*, *The Ambassadors*, and *The Golden Bowl*. The cornerstone of narrative structure in each of these novels is the scene. His subjects, James observes in the preface to *What Maisie Knew*, "keep conforming to the 'scenic law.' " They present themselves "as little constituted dramas, little exhibitions founded on the logic of the 'scene,' the unit of the scene, the general scenic consistency" (11:xxi). The march of the character's vision, the journey forward from ignorance to knowledge, is represented by a succession of tightly connected scenes, each constructed to accomplish a certain purpose, to carry the action to a certain point. How clearly James conceived of his novels as a series of interlocking parts, each part performing its own particular function, is evident in the "detailed scenario" for *What Maisie Knew*. Here the action of the novel is blocked out chapter by chapter to form a "series of moments," each linked to what precedes and follows it, testimony to James's conviction that the "intensely structural, intensely hinged and jointed preliminary frame" was "indispensable for a straight and sure advance to the end."[10]

As the last phrase implies, James's subject requires in the novel a steady forward movement in time. The framework, of course, is flexible, capable of expanding or compressing time; no one was more conscious than James of the necessity of foreshortening—but usually there are no dislocations in the time framework. When characters meditate on the past, their reflections are not flashbacks but part of the narrative of immediate experience; and the characters themselves, like the novelist, are conscious of perceptions and impressions as links in a sequence unfolding in time. In *The Golden Bowl* Maggie recognizes the importance of the request to her father that Charlotte be invited to Fawns as the source "from which the chain of causes and consequences was definitely traceable." In retrospect a climactic encounter with the prince falls for Maggie "into a succession of moments that were *watchable* still; almost in the manner of the different things done during a scene on the stage" (24:23, 11).

To represent the "chain of causes and consequences" and at the same time to give "the sense of duration, of the lapse and accumulation of time,"[11] James created a structure in which fully dramatized scenes, often of great emotional intensity, alternate with passages that summarize a character's reflections and impressions over a period of days or weeks. Yet another kind of episode contributes to the structure of *The Ambassadors* and *The Golden Bowl:* the conversation with the confidante at regularly recurring intervals, at which the meaning of events up to that point is articulated and the feelings and impressions gathering force in a character's mind resolve themselves into statements providing a basis for further deduction and inference. It is clear that all aspects of the structure of James's late novels—the forward movement of time, the tightly connected sequence of dramatic scenes and passages of analysis and reflection upon those scenes, and the dialogues of confidante and another character—all conduce to the treatment of James's central concern. Indeed the structure of the novel is itself the expression of James's subject: the process of a character's vision, by which a series of connections is established and the concealed is made manifest.

Like the process of vision represented in James's novels, Marlow's narration in "Youth," *Heart of Darkness*, *Lord Jim*, and *Chance* is analogous to the process of artistic creation. The analogy is even more obvious, for Marlow as the narrator performs within the novel an act of creation as he constructs or shapes the stories of Kurtz and Jim and others and relates them to a group of listeners. As the artist seeks to bring "to light the truth, manifold and one," underlying all he sees (3:xi), so Marlow in telling of his experience seeks to give "its very existence, its reality—the truth disclosed in a moment of illusion" (4:323). Marlow is chiefly preoccupied not with the process of creating form, however, but with the function of language, with the power of words to re-create experience. Reflecting something of his creator's agonized sense of struggle, Marlow confesses not only to the impossibility of seeing Jim clearly but also to the impossibility of conveying the essence in words: "I am missing innumerable shades—they were so fine, so difficult to render in colourless words" (4:94).

In seeking to express truth, Marlow does not fail to exercise his considerable powers of analysis and generalization. Like Strether he induces general truths from facts, tests his ideas by observation, and proceeds deductively from the known to the unknown.[12] In *Chance* he calls himself "a man of deductions" (13:326), and in the first edition, in a passage omitted by Conrad from later editions of the novel, he declares that a glimpse or a sudden insight followed by "a series of logically deducted verisimilitudes" is the road to truth.[13] But what Marlow constructs in his narratives is not a linked chain such as that forged in *The Ambassadors* by insight and analysis. Instead of the framework of chronological time, essential to James's representation of a process of vision, Conrad constructs narratives which, in their backward and forward movements in time, reflect the associative, not the logical, processes of Marlow's mind. Instead of a forward movement from one point to another, Marlow's narratives, especially in *Heart of Darkness* and *Lord Jim*, create the picture of the mind circling about its subject, suddenly plunging below the surface, then rising to repeat the act from a succession of different vantage points.

Disruptions of chronological sequence are equally striking in Conrad's novels which do not focus upon the consciousness of one narrator like Marlow. One recalls *The Secret Agent*, in which the journey to the almshouses, undertaken by Winnie's mother to protect Stevie, is portrayed after the news of Stevie's death is made known; *Under Western Eyes*, in which the circumstances of Razumov's employment by the Russian police are revealed only after he has been seen in Geneva in his role as a double agent; *Nostromo*, in which the picture of Ribiera's ignominious collapse, literally a

fall from the back of an expiring mule, precedes the scene on shipboard six months earlier when Ribiera, flanked by emissaries of
foreign powers, celebrates the beginning of the railroad. Like the
house of the Violas, which "seemed to be the centre of a turmoil
widening in a great circle about its closed-up silence" (7:19), the
shipboard ceremony in *Nostromo*, Jim's desertion of the *Patna*, and
the destruction of Stevie in Greenwich Park are focal points, not
stages in a chronological sequence, but centers from which actions,
both past and future, seem to flow.

In all these novels Conrad enables the reader to place events in
chronological order and to determine the length of time between
one event and the next. The action of *The Secret Agent*, from Verloc's interview with Mr. Vladimir to Winnie's suicide, consumes
roughly one month. Three years elapse between Jim's desertion of
the *Patna* and his journey to Patusan; Marlow visits Jim two years
later, and Jim dies the following year.[14] *Heart of Darkness* in particular abounds in terms of measurements which imply chronological sequence. Marlow crosses the channel "before forty-eight
hours"; the voyage to the mouth of the river lasts "upward of thirty
days"; he takes passage to the Company Station "thirty miles
higher up"; then endures the "two-hundred mile tramp" which
ends at the central station "on the fifteenth day." Work on the
wrecked steamer consumes three months, the journey to the inner
station three days. At the same time, however, the effect of the
experience, dreamlike and absurd, induces in Marlow a profound
sense of disorientation which renders meaningless the conventional measurements of space and time and subjects him to the
illusion of eternal recurrence. The journey to the Congo, during
which "everyday the coast looked the same, as though we had not
moved," foreshadows the even more dreamlike journey up the
river, past "long reaches that were like one and the same reach,
monotonous bends that were exactly the same" (5:61). Struggling
to maintain his hold on "the redeeming facts of life," Marlow struggles to preserve the sensation of moving forward—"sometimes I
would pick out a tree a little way ahead to measure our progress
toward Kurtz by"; but in this world without landmarks motion ob-

literates the point of reference: "I lost it invariably before we got abreast" (5:100).[15]

Ultimately Marlow has the illusion of transcending the categories of space and time. To go up the river is not only to travel back to "the earliest beginnings of the world" but to enter a timeless realm in which all ages are simultaneously present. Then one glimpses, however fleetingly, unchanging realities, "truth stripped of its cloak of time"; one understands that "the mind of man is capable of anything—because everything is in it, all the past as well as all the future" (5:97, 96).[16] The dominant effect of the experience of timelessness is not, however, to induce in the character— or the reader—a sense of tranquillity or a vision of unity in which all opposing forces are harmonized; instead, the obliteration of temporal and spatial sequences intensifies the character's sense of disorientation and disquiet. For the reader the dislocations in the time framework either emphasize the futility of the characters' efforts, as in *The Secret Agent* and *Nostromo*, or help to represent the experience of confusion and uncertainty which leads Marlow in *Lord Jim* to the conviction that complete knowledge of another person's nature and motives is impossible. In other words structure is an expression of theme in Conrad's novels no less than in James's. The time shifts in *Lord Jim* and the viewing of the same event from different perspectives help to produce what Najder terms "sceptical realism,"[17] a way of seeing and a method of narrating which in themselves dramatize the impossibility of attaining absolute certainty.

Emphasis upon Conrad's methods of representing states of doubt and bewilderment should not imply that James failed to portray the mental processes of his characters as they are baffled or confounded by what they see. Jane Tompkins, in a study of style in *The Beast in the Jungle*, discusses in detail the ways in which the structure of James's sentences—their inversions, placement of adverbs, and insertion of parenthetical phrases and clauses—obliges the reader to weigh alternatives, ponder new aspects of an idea and postpone conclusions "until the last possible moment."[18] That James's style reflects the mental processes of characters engaged in similar mental acts is evident in countless passages in the late novels. In *The Ambassadors*, for instance, the movement of sentences often mirrors the movements, deliberative and impulsive, of Strether's mind as he gropes in his maze of mystifying allusions. The passage portraying Strether's efforts to divine the intentions and foresee the actions of Sarah Pocock suggests in its alternation of question and statement the shifting forces of certainty and doubt within Strether—and by virtue of his power to imagine her consciousness—within Sarah Pocock as well.

Strether, watching, after his habit, and overscoring with thought, positively had moments of his own in which he found himself sorry for her—occasions on which she affected him as a person seated in a runaway vehicle and turning over the question of a possible jump. *Would* she jump, could she, would *that* be a safe place?—this question, at such instants, sat for him in her lapse into pallor, her tight lips, her conscious eyes. It came back to the main point at issue: would she be, after all, to be squared? He believed on the whole she would jump; yet her alternations on this subject were the more especial stuff of his suspense. (22:162)

In its way Strether's sense of anxiety and unrest is as keen as Marlow's, but one notes in this passage and throughout the novel that the effort of the author and usually of Strether himself is to clarify the situation by analyzing the sense of uncertainty or the sources of doubt. Whereas Conrad strives in several of his novels, notably in *Heart of Darkness*, *Lord Jim*, and *The Rescue*, to deepen the sense of mystery engulfing the characters in their struggle with the unfathomable and the inexplicable, James converts even the experience of bewilderment into occasions for acts of analysis and clarification. Not surprisingly, then, the mind's groping movements which in Conrad's novels are reflected in the structure of the whole work are in James's novels reflected only in the structure of the sentence or, at most, of the paragraph, and the movement of the sentence is usually toward clarification, if only of the nature of the enigma.

Because we have been considering James's third-person narratives and Conrad's novels in which a first-person narrator recalls past events, one might think that the differences in structure result simply from this fact: that James's characters like Strether, Maisie, and Maggie are registers of present action as it moves to its conclusion, whereas Marlow commands the view of an action concluded, if inconclusive. Because Marlow is separated from his experience by months or years, he can juxtapose events and impressions in a way impossible to James's characters who register action unfolding in the fictional present. Even when James narrates in the first person through a character who is recalling a concluded action, he adheres just as firmly to his principles of scenic construction, making the framework of the tale a chronological sequence of causally connected acts and endowing the narrator with his own conception of action as a sequence of related phases. The governess and main narrator of *The Turn of the Screw* recalls her experience as a "succession of flights and drops" (12:158). The narrator of *The Sacred Fount*, James's longest first-person narrative, emphasizes the chainlike pattern of the action he reconstructs: "I recover . . . a full sequence of impressions, each of which, I afterwards saw, had been appointed to help all the others. If my anecdote . . . had begun, at Paddington, at a particular moment, it gathered substance step by step and without missing a link."[19]

That James's sense of causal connection was strong to the point of governing the structure of his novels is evident in both his first-person and third-person narratives. Conrad's fiction is not devoid of sequences created by the power of one act to cause another: for instance each of Jim's decisions—to stand trial, to go to Patusan, to give Brown a clear road, and to die at the hands of Doramin—springs from the effects of choices already made. But the view of perception which Marlow expresses differs radically from the view which governs the construction of James's novels. Whereas James sees perceptions springing irresistibly one from another, Marlow, in a passage that looks forward to Camus's statement in "The Myth of Sisyphus," sees the "moment of vision . . . when we see, hear, understand ever so much—everything—in a flash," not as a link in a chain but as an isolated point followed by return "into our agreeable somnolence" (4:143). On occasion, in Conrad's novels, the moment illuminates a reality so terrifying or shocking to the moral nature that far from leading the observer to further insight it forces

him backward, as if from a precipice. When Marlow in listening to
Jewel's story suddenly glimpses "a world that seemed to wear a
vast and dismal aspect of disorder," he retreats at once: "I went
back into my shell directly. One *must*—" (4:313). In *Heart of
Darkness* evidences of Kurtz's degeneration—"intolerable to
thought and odious to the soul"—are too monstrous to be contemplated long. As Marlow focuses the glass to bring near the
heads on the posts and then causes them to "[leap] away . . . into
inaccessible distance" (5:131), so he can focus his mind to bring the
remembered experience into close range, then let it recede. In
contrast James's characters move forward from perception to perception, often pausing to look back and let the full meaning of an
impression fill their minds: Maisie's most disturbing experience,
her passage with her father and the grotesque countess, remains
"for days and weeks, ineffaceably illumined and confirmed; by the
end of which she was able to read into it a hundred things that had
been at the moment mere miraculous pleasantness" (11:179).

   The characteristic action of James's novels is therefore basically
different from that of Conrad's. Action in most of James's novels
begins when the protagonist enters a world strange to him, more
complex than he has known, and slowly begins to comprehend the
situation into which he has been drawn. Action in most of Conrad's
novels begins with the sudden disruption of a character's everyday
routine life, disruption which destroys those illusions of self and
the world in which he had found security. The disruptive force
comes in different forms—disaster at sea (*Lord Jim* and *The Rescue*) the intrusion of a fugitive from justice (*Under Western Eyes*
and "The Secret Sharer"), the command of a superior (*The Secret
Agent*), the assault of sexual passion (*An Outcast of the Islands*).
In each of these novels, however, the scene which marks the turning point in the character's life (e.g. the disabling of the *Patna*, the
intrusions of Leggatt and Haldin) comes early in the action. In
James's novels, on the other hand, the climactic scene of revelation
usually comes toward the end: the process of vision culminates in
the fully dramatized recognition scene such as Isabel's midnight
vigil before the fire, Olive Chancellor's walk on the shore after
Verena's desertion, Strether's sight of Chad and Madame de Vion-

net on the river. The function of each of these scenes is to reveal to reader and character what has hitherto been hidden or not fully seen, to "dry up the mists and ambiguities of life."[20]

In Conrad's novels, as Peter Garrett has pointed out, the horror of the truth to be disclosed forbids such scenes of recognition and allows instead only "brief, peripheral glimpses of a hidden central meaning." According to Garrett the "wandering circling movements" of Marlow's consciousness are produced by the tension of conflicting impulses, to discover the truth and to protect the self from the truth.[21] James's characters also experience the tension of conflicting impulses—to know and to shield themselves from knowledge. For all her presumed desire for knowledge Isabel Archer almost consciously clings to illusions: "She had a natural shrinking from raising curtains and looking into unlighted corners. The love of knowledge coexisted in her mind with the finest capacity for ignorance" (3:284). But James's protagonists shrink not from the horror of a perceived reality as Marlow does, but from the dangers of a reality not yet discovered; and once Isabel is "in the secret," once she knows the facts of Madame Merle's and Osmond's relation, the knowledge fills her consciousness, creating a structure, self-contained and complete, like the novel itself: "The truth of things, their mutual relations, their meaning, and for the most part their horror, rose before her with a kind of architectural vastness" (4:391).

This is not to say that all questions are answered at the end of James's novels: surely no character's destiny has been the subject of more speculation than have Isabel Archer's final acts and probable future. Conrad was right when he said of James's novels: "His books end as an episode in life ends. You remain with the sense of life still going on" (18:19). By the end of James's novels, however, certain truths once obscured have been revealed, the situation has been sounded and resolved by a sequence of tightly connected scenes leading the central character to an ever-fuller comprehension of the unfolding drama. In one way Conrad's novels have a finality absent from James's; one thinks of the deaths of Willems, Jim, Nostromo, Verloc, and Heyst; the degeneration of Almayer; the maiming of Razumov; the sacrificial departure of Peyrol. And yet, in certain novels, notably *Lord Jim* and *Heart of Darkness*, death merely increases the urgency of the questions the narrator asks and deepens the aura of mystery that he can never penetrate. James portrays characters in the process of discovering that which can be known; Conrad portrays characters vouchsafed glimpses of that which cannot be fully revealed or understood.

III

Since James and Conrad use imagery to create thematic pattern and structure, differences in their principles of composition are reflected in the varying ways in which images originate and function within the novels. Before pursuing the points of contrast, however, let us remind ourselves again of the fundamental affinities in their methods. The power of both novelists to convey meaning through figurative language and to endow objects and images with symbolic value creates an important bond between them. Of all the novelists writing in England in the late Victorian and Edwardian periods only James and Conrad have produced fiction calling for book-length studies of their imagery.

The fiction of both James and Conrad reveals the twofold power of imagery: to give concrete expression to ideas and to evoke states of feeling or the power of hidden realities. In James's works which portray the journey of characters from ignorance to knowledge, the characteristic function of imagery is to assist the protagonist—and the reader—in understanding the situation. Character and narrator employ images primarily to define ideas and analyze situations in concrete terms. In those novels of Conrad in which the effect of observation and analysis is to intensify the character's sense of doubt or bewilderment and to render his world increasingly baffling and mysterious, the characteristic function of imagery is to evoke the incomprehensible and the unseen and to heighten the sense of mystery. Whereas James habitually moves from the general and the intangible to the specific and the concrete, Conrad moves from the object or image outward—to the intangible and the abstract.

One may conveniently divide James's images into two categories. One includes those images that seem to rise spontaneously from the depths of the character's mind: Strether's image of Gloriani as the magnificent tiger, for example, or Maggie's image of Charlotte, "the splendid shining supple creature" (24:239), out of the cage and at large. The other category includes those images which serve as vehicles of metaphors, constructed sometimes by the characters but more often by the omniscient author to translate an idea into concrete terms. Strether and Maria Gostrey, for instance, initially confront each other "over the mere laid table of conversation"; their failure to discover a bond in a mutual acquaintance "had rather removed than placed a dish, and there seemed nothing else to serve. Their attitude remained, none the less, that of not forsaking the board" (21:7). The primary function of the images of the first category is to express feelings; the primary function of the images of the second, to define relationships. In contrast to the images of the first group, evoked and understood without conscious acts of comparison, the metaphors, often extended through several points of resemblance, exercise the analytic faculties of both narrator (or character) and reader. Both kinds of image, however, make concrete the abstract or the intangible (Maggie's fear, Strether's and Maria Gostrey's relation). Both kinds focus the mind on the object or scene, even as the evocative power of the image works to expand the range of meaning.[22]

Once the image is introduced into the world of the novel it may give rise to a chain of metaphors which mark the stages in the development of an action. In *The Ambassadors*, for instance, Strether's progress is represented in several sequences of metaphors which reinforce the structure of the novel: the journey by water, sacrifice on a scaffold, and performance in a theater. Changes in the relationships among the characters in *The Golden Bowl* are marked by changes of the metaphors of actors and spectators, partners and opponents, and hunters and hunted. Like the plot to which it corresponds, the sequence of metaphors is an unfolding in concrete language of the idea which informs the novel.

On occasion a metaphor is developed to the point that characters become like figures in an allegory, actors in a dramatic scene. At the beginning of the second half of *The Golden Bowl*, for instance, Maggie confronts "in the garden of her life" a pagodalike structure, the highly visible, even obtrusive, symbol of a situation the truth of which is concealed from her; she circles the structure, looks in vain for a door, knocks tentatively, and hears response from within (24:3–5).

Whether or not the image of the pagoda originates in Maggie's mind is impossible to determine. In fact, as Peter Garrett has observed, in all the late novels of James, the reader is often unable to determine whether images developed by the author are also present in the consciousness of the characters.[23] The effect of the metaphors and analogies, however, is to suggest mental exertion on the part of the characters. Although James's statement that the pagoda "figured the arrangement" seems to identify the image as the narrator's, not Maggie's, the reader in following the development of the metaphor feels that Maggie is performing a mental act analogous to, if not identical with, that of the narrator. Indeed, in all James's novels from *Maisie* on, the development of metaphors contributes to the impression of characters constantly seeking to explain and clarify, to identify motives and see connections. It is no accident that the first chapter of the second half of *The Golden Bowl*, which contains the densest concentration of highly wrought metaphors in the novel, is also the chapter which represents the protagonist's most sustained mental effort. Whether or not Maggie compares herself, as does the narrator, to a figure circling a pagoda, a spaniel shaking water from its ears, a young mother clinging to her child, a housemaid thrusting objects into an unused room, and a rider in a carriage, she is clearly experiencing intense mental activity. One may regard the mental energy James expends in creating the images to define Maggie's situation as an analogue to the mental energy Maggie expends in analyzing the words and gestures and expressions of Charlotte and the prince and in achieving her first important perception, that as regards herself and her father, the prince and Charlotte act from identical motives.

Like James, Conrad often expresses the ideas and emotions of his characters in figurative language, moving as James does from the abstract and intangible to the concrete image. In *Lord Jim*, for instance, Marlow successively compares Jim with his flaw to a sovereign with "some infernal alloy in his metal" (4:45—one of the few images of money in Conrad); his wounded spirit to a bird with a broken wing, which will "hop and flutter into some hole to die quietly of inanition there" (4:184–185); his sudden agitation to that of a "dry leaf imprisoned in an eddy of wind" (4:185). But Conrad hardly ever extends the comparison beyond the single sentence. The development of a conceit through several paragraphs, such as we find in *The Golden Bowl*, is completely foreign to Conrad's method. Nor does Conrad represent the progress of an action by a series of logically related metaphors as James does in the late novels. Instead Conrad's images often create patterns of contrasts —light and dark, height and depth, sea and land, spirit and flesh —which, as the images accumulate, assume ever wider implications. If James's images move the reader forward from point to point, Conrad's images create movement outward, like circles in water. Just as Stein passes "out of the bright circle of the lamp into the ring of fainter light—into the shapeless dusk at last," so Marlow's mind moves toward the abstract and unlimited. The "distant mirrors" in Stein's apartments become in Marlow's sight "the depths of a crystalline void"; to feel the force of Jim's "imperishable reality" Marlow must move from the image of the man to the abstract and unattainable, to "absolute Truth" ungraspable as the reflection of flickering candlelight in the mirror (4:213, 216).

In *The Beast in the Jungle* and *Heart of Darkness* one can see within the work itself the way the controlling image originates and develops, in the mind of the protagonist. As James moved from the idea to the action which expressed the idea, so Marcher, within the tale, first conceives of his rare destiny in general terms: he has the sense "of being kept for something rare and strange," something "to wait for—to have to meet, to face, to see suddenly break out in my life" (17:71, 72). The force of the conception suggests the image of the beast, which is introduced in a simile: "Something or other lay in wait for him, amid the twists and the turns of the months and the years, like a crouching beast in the jungle." Here it is clear that the image issues from the protagonist's mind: "Such was the image under which he had ended by figuring his life" (17:79). Having found his term of comparison, having brooded on it for months, Marcher begins to feel the image as a living presence in his life. The imagined destiny, upon which he and May Bartram have speculated, has "its incalculable moments of glaring out, quite as with the very eyes of the very Beast" (17:87). After this point the image appears repeatedly as the vehicle of a metaphor, indicating that the identity of Marcher's destiny and the image has become complete: the result of May's last words to Marcher is that "the Jungle had been threshed to vacancy and that the Beast had stolen away. . . . poor Marcher waded through his beaten grass, where no life stirred, where no breath sounded, where no evil eye seemed to gleam from a possible lair" (17:116). At the end the idea of Marcher's destiny is wholly subsumed in the image, just as Marcher himself is soon to be overwhelmed by the being his mind has created. "He saw the Jungle of his life and saw the lurking Beast." What existed first as a figure of speech is now in Marcher's mind a terrifying reality which he sees, "in his hallucination," rise "huge and hideous, for the leap that was to settle him" (17:127).[24]

In its final manifestation as the product of Marcher's obsessed mind, the beast becomes a symbol whose meaning is not to be confined to the terms of a single conception. Readers have seen the beast both as a symbol of Marcher's predatory and exploitative impulses and as a projection of his repressed fear of sexual passion.[25] The symbol has its origin, however, in a clearly formulated idea which called forth the metaphor, and at every point in the story the symbol is referable to the initial conception. The story is a fable in which everything—characters, setting, dialogue, imagery, and plot—bodies forth this initial conception, the idea of the man who achieves the rare fate to which he believes himself destined when he discovers himself to be the man "to whom nothing on earth was to have happened" (17:125).

Conrad's method in *Heart of Darkness* is markedly different. The unifying metaphor of the story, the heart of darkness, originated not from an idea, as did James's metaphor of the beast, but in impressions of particular places, "definite images," such as Marlow's vision of Britain as a darkness conquered centuries ago by the Romans; and his memory of the "blank space" on the map of Africa which time transformed into "a place of darkness." Whereas James works from the idea to the image, Conrad converts the physical reality, the unexplored wilderness at the center of Africa, into the metaphor of the heart of darkness, thus moving from the tangible to the abstract. When Marlow sees the two knitters in the company office as guardians of "the door of Darkness" (5:57) he converts his journey to the center of a continent into a passage to infernal regions of ghosts and shades. When he compares the smile of the manager to a "door opening into a darkness" (5:74) and when he senses the mind of Kurtz as an "impenetrable darkness" (5:149), his journey becomes a descent into the depths of the human mind. Instead of moving from idea to simile to metaphor to hallucinatory image as James does in *The Beast in the Jungle*, Conrad creates from the image a succession of metaphors for realities—natural, human, and supernatural—that cannot be visualized or clearly defined. In contrast to James's metaphor of the beast, which at every point can be comprehended in terms of the germinal idea, Conrad's metaphor of the heart of darkness leads the mind outward, from the known to the unknown, from the formed to the formless. Its purpose is not to express one particular idea but to evoke unseen realities, mysterious and inexpressible, to be sensed in fleeting moments but never to be scrutinized or defined. At the end of *The Beast in the Jungle* Marcher receives illumination which, once begun, "blazed to the zenith" (17:125), revealing him to himself in pitiless clarity. All that Marlow can say of the "culminating point" of his experience is that "it seemed to throw a kind of light on everything about me—and into my thoughts . . . not extraordinary in any way—not very clear either. No, not very clear" (5:51).

As *The Beast in the Jungle* and *Heart of Darkness* suggest, James and Conrad can be identified with different traditions in their use of image and symbol. Conrad's statement of aesthetic principles and his symbolic works have led several critics to associate his art with that of the French Symbolists. Not only do Conrad's references to Baudelaire in letters, his use of Baudelaire's words as the epigraph to *The Shadow Line*, and his probable indebtedness to Villiers de l'Isle Adam in the creation of Axel Heyst suggest Conrad's strong sense of affinity with his French contemporaries; as

Donald Yelton has emphasized in his excellent study, Conrad's novels recall Symbolist poetry in their repeated stress upon "mystery" and in their evocation of the indefinite and the unknowable— in Yelton's words "a realm of arcana behind the veil of surface appearances";[26] or, as Conrad expresses it in *Lord Jim*, the "silent still waters of mystery" in which "absolute Truth . . . like Beauty itself, floats elusive, obscure, half submerged" (4:216). Yelton also asserts that Conrad in his aesthetic theory and artistic aims betrays "the most striking congruence" with the Symbolist writers, especially in his celebration of music as the "art of arts" and in his stress upon the "magic suggestiveness" of words (3:xiii).[27] We must note, however, that Conrad rejects a central idea of the Symbolists, their conception of the artist as an isolated figure, remote from the concerns of ordinary life, who expresses through private symbols feelings unique to himself and perhaps uncommunicable to others. Conrad's idea of the novelist as a man, like other men, who claims no special nature or "superior essence" (18:9), and whose "high desire" is to touch "the secret spring of responsive emotions" in others (3:xiii) is much closer to Wordsworth's poet, "a man speaking to other men," than to Mallarmé's artist in the ivory tower.

James's essays on Flaubert and Baudelaire and his allusions to Maeterlinck in *The Wings of the Dove* testify to James's interest in the writers with whom Conrad has been compared. James is not, however, a symbolist, as F. O. Matthiessen has emphasized. The main images and symbols of a novel were usually not part of James's initial conception of a work but emerged later, as if released by the novelist's probing scrutiny of his subject. James "did not, like Mallarmé, start with his symbol. He reached it only with the final development of his theme, and then used it essentially in the older tradition of the poetic metaphor, to give concretion, as well as allusive and beautiful extension, to his thought."[28] James defines his own practice and places himself as well as Hawthorne in "the older tradition" when he observes that Hawthorne is "perpetually looking for images which shall place themselves in picturesque correspondence with the spiritual facts with which he is concerned." The "correspondence" to which James refers, it is clear, is not Baudelaire's *correspondance* but the conjunction of idea and image, which was to James "of the very essence of poetry."[29]

If James is to be described as a symbolist writer, his method can also be compared to that of Ibsen. As Michael Egan convincingly demonstrates, James's method of developing an idea through a pattern of related images which at critical points connect to the physical action is essentially the method of symbolic works like *Rosmersholm* and *The Wild Duck*. One need not embrace Egan's assertion that James "borrowed" his method from Ibsen or that *Hedda Gabler* is the "main source" for *The Wings of the Dove* to see the resemblances he notes in the symbolic structures of these two works.[30] Certainly there is no question of James's recognition of Ibsen's power and importance. He hailed Ibsen as a writer who "constitutes an episode"; as a dramatist who achieved the "perfect practice" of his art and produced "an intensity of interest by means incorruptibly quiet"; as a symbolist whose plays exhibit a "large, dense complexity of moral cross-references."[31]

In none of his published letters or essays does Conrad express a particular interest in Ibsen. But in important ways Conrad's art, like James's, bears a closer resemblance to the dramas of Ibsen than to the poetry or drama of the French Symbolists. Despite Conrad's evocation of the mysterious, the unfathomable, and the inconclusive, the backbone of his novels is always an action. As James consistently guided himself by the principle that he expressed in one of his first reviews—that the "soul of a novel is its action,"[32] so Conrad in every novel expressed his ideas and themes and convictions through conflicts of characters, often as dramatic as those of Ibsen's plays, conflicts in which the whole essence of a character's nature seems distilled. Indeed, when James described the picture evoked by Ibsen's plays—"Well in the very front of the scene lunges with extraordinary length of arm the Ego against the Ego, and rocks in a rigour of passion the soul against the soul,"[33] one might well think of the fateful struggles of Kurtz and Marlow, Richardo and Lena, Aissa and Willems, Verloc and Winnie, Jim, and Brown.

For all their interest in modes of perception and in the effects of events upon the individual sensibility, both James and Conrad are concerned primarily with characters. They build their novels upon a central relationship involving a small group of characters at a time of crisis, and the nature of the protagonist's development always depends upon the kind of relationships that he establishes with other people.

IV

Important as it is, the discovery of facts hitherto concealed is only part of the central character's experience in James's novels. The chief value or reward of Strether's journey from ignorance to understanding, for instance, lies not in the possession of facts but in the extension of consciousness, the fruit of his effort to participate imaginatively in the lives of others. What makes Strether "a man of imagination" is above all his intuitive sense of others' feelings and his power to re-create for himself the experience of others as he feels it. Almost from the beginning Strether feels as an essential part of his mission the effort to "reconstruct," to put himself imaginatively in Chad's place: "He was there on some chance of feeling the brush of the wing of the stray spirit of youth. . . . He reconstructed a possible groping Chad of three or four years before" (21:94). What crowns Strether's search for truth is not the solution of the mystery but his sense of having lived more fully, through having known "a little supersensual hour in the vicarious freedom of another."[34]

The power of imagination, which Strether misses in Chad but feels to be developed in excess in himself, is the very power Marlow declares wanting in himself but present in excess in Jim. But by "imagination" Marlow here means not the power of sympathetic identification but the "faculty of swift and forestalling vision," which paralyzes the will in a crisis. Nor does Marlow lack the power to re-create the experience of others. He has enough imagination of the Jamesian kind to visualize the situation on the *Patna* when Jim describes it: "I can easily picture him to myself," and to express the situation from Jim's point of view, to render the last minute on board the *Patna* as Jim had felt it, "crowded with a tumult of events and sensations which beat about him like the sea upon a rock" (4:96, 84, 108). In *Chance* Marlow goes even farther, constructing the personality and motives of a man, Roderick Anthony, whom he has never seen.[35] But in no novel or tale does Marlow enjoy the vicarious experience of another's mental life. Marlow may feel that it was Kurtz's "extremity that I seem to have lived through," but Kurtz remains an "impenetrable darkness" (5:151, 149) forever separated from Marlow by the fact that Kurtz has passed beyond the threshold, has descended into the abyss, whereas Marlow has halted at the edge. The teacher of languages in *Under Western Eyes* shows astonishing knowledge of Razumov's inner life in the passages which dramatize Razumov's consciousness, but here Conrad simply allows his narrator to assume a novelist's omniscience; when omniscience is withdrawn, the teacher sees Razumov as a mysterious figure whom he does not profess to understand.

In their doubts and uncertainties Conrad's narrators stand in marked contrast to most of James's characters who serve as "most polished of possible mirrors" (5:xv). The function of these characters is indicated by the role which James assigns to Rowland Mallet, the central consciousness of his first long novel, *Roderick Hudson*: the office of Rowland is above all "to feel certain things happening to others"; after a month with his protégé, he feels that "he had really been living Roderick's intellectual life . . . as well as his own" (1:xviii, 88–89). James's characters, it is true, are sometimes wrong in their inferences, and the feelings they impute to others and the experiences in which they think they participate are often the creation of their own imaginations. The line between intuition and fabrication is sometimes difficult, if not impossible, to draw. For instance the narrator of *The Sacred Fount*, the character of James who goes farthest in the imputing of motives and constructing of relationships, is finally left, like the reader, in a state of uncertainty as to the validity of his speculations. In contrast Marlow in *Chance* betrays no uncertainties in his analysis of the relationship of Flora and Anthony; nor is the reader provoked into questioning the conclusions Marlow draws about situations as inherently mysterious as those which preoccupy the narrator of *The Sacred Fount*. Is it not James rather than Conrad, then, who most dramatically represents the unknowableness of persons? Is it not in Conrad's *Chance* rather than in James's novels that a character enjoys the fullest knowledge of a situation?

James's narrator in *The Sacred Fount* is baffled and tormented, and Marlow in *Chance* is not. The questions James's narrator puts to himself and other characters, however, *can* be answered in precise terms, even if he does not get the answers: Is May Server the mistress of Gilbert Long? Are Long and Mrs. Brissenden lovers? The narrator is thwarted, paradoxically, because he asks questions of this kind, because he seeks information which it would be possible to obtain. Not content with intuitive knowledge, expressed in his idea of the sacred fount, he tries to reduce what he himself acknowledges as a mystery to the limits of an equation or a diagram. In contrast Marlow begins not with an hypothesis but with facts provided by other characters who cannot see the psychological significance of what they observe; then, like a novelist, he imagines the central situation of the novel, the relation of Flora and Roderick Anthony. In *Chance*, as in *Under Western Eyes*, Conrad grants to his narrator what James withholds from the narrator of *The Sacred Fount* and from all the central characters of his novels: the authority of the omniscient author. Throughout much of *Chance* Marlow is not a character in a novel as are Strether and Maisie and Marlow in *Heart of Darkness* and *Lord Jim*. At times he serves, like the narrator of some of James's short stories, as "the unwarranted participant, the impersonal author's concrete deputy or delegate, a convenient substitute or apologist for the creative power otherwise so veiled and disembodied" (23:v).[36]

James's protagonists do not enjoy the novelist's omniscience—indeed James warned against "the danger of filling too full any supposed and above all any obviously limited vessel of consciousness" (5:ix)—but the protagonists do slowly gain a fuller knowledge of themselves and their associates, if they do not sound the very depths of human character. The fact that James's reflectors like Rowland, Isabel Archer, Hyacinth Robinson, and Strether are deceived in the persons to whom they attach themselves does not prevent them from feeling that they live more fully as they live through the lives of others or of eventually seeing the once mysterious figures clearly. If in the first half of *The Portrait of a Lady* Isabel sees only a part of Osmond's nature "as one saw the disk of the moon when it was partly masked by the shadow of the earth," by the end "she saw the full moon . . . she saw the whole man" (4:191). On the other hand Marlow is aware that Jim, like everyone else, possesses that side "like the other hemisphere of the moon, [which] exists stealthily in perpetual darkness, with only a fearful ashy light falling at times on the edge" (4:93). Even when James's characters feel the mysterious nature of another most keenly they experience their bafflement in sensations of absorption in the mysterious element. Chad's manner is the "fathomless medium" in which Strether, in his "deep immersion" (21:172), is held. Marlow is separated from Jim, whose motives shimmer "like a pool of water in the dark . . . which I despaired of ever approaching near enough to fathom" (4:183).

As the comparison of *The Ambassadors* and *Lord Jim* suggests, the nature of the bond which joins characters in James's and Conrad's novels is essentially different. What binds Strether to Chad is Strether's sense that he recovers through Chad his own lost opportunities, that Chad and Madame de Vionnet are "my youth" since "somehow at the right time nothing else ever was" (22:51). What compels Marlow's fidelity to Jim is initially "the fellowship of the craft" but ultimately Marlow's sense that Jim, possessing weakness latent in all men, shadows forth truths about human nature "momentous enough to affect mankind's conception of itself" (4:93).[37] In James's novels the bond between characters is created when one enters imaginatively into the experience of the other; in Conrad's novels the bond is forged when one recognizes in others qualities and impulses latent in oneself. Consciousness in James moves out to encompass what is not itself; consciousness in Conrad discovers that it comprehends the whole within itself: "the human heart is vast enough to contain all the world" (4:323). The difference suggests James's idea of the novelist entering into or "assimilating" the consciousness of each character he creates and Conrad's conception of the novelist bound to characters and readers by the shared experience of universal feelings, by "the subtle but invincible conviction of solidarity that knits together the loneliness of innumerable hearts" (3:xii).

The implications of these different conceptions of the novelist's art are evident in the moral concerns of the two writers. To James, fascinated by the assimilative powers of the mind, by the "grasping power" of the imagination, the virtue of characters resides in their power to enter imaginatively into the experience of others, and yet to feel the personality of the other as sacred and inviolable. What James prizes above all in his characters is the capacity for sympathetic identification with other characters, a power similar to that which manifests itself in the artist's "unprejudiced intellectual eagerness to put himself in other people's place, to participate in complications and consequences."[38] To Conrad, who in his most important preface celebrates the "feeling of solidarity . . . which binds men to each other and all mankind to the visible world" (3:xiv), the virtue of characters manifests itself in their fidelity to each other and to the codes which order the lives of men in a community. The fact that egoism is the "fount and origin" (4:152) of sympathy does not negate the value of that sympathy which expresses itself in a sense of kinship with others. In James's fiction the greatest evil, the unpardonable sin, is committed by those, like Osmond and Marcher, who exploit others and violate their integrity; in Conrad's novels the act which places upon the doer the heaviest burden of guilt and subjects him to the keenest anguish is the act of betrayal, a "breach of faith with the community of mankind" (4:157). James portrays the consciousness of characters who achieve growth through their relations with others but who at the end usually stand alone, separated from those to whom they were once bound. Conrad, while emphasizing the separateness of persons and the impossibility of ever knowing fully the nature of another, portrays characters who can realize their ideal of self only in securing their place in the human community.

James and Conrad place questions of conduct at the center of their novels. Psychological forces are not to be separated from moral issues; the value of a character's knowledge is measured by the kinds of attitudes and actions to which it gives rise, and the strengths and weaknesses of characters are revealed primarily through their relationships with others. Although the organizing principles and the ideas underlying these principles are different in James's and Conrad's novels, for both novelists human consciousness and human action remain the primary values. Their central characters suffer betrayal and disillusionment, mental anguish and loss; but the very capacity of characters like Strether and Marlow to feel and suffer and care for a standard of conduct—whether it governs the actions of men at sea or of men and women in a private relationship—imparts to their lives those values which make it fitting to apply to both novelists Conrad's praise of James as the "historian of fine consciences" (22:17).

4

Romance · I

For well over a hundred years before James and Conrad began to publish fiction and criticism, writers had addressed themselves to these questions: What is romance? How does a romance differ from a novel? How is romance to be distinguished from realism? By the 1860s, when James published his first stories—among them "De-Gray: A Romance" and "The Romance of Certain Old Clothes"—the terms *romance* and *romantic* had acquired a range of meanings, at the same time that certain distinctions—between the romance and the novel, the romantic and the realistic, and the ideal and the real—had become commonplace. Although both James and Conrad disliked labels like *romantic* and *realistic*—"the clumsy separations" James called such distinctions[1]—both novelists in their later years formulated their own definitions of romance. They used the terms *romance* and *realism* in their essays and letters; and in their fiction they drew from and contributed to traditions which had begun to emerge by the middle of the eighteenth century.

I

With the publication of *The Castle of Otranto* in 1764 Horace Walpole introduced a kind of fiction, the Gothic romance, popular to this day. In the preface to the second edition (1765), when he defined the two kinds of romance he had attempted to blend—the "ancient," in which "all was imagination and improbability," and the "modern," in which nature is the model to be copied—he made a distinction which many writers after him were to develop.[2] In 1785 Clara Reeve, the author of *The Old English Baron* (written in acknowledged imitation of *The Castle of Otranto*), elaborated upon

Walpole's definitions of ancient and modern romance to differen-
tiate the romance from the novel. "The Romance is an heroic fable,
which treats of fabulous persons and things.—The Novel is a picture of real life and manners, and of the times in which it is written.
The Romance, in lofty and elevated language, describes what
never happened nor is likely to happen. The Novel gives a familiar
relation of such things, as pass every day before our eyes."[3]

It would be hard to find a clearer statement of a distinction to be
made repeatedly in the nineteenth century: the romance pictures
the remote, the strange, the marvellous, the improbable; the
novel, the familiar, the ordinary, the contemporary, the probable.
To these definitions Walter Scott, the "first English prose story-
teller" as James identified him,[4] lent the force of his authority. In
his important "Essay on Romance" (1824), he distinguished between the romance, "the interest of which turns upon marvellous
and uncommon incidents," and the novel, in which "events are
accommodated to the ordinary train of human events, and the
modern state of society."[5] Scott does not use the word *realism* in
his essays, but in praising the "force and precision" with which
Jane Austen presented incidents "from the current of ordinary life"
and in describing her pictures of characters as "finished up to nature," comparable in their "minute detail" to the works of the
Flemish painters,[6] he was identifying some of the qualities by
which later writers were to define realism in fiction.

Insofar as the realist is one who nourishes his mind and imagination upon observable realities and strives to render their form and
substance—"to make you see"—both James and Conrad are
realists. James's declared prejudice "in favour of a close connota-
tion, or close observance of the real"[7] was shared by Conrad, who
praised Maupassant's "scrupulous, prolonged and devoted attention to the aspects of the visible world" (18:28) and, in his essay on
James, defined fiction as history "based on the reality of forms and
the observation of social phenomena" (18:17). Both novelists, however, rejected the kind of realism which seeks a photographic imitation of life and remains content with the depiction of surfaces.
The artist, in James's words, strives to "render the look of things,
the look that conveys their meaning"; he seeks to capture the "sub-

stance" as well as the "surface."[8] Conrad's effort to express the essential or enduring qualities of his subject, to render "the highest kind of justice to the visible universe" (3:xi), led him to declare that "all my concern has been with the 'ideal' value of things, events and people. That and nothing else. The humorous, the pathetic, the passionate, the sentimental *aspects* came in of themselves."[9] The failure to render the ideal value of the subject led Conrad to criticize the realism of Arnold Bennett's *A Man from the North*: "You stop just short of being absolutely real because you are faithful to your dogmas of realism. Now realism in art will never approach reality. And your art, your gift, should be put to the service of a larger and freer faith."[10] The "road to legitimate realism," Conrad declared in his essay on Fenimore Cooper, "is through poetical feeling" (18:56).

Clearly terms like "real life," "probability," "fidelity," and "accuracy"—terms commonly used to distinguish realism from romance—do not describe all the elements of James's and Conrad's art. In his prefaces James not only distinguishes between "the air of romance," which may "surround" a subject and "the element of reality" in which a subject may be steeped (2:xiv); but he describes as "romantic" many aspects of his own art. In *The Tragic Muse* he strove to invest Nick Dormer's sacrifice of a political career with "a certain romantic glamour" (7:ix). In portraying the ghosts in that "sinister romance" *The Turn of the Screw*, he departed from convention and "cast my lot with pure romance, the appearances conforming to the true type being so little romantic" (12:xvi, xx). Most important perhaps is his reply to the critic who objected to the grace and pathos with which he had invested the figure of Daisy Miller: "My supposedly typical little figure was of course pure poetry" (18:viii). His defense, which could be applied to other characters, like the "supersubtle fry" of artists criticized for not being true to life (15:ix), recalls Cooper's defense of his "poetic view" of Leatherstocking: "It is the privilege of all writers of fiction, more particularly when their works aspire to the elevation of romances, to present the *beau ideal* of their characters to the reader. This it is which constitutes poetry."[11]

Like James, Conrad was aware of elements in his own work to

which it was fitting to apply the terms *romance* and *romantic*. He subtitled *Lord Jim* "A Romance" and *The Rescue* "A Romance of the Shallows." The "hawk-eye for hard facts and precise details," which Edward Garnett noted in Conrad,[12] did not destroy "the romantic feeling of reality" which Conrad recognized as "an inborn faculty" in himself (14:vii). Like James, Conrad exemplifies the artist, who, in James's words, "commits himself in both directions," and whose "current remains therefore extraordinarily rich and mixed, washing us successively with the warm wave of the near and familiar and the tonic shock . . . of the far and strange" (2:xv).

In analyzing this current "rich and mixed," we do well to recall at the start an important distinction, which James emphasized in his preface to *The American*, between a work called a romance and a character with a romantic cast of mind: "It would be impossible to have a more romantic temper than Flaubert's Madame Bovary, and yet nothing less resembles a romance than the record of her adventures" (2:xvii). Most of James's and Conrad's novels in which the likeness to romance is strongest center on characters of romantic temper.

There are appropriate examples to serve as a basis for generalization in the works of romantic fiction of greatest interest to James and Conrad. For both novelists, a list would include the works of Walter Scott, Robert Louis Stevenson, and Victor Hugo. (James reviewed both *Ninety-Three* and *Toilers of the Sea*—one of the works, Conrad recalls in *A Personal Record*, that his father translated.) James's list would also include the novels of Hawthorne and the Gothic romances of Ann Radcliffe and her school; Conrad's list, Flaubert's *Salammbô* and *The Temptation of St. Anthony*, as well as the sea novels of Cooper and the tales of Captain Marryat to which he pays tribute in his "Tales of the Sea." We must also include the most important product of Conrad and Ford's collaboration— the five-part narrative *Romance*.

Judging by the common definitions, most readers would probably say that what make novels romantic are exciting adventures in remote places, creating in characters and readers states of wonder and suspense. Royalists slaughtering besiegers of a castle, two brothers fighting a duel in the dead of a winter night, prisoners

with guttering candles escaping through subterranean passages—
these are the scenes that readers of *Ninety-Three*, *The Master of
Ballantrae*, and *The Mysteries of Udolpho* are likely to recall. Certainly *Romance* contains the elements of high-colored incident
which inspired Scott's catalogue of the conventional materials of
romance: "Robbers, smugglers, bailiffs, caverns, dungeons and
madhouses."[13] The narrator of *Romance*, a young Englishman
named John Kemp, goes to the West Indies in quest of romance,
and for him "romance" is primarily adventure. "I was in search of
romance, and here were all the elements; Spaniards, a conspirator,
and a kidnapping" (6:95)—to which list one could add: smugglers,
pirates, bandits, priests, a beautiful heroine, an aged aristocrat, a
Spanish palace, fabulous wealth, a murder, a death-bed scene, a
proposal on bended knee, near starvation in a cavern, and rescue at
the eleventh hour. To Pinker, Conrad described *Romance* as a
"story of adventure" and "a serious attempt at *interesting, animated Romance* with no more psychology than comes naturally into
the action."[14]

In "The Art of Fiction" James rejects the idea that "adventure" is
necessarily a matter of duels and pirates and buried treasure. A
"psychological reason," he asserts, can be as rich in pictorial value
and dramatic interest as a kidnapping or a shipwreck.[15] Elaboration
of this point in the preface to *The American* leads James to his
fullest definition of romance. Observing that many people have
identified romance simply by the presence of caravans or ghosts or
forgers or wicked women, he contends that "the idea of the facing
of danger," to which these elements are reducible, is not of itself
romantic. "The panting pursuit of danger is the pursuit of life itself,
in which danger awaits us possibly at every step and faces us at
every turn" (2:xvi).

Since conflict and danger are confined to no one kind of action
romance is to be identified, James argues, not by the situation it
presents but by the premises on which the picture of the situation
is based.

The only *general* attribute of projected romance that I can see . . . is the
fact of the kind of experience with which it deals—experience liberated,

so to speak; experience disengaged, disembroiled, disencumbered, exempt from the conditions that we usually know to attach to it and . . . drag upon it, and operating in a medium which relieves it, in a particular interest, of the inconvenience of a *related*, a measurable state, a state subject to all our vulgar communities. (2:xvii)

Instead of proposing to depict the reality we know, with its confusions and complexities and inconsistencies, the romancer creates what Samuel Hynes has termed the "world-of-the-work,"[16] a contrived reality which may be governed by principles different from those which order the reality we know. The defining attribute of the contrived world is suggested in *The Ambassadors*, when Strether, sitting alone in Notre Dame, tries "to reconstitute a past, to reduce it in fact to the convenient terms of Victor Hugo" (22:7). The key word is "reduce"; the world of the romance is a simplified world—an idealized world in which, in Northrop Frye's words, "heroes are brave, heroines beautiful, villains villainous, and the frustrations, ambiguities and embarrassments of ordinary life are made little of."[17]

Some of the ways by which the reduction or simplification is accomplished can be illustrated by Conrad and Ford's *Romance*. Of first importance is the epigraph "Romance," which affirms the power of time to transform the mundane workaday present into memories that become "romantic in dimn'd hours." In their belief that "the feeling of the romantic in life lies principally in the glamour memory throws over the past,"[18] Ford and Conrad remind one of Hawthorne, who associated romance and the past in the preface to *The House of the Seven Gables:* "The point of view in which this tale comes under the Romantic definition lies in the attempt to connect a bygone time with the very present that is flitting away from us."[19]

In his prefaces Hawthorne emphasizes another method of ordering and simplifying reality: the placing of a group of characters in a setting connected to the mainstream of a nation's life yet separated from it. What Hawthorne found in the Blithedale community, a "theatre, a little removed from the highway of ordinary travel,"[20] writers of romance have sought in a wide variety of settings: lonely ruined castles, ships at sea, treasure islands, and country estates. In *Romance* Ford and Conrad place their characters in "theatres, a little removed," by isolating them first in the Casa Riego, the palace of the heroine's father; then on the ships to which they escape, then in the cavern where Seraphina, who is both heir to the land and "a fugitive princess of romance," sits "concealed in the very heart of her dominions" (6:364).

The immutable love of the narrator and Seraphina illustrates another way in which the romancer simplifies or reduces the complexities of existence: he creates characters without complexity, often ruled by a single passion or obsession. O'Brien, the villain and archenemy of Kemp, lives only to seek Seraphina and her fortune; Don Carlos, to protect his cousin Seraphina from O'Brien; Tomas Castro, to serve his master Don Carlos. In worlds where stainless good confronts unremitting evil, the happy ending, in which the virtuous triumph and the evil perish, is a literary convention. In *Romance* the narrator's chivalrous refusal on two occasions to kill his enemies might, without the protection of romance, have resulted in his and Seraphina's deaths, but in the romance, "nearest of all literary forms to the wish-fulfillment dream,"[21] the hero is rescued at his court trial on the eve of his conviction.

In its sympathetic uncritical view of the protagonist, *Romance* is characteristic of novels like *Ninety-Three* and *The Mysteries of Udolpho*, which are never ironic or sardonic in tone. This is not to say that the sordid and ugly and grotesque have no place in romance. Indeed, as Hugo points out, the ugliness of the flawed and the corrupt heightens by contrast the beauty of the ideal.[22] In *Romance* the purity of Seraphina and the chivalry of Kemp are highlighted by the appearance and acts of the two grotesques symbolized by the title of part 4, "Blade and Guitar": the misshapen Castro with his steel blade for an arm, and the revolting Manuel de Popolo, whose ravings incite his "sordid, vermin-haunted crowd" (6:267) to pillage and slaughter. But knowing that wit and irony are foreign to the spirit of their romance, Conrad and Ford suppressed those elements, creating in Kemp a narrator who does not invite critical scrutiny and whose words are to be accepted at face value.

Since this is the case, Kemp's own romantic view of the world is an integral part of the romance. We have noted James's distinction between romance and a character of romantic temper but the distinction ceases to matter when a romantic character's view reflects his world without distortion. Throughout the first three chapters and the final chapters of *Romance* John Kemp brings to his experience no clearly defined point of view, save his craving for adventure. But in the "matchless Fourth Part"—as Ford described Conrad's work[23]—romance is created not only by the adventures but by the way the narrator sees his world, by the sense of wonder or joy or despair, which heightens the intensity of what he views. He illustrates that romanticism which Conrad defined as "a point of view from which the very shadows of life appear endowed with an internal glow" (14:viii). On board ship the morning after his rescue, for instance, the narrator sees revealed in the clear air "a new world—new and familiar, yet disturbingly beautiful. I seemed to discover all sorts of secret charms that I had never seen in things I had seen a hundred times"(6:308). The wonder of discovery is expressed in sharp visual images suggestive of qualities seen for the first time: a sailor's forearm, like a "billet of red mahogany"; the white speck of a distant schooner like a fallen snowflake; the curve of sails "soothed into perfect stillness by the wind" (6:308–309).

By Conrad's definition romance is a heightening of experience. What results is not necessarily a distortion of reality, for the "romantic feeling of reality," he asserts, can survive "recognition of the hard facts of existence" and is "none the worse for the knowledge of truth" (14:vii–viii). The "romantic feeling of reality" was certainly present in James no less than in Conrad. Several of his most important characters—Strether, Isabel Archer, Hyacinth Robinson, and Milly Theale—like Conrad's narrator in *Romance*, see in their world "secret charms" to which others are blind. But it is worth stressing that James in his fullest discussion of romance separates the real from the romantic, seeing them in contrast to each other. Conrad defines a romanticism which is not in opposition to the truth, but is a way of seeing in the hardness of truth "a certain aspect of beauty" (14:vii); James defines romance as experience disconnected from the exigencies of actual life, "uncontrolled by our general sense of 'the way things happen'" (2:xviii). If experience is figured as a balloon tied to the earth, the act of the romancer is to "cut the cable," to free the balloon from the earth (2:xviii). Some eight years before James used his metaphor in the preface to *The American*, Conrad in *Lord Jim* described the romantic like Jim—not as one released by the cutting of the cable—but as swinging "farther in any direction, as if given a longer scope of cable in the uneasy anchorage of life" (4:224). James's definition of romance suggests an awakening on the part of the character to the facts of existence which romance ignores or falsifies; Conrad's definition suggests a way of feeling the world which may work to a character's destruction but against which there may be no clear-cut "real world" to be juxtaposed.

We have already seen one important difference in the two novelists' work which is consistent with this difference: the gradual revelation of hidden reality to one character, such as that dramatized in *The Ambassadors*, as contrasted with the many views of an enigmatic figure like Jim, none of which is affirmed as the truth. Other differences implicit in the two writers' definitions of romance will become evident as we compare their use of romantic conventions and their portrayal of romantic protagonists.

II

Elements of romance in James (excluding the tales of the supernatural) are most prominent in those fictions which dramatize a character's entrance into an unfamiliar world, alluring yet treacherous. A list of such works devoted to the theme of discovery would include most of James's important novels: *Roderick Hudson*, *The American*, *The Portrait of a Lady*, *The Princess Casamassima*, *The Ambassadors*, *The Wings of the Dove*, and *The Golden Bowl*. *The American*, however, is the only novel of which James said, "I had been plotting arch-romance without knowing it" (2:ix), and it is the novel in which romantic conventions do most to determine the reader's response to characters and events.

In the preface James traces the "consistently, consummately" romantic character of the novel to the lapses from verisimilitude, noticeable to the reader because the romancer had not succeeded in "cutting the cable" with sufficient skill to keep the reader from perceiving that "the way things happen is frankly not the way in which they are represented as having happened, in Paris, to my hero" (2:xviii). In particular James cites the presence of Newman alone at the opera immediately after his engagement is announced; the obscurity of Madame de Cintré's motives in backing out; and above all the rejection of Newman by the impoverished Bellegardes, who, James argued, in reality "positively would have jumped . . . at my rich and easy American" (2:xix).

James's statements suggest that he had proposed to write a realistic novel and unwittingly produced a romance. But other elements in the novel, of which James surely was conscious, do as much as the lapses from verisimilitude to unfurl "the emblazoned flag of romance" (2:ix) over the work. Of all James's novels *The American*, with its duel, its dark family secret, its ancient castle and convent, and its hero strong in the "general easy magnificence of his manhood" (2:2), is most indebted in its plot to the motifs and situations of Gothic romance. If the fabulous business exploits of Newman's past life link him with the heroes of American folklore and tall tales, his adventure in Paris is the archetypal adventure of the hero of romance and fairy tale: to win his reward and his heart's wish he must survive an ordeal and pass a test; he must rescue his beloved from the spell cast upon her.[24]

Several times identified with the princess of a fairy tale, Claire de Cintré, like the heroines of Gothic romances, is a pure and incorruptible victim of evil forces, here embodied in her mother and elder brother, guilty of one murder and willing to exert the psychological pressure (in scenes left to the reader's imagination) which compels Claire to entomb herself for life. Together, the evil Bellegardes and their opposites, the saintly Claire and the virtuous Newman, come as close as any characters in James to representing the conflict of pure good and pure evil which the contrived world of romance sustains. As if to forestall possible objections of readers, James lets the characters themselves call attention to the melodramatic nature of the situation. To Newman, Claire's secluded life is "like something in a regular old play. . . . That dark old house over there looks as if wicked things had been done in it and might be done again" (2:111). In Valentin's words Claire's marriage to a corrupt and aged nobleman was "a first act for a melodrama" (2:152).

Such awareness on the part of the characters distinguishes them from the characters of Gothic tales who do not see their world as theatrical or contrived. From the portrayal of characters aware of the conventions which their situations illustrate, it is but a step to the criticism of these conventions—to comedy and wit and satire. Richard Poirier has shown how James in his first full-length novel, *Roderick Hudson*, transformed melodrama into an instrument of satire—by making comic those melodramatic poses and gestures which are the index of a character's egotism and blindness.[25] In *The American* the evil Bellegardes are at once sinister connivers guilty of betrayal and murder, urbane figues whose wit exposes the naiveté of Newman, and comic figures whose pretensions are targets of James's satiric wit.

The relation of Newman to the conventions and proprieties of the world of the novel is complex. He is romantic in that he is an idealized figure who resembles archetypal figures of romance. As the idealized hero in the American mould he is a vigorous opponent of certain practices such as the duel glorified in romantic fiction. Newman is romantic in another sense, in that his view of life simplifies or falsifies reality: to his unsophisticated eyes "the complex Parisian world" is "a very simple affair" (2:39). Above all Newman is romantic in his faith in the boundless power of his will. Until he is thwarted by the Bellegardes, he rests confident in that "view of his effective 'handling' of life to which, sooner or later, he made all experience contribute" (2:325).

The turning point in Newman's adventure, when for the first time in his life he is absolutely checked by forces against which he seems powerless, confronted James with the question of his hero's ultimate relation to the conventions of romance. When romantic heroes such as Quentin Durward or Ivanhoe are thwarted or betrayed, they defeat their enemies, rescue the heroine, and receive the reward of a happy marriage. Although Quentin Durward is told by his captor that he must face reality after "a happy journey through Fairy-land—all full of heroic adventure, and high hope and wild minstrel-like delusion, like the gardens of Morgaine la Fée,"[26] he goes on to every reward the world of romance can give. Instead of allowing Newman to follow the path of Scott's heroes, James contrived a situation in which Newman himself should renounce his effort to win Claire de Cintré from his enemies. When the Bellegardes' servant Mrs. Bread reveals the secret of Madame de Bellegarde's murder of her husband, she gives Newman the weapon that he may use to threaten his enemies and perhaps force their surrender. For a time he unquestioningly travels the avenger's path; then, as if perceiving that revenge on the Bellegardes, no less than Valentin's duel, is a "wretched theatrical affair" (2:359), he abjures his attempt, not because he forgives the Bellegardes, James emphasizes, but because "the very force of his aversion" (2:vii) compels him to reject both conventional alternatives: to seek vengeance or to devote his life to hopeless longing for the unattainable.

Newman fails but he is not defeated. By accepting at last the limits imposed by circumstance, he escapes finally the self-defeating passions of revenge and regains his self-possession, which in itself affirms the vitality of the will and marks a victory over circumstance. Such at least appears to be James's view of Newman at the end, but several readers have criticized Newman's behavior on the grounds that his willingness to expose family secrets for his own gain is ignoble and that in destroying evidence of crime he is as guilty as Urbain de Bellegarde, who concealed knowledge of his mother's responsibility in his father's death.[27] Readers who agree with these criticisms of Newman, having at first accepted his view of himself as simply "a good fellow wronged," may feel that James at this point has "cut the cable" without being detected, that their impulse to judge Newman critically had been "skilfully and successfully drugged" (2:xviii). If this is true, then surely the most potent "drug" is the romantic melodrama itself, which induces one to assume that the opponent of evil must himself be flawless. In any case the majority of critics have followed James's lead in seeing

Newman as a guiltless victim, who in sparing his enemies continues, like the hero of romance, to embody an ideal, an ideal here realized not in vengeance but in renunciation.

"A tradition is kept alive only by something being added to it,"[28] James observed in an essay on Stevenson. *The American* foreshadows the ways in which James in his later novels adds to and maintains the tradition of the romance. Perhaps the most important departure in *The American* from the "usual formula" lies in the point of view which enables James to blend melodrama and comedy and to question the assumptions upon which certain conventions of romance are based. When compared to mature works like *The Portrait of a Lady* and *The Ambassadors, The American* may well seem an imperfect fusion of elements. The Bellegardes, for instance, are depicted with too much realistic detail to be simply conventional figures of melodrama, but they are too much simplified to be wholly realistic representatives of nineteenth-century French society. Newman himself may be criticized as an inconsistent mixture of the ideal and the imperfect. His repeated failures of perception, which many readers have noted, seem inconsistent with the consummate shrewdness which James attributes to his ideally successful businessman.

In its ending, however, *The American* anticipates James's later works in which motifs and conventions of romance are used to dramatize his central theme: the journey from ignorance to knowledge. Newman's renunciation of his revenge clearly foreshadows those mental acts through which James's later protagonists in the face of outward defeat achieve inward growth. Although Newman is too little susceptible to impressions and although his character is too much formed at the start to undergo any fundamental change, he is different at the end from the man who once proposed to win "the greatest victory over circumstances" (2:50). He has been obliged to recognize limits, to confront and yield to forces which cannot be circumvented. The convent wall which at the end separates him from his dream is a symbol not only of cultural barriers but of all realities that must be recognized. Such recognition is the destiny of all James's protagonists, from Rowland Mallet to

Maggie Verver, who try to shape a world to meet their own need.

Of James's novels *The American* relies most heavily upon romantic melodrama for its plot. This source of interest is not absent from James's later novels, but in them the world of romantic adventure is evoked chiefly by figurative language. John Paterson has shown that in *The Ambassadors* Strether's impressions are rendered through imagery of shipwrecks, pirates, labyrinths, and caves,[29] and one might make a similar study of Gothic images of prisons, haunted chambers, and instruments of torture in *The Golden Bowl*. The first edition of *The American* offers little illustration of the method but in the revision for the New York Edition James heightened the inward drama through the imagery of adventure. When Newman realizes the poverty of a life of "mere money-getting," for instance, he sees it, "in its ugliness, as vast and vague and dark, a pirate-ship with lights turned inward" (2:102). Through imagery of this kind James seeks not only to illuminate essential resemblances between the mundane and the exotic, the socially sanctioned and the outlawed, but also to show that the inward life may be as rich in suspense and danger as a tale of robbers and murders. Instead of making a distinction as Stevenson did between the exciting and the tame—between "incident" and the "clink of teaspoons"[30]—James sought to invest the normal, the usual, the unspoken, and the inward with the climactic force of high adventure.

James's use of romantic convention is inseparable from his portrayal of characters. Not only does he represent their inward states by imagery of romantic adventure, but he often presents his central action, the journey from ignorance to knowledge, as the passage from romantic illusion to perception of realities which call into question the basic premises of romantic fiction on which the characters' romantic illusions have in part been nourished. In other words, if the worlds in which James places his characters have characteristics of the contrived world of romance, many of the characters themselves seek what they define as "romance"—a word with which characters associate certain values which may or may not be shared by James.

III

All the characters James identifies as romantic illustrate his definition of romance as that which is distinguished from the real, and
opposed to "our general sense of the way things happen." Whether
the experience liberated and disengaged takes the form of daydreams and fantasies or of ideas which the characters accept as
truth; whether the characters fail to see or whether they willfully
ignore the limits reality imposes, the vision of those whose view of
life is termed romantic in some way distorts realities perceptible to
the reader and usually to other characters.

James's characters of romantic temper can be easily divided into
two groups: those comic figures who do not change and whose
romanticism is a fixed attribute to be satirized; and the protagonists
whose romantic ideas, although they may call forth the author's
satiric darts, are an expression of a rich and complex nature capable
of development.

Foremost in the first group are Mrs. Penniman (*Washington
Square*) and Mrs. Wix (*What Maisie Knew*), who despite the
marked differences in the tone and method of the two novels, bear
resemblances to each other. Both are widows in positions of
dependence—Mrs. Penniman as the companion of her brother's
daughter Catherine, and Mrs. Wix as the governess of the child
Maisie. Both are inferior in mind and character to the child they
propose to instruct; both become infatuated with the young man to
whom the heroine is attached; both represent a point of view, sentimental, self-interested, and uninformed, which helps to mark the
growth of the heroine, who by the end perceives truths inaccessible to her mentor.

The romanticism of both aunt and governess is fed by the popular fictions of sentiment and adventure. Mrs. Wix regales Maisie
with stories from novels "all about love and beauty and countesses
and wickedness. Her conversation was practically an endless narrative, a great garden of romance, with sudden vistas into her own
life and gushing fountains of homeliness" (11:27). The salient trait
of Mrs. Penniman is her "mock romanticisim,"[31] her penchant for

seeing herself and others as figures in thrilling dramas of the kind depicted in the "light literature" (p. 15) to which she is addicted. Of the two figures Mrs. Wix is the product of the subtler art; indeed she is one of James's memorable portraits, a richly conceived figure whose romanticism is but one strain in a nature capable of self-pity, maternal devotion, sexual provocation, and moral righteousness. Mrs. Penniman is conceived in much simpler terms, her character expressed almost entirely in her foolish fondness for secrecy and melodrama. Dr. Sloper, her brother, remarks the "crudity" of her talk; her sister the poverty of her "artificial mind" (p. 48), and even Catherine in her most unillumined state perceives Mrs. Penniman as a limited figure: "Catherine saw her all at once, as it were, and was not dazzled by the apparition" (p. 19). But the very simpleness of the figure enables us to isolate the lineaments of the type for analysis.

Like the characters of *The American* the four main characters of *Washington Square*, including Mrs. Penniman, are conceived in relation to a plot which, as several critics have observed, is that of a melodramatic fairy tale. Richard Poirier has identified the archetypes of the characters: the Cruel Father, the Motherless Daughter, the Handsome Lover (who here schemes for the heroine's fortune) and the Fairy Godmother, here the aunt who becomes the rival of her niece for the Lover's attentions.[32] As in *The American* the expectations created by these elements of conventional romance are not met; in Poirier's words, *Washington Square* exemplifies the "vital art of turning the anticipated into the unexpected response."[33] But whereas Newman eventually rejects melodramatic acts, each of the three main figures surrounding Catherine—her father, her suitor, and her aunt—sees the action as an entertainment with Catherine at the center and consciously exploits the melodramatic possibilities of the situation. Morris Townsend, whose handsome appearance suggests to Catherine "a young knight in a poem," is a hypocrite, posing as her rescuer and exulting in "my power to break in upon your cruel captivity" (pp. 44, 114). Dr. Sloper is not a hypocrite but a speaker of truths, who, as Poirier observes, is eventually blind to truth, forbidden by his intellectual pride from ever seeing Catherine in any role but the one he has cast for her. The readiness of the two men to create situations by which they may profit at Catherine's expense has its comic and eventually its corrupt extension in the sentimental and theatrical fantasies of Mrs. Penniman. She does not lie to Catherine as Townsend does, or mock her as the doctor does; but she seeks gratification through Catherine as surely as the others do. When she indulges in a wish-fulfilling fantasy of Townsend's marriage, Catherine of necessity is the bride but she, Mrs. Penniman, is the heroine of the occasion.

Mrs. Penniman's real hope was that the girl would make a secret marriage, at which she should officiate as bride's woman or duenna. She had a vision of this ceremony being performed in some subterranean chapel— subterranean chapels in New York were not frequent, but Mrs. Penniman's imagination was not chilled by trifles—and of the guilty couple— she liked to think of poor Catherine and her suitor as the guilty couple— being shuffled away in a fast-whirling vehicle to some obscure lodging in the suburbs, where she would pay them (in a thick veil) clandestine visits; where they would endure a period of romantic privations; and when ultimately, after she should have been their earthly providence, their intercessor, their advocate, and their medium of communication with the world, they would be reconciled to her brother in an artistic tableau, in which she herself should be somehow the central figure. (p. 117)

This fantasy is so absurd, so remote from the probable actions of all the characters, that the woman who conceives it seems a harmless fool. But Mrs. Penniman, who not only daydreams but makes herself the confidante and advisor of Catherine's suitor, is not simply a comic excrescence on the surface of the novel. As Catherine's increasingly critical judgments of her aunt indicate, the romantic fantasies of one character may force another character to ever clearer perception of the real nature of what surrounds her: eventually Catherine perceives her aunt guilty of "meddlesome folly" and is "sickened at the thought that Mrs. Penniman had been let loose . . . upon her happiness" (p. 230). For the reader Mrs. Penniman's absurd fantasies, as Poirier notes, transform into comedy the melodrama latent in the situation, thus inviting one to look critically at all the characters. Finally the resemblances between Mrs. Penniman and her brother, seeming opposites, indicate what unchecked romanticism and cold intellectualism have in common: inflexibility, blindness, and the will to control others' destinies. Only Catherine respects "untested functions" and instead of forcing a role upon herself "watched herself as she would have watched another person, and wondered what she would do" (p. 113). To Catherine Dr. Sloper seems infinite and all powerful, but it is Catherine alone who is not constricted, who alone has the capacity to develop beyond present limits.

The qualities that attend unbridled romanticism are also exhibited by a group of characters of romantic temper who occupy a middle ground between comic figures like Mrs. Penniman and "the free spirits" of the major novels. Such characters as the Princess Casamassima and Olive Chancellor are comic in their view of poverty as romantic and in their dedication to "the people," which enables them to exalt themselves and rationalize meddling as benevolence. At the same time the intelligence, taste, and power to charm others exhibited by both the princess and Olive—the most and the least alluring of James's women—set both characters apart from comic figures like Mrs. Penniman. These "middle" characters, however, lack the capacity for growth which marks the "free spirits," whose romantic tendencies, although they may lead them to falsify reality and interpose blindly in the lives of others, are inseparable from generous impulses and intuitive power.

The complexity of the romantic personality is evident in Rowland Mallet, first named in James's list of characters who serve as "most polished of possible mirrors" in his fiction (5:xv). It might first appear that Rowland, sober, deliberate, and judicious as he seems, is created simply as a contrast to Roderick Hudson, who with his flowing locks, passionate utterances, defiance of restraints and visions of doom, seems a caricature of the romantic artist. But Rowland, like Newman, is romantic in his faith in his power to shape another's destiny. Rowland is not a vicious meddler like Mrs. Penniman; he does not subject people to impossible roles in absurd daydreams, but he too suffers a sense of emptiness in his life; long-

ing for "some absorbing errand" (1:7), he sets Roderick up in
Rome, proposes the course Roderick should take, then clings to his
ill-fated plan with a determination that he himself describes as "in-
sanely romantic" (1:293).

Like Valentin and Claire de Cintré, Roderick confounds the
hopes of the would-be rescuer not by departing from the conventional patterns of romance but by conforming to them. Enchanted
by the charm of Christina Light, James's chief exemplar of the fatal
woman, who is herself the victim of romantic illusions, Roderick
succumbs to his passion, abandons his art, and suffers "in thrall"
until he falls to his death in the Alps. As Newman before the convent wall faces the reality of his loss, so Rowland, as he watches by
the dead body of his friend, sees the truth of his life, understanding
as never before the full measure of his emotional dependence upon
Roderick, "how up to the brim, for two years, his personal world
had been filled" (1:526).

James's portrayal of Rowland illustrates what is to be observed in
most of his major novels: the difficulty in distinguishing between
the romantic vision of the characters and the romantic nature of the
world in which the characters are placed. Rowland is quick to feel
himself in an enchanted place, as when at the Villa Ludovisi with
Roderick he knows "the spell . . . of supreme romance," and when
at Frascati he feels the scene "rich in the romantic note" (1:84,
227). But a world which contains Christina Light, "a figure radiant-
ly romantic" (1:375), of fabulous beauty and mysterious origin,
has in itself all the potentiality of romance. Nor can one separate
the romantic power of European landscapes from the romantic
tendencies of characters who view the scenes. It does not require
the protagonist of "A Passionate Pilgrim" to feel that he stands "in a
dream, in a world quite detached" (13:408) to endow the ancestral
English house with the aura of legend and tradition. In James's
novels romantic settings and characters act upon each other; as the
setting intensifies the nostalgia and yearning of the observer, so the
observer infuses the scene with his own emotion, and the romantic
world becomes one which the characters half perceive and half
create.

None of James's novels exemplifies this truth more vividly than *The Ambassadors*, which presents in Strether the protagonist quickest to feel the romance of scenes which evoke the beauty and grandeur of the past. If Rowland and Newman represent the active side of the romantic personality, its will to arrange and control, Strether represents its more passive side in his surrender to scenes and characters that appear to him as if bathed in a magic substance. Strether's imagination of Chad's artistic days in the Latin Quarter inspires "an almost envious vision of the boy's romantic privilege" (21:91). In Little Bilham's rooms Strether is quick to "read into the scene" "the legend of good-humoured poverty, of mutual accommodation fairly raised to the romantic" (21:127). Gloriani is crowned with "the light, with the romance, of glory" (21:196), while Madame de Vionnet, as various as Cleopatra and the legatee of the "great legend," is "romantic for him far beyond what she could have guessed" (22:9).

Heightening the romantic charm of all he sees is Strether's fondness for seeing the people in his world as characters of romantic fiction come to life: "It was the way of nine tenths of his current impressions to act as recalls of things imagined" (22:6). Before he meets Chad Strether imagines him the victim of a wicked woman in a melodrama such as he sees at the London theater. When no "bad woman in a yellow frock" (21:53) appears in the drama enacted in Paris, Strether abandons one romantic stereotype for another. Meeting Madame de Vionnet at Notre Dame, where the charm of his favorite romancer Victor Hugo is most potent, he casts her in a new role, as "some fine firm concentrated heroine of an old story" (22:6). Like an artist conceiving a character, Strether imagines a life for Madame de Vionnet, an ordeal of unremitting self-restraint and sacrifice which the "virtuous attachment" with Chad demands—sacrifice of the kind to which Conrad's Roderick Anthony in *Chance* actually subjects himself and Flora, with such painful consequences.

Strether's romanticism has concealed truth from him; at the same time his imagination enables him to perceive values which if never acknowledged by the Pococks and the Waymarshes of the world are not less real for that. As clearly as any novel, *The Ambas-sadors* dramatizes the strengths as well as the weaknesses of the romantic imagination and demonstrates the impossibility of isolat-ing at all times the true vision from the false. James asserted that it was "as difficult . . . to trace the dividing-line between the real and the romantic as to plant a milestone between north and south" (2:xx). In *The Ambassadors* it is sometimes equally difficult to say whether Strether's impressions more nearly conceal or reveal the truth of what he observes. When the narrator of "A Passionate Pil-grim" confesses himself unable when observing his friend "to fix the balance between what he saw and what he imagined" (13:415), he describes the problem posed by the vision of Lambert Strether.

Of all James's novels *The Ambassadors* most fully expresses the values of the romantic imagination. But undoubtedly the most complete study of the romantic personality is the analysis of Isabel Archer, the protagonist of *The Portrait of a Lady*, the fiction gen-erally regarded as James's first masterpiece, the novel which James declared would be to *The American* as wine is to water.[34] The sixth chapter of *The Portrait* presents the fullest delineation of the romantic temperament that James was ever to make. The heroine's most important faculty, her "remarkably active" imagination is both her strength and her weakness, a power "which rendered her a good many services and played her a great many tricks" (3:68). James described Isabel as a "feminine counterpart to Christopher Newman"[35]—one notes James's fondness for identifying characters with the great rulers and explorers—and Isabel shares Newman's romantic belief in the boundless power of the self: "She had a fixed determination to regard the world as a place of brightness, of free expansion, of irresistible action." Like Newman she cherishes at first the illusion that if one is guiltless of any devious intent, one cannot suffer from the possible treachery of others. Her energy and will to act express themselves not in the attempt to direct others' lives but in the effort to form herself: "She was always planning out her development, desiring her perfection, observing her prog-ress." The root of her personality is self-esteem: "She had an un-quenchable desire to think well of herself" (3:68, 72, 68), but generosity, courage, fidelity, and integrity are components of her ideal image of herself. Self-esteem also leads her to idealize persons who admire her, so that the pleasure she takes in their admiration may be enhanced. As the only character in the novel whose future is not in great measure determined from the beginning, she engages the attention of all the characters, who like Isabel and her creator, see her development as a drama to be enacted.

In *The Portrait of a Lady* James draws his most detailed portrait of a romantic personality, and in so doing he creates the narrative which best exemplifies his power to transform the plot of romantic melodrama into a drama of inward action. Not only does *The Portrait* present James's most extensive use of Gothic imagery to render a character's consciousness; in Isabel Archer he creates the protagonist whose view of life is most deeply colored and whose fate is most critically affected by response to the romantic tradition upon which he draws. By observing the ways in which Isabel's history parallels and diverges from that of the typical heroine of romance, one sees more clearly perhaps than in any other novel the intricate relation between James's use of romantic conventions and his portrayal of the romantic temperament; one most fully perceives the ways James sustained a tradition by adding to it.

We can readily appreciate James's accomplishment if we briefly compare *The Portrait of a Lady* with the romances it most closely resembles. The novels of Ann Radcliffe, especially *The Mysteries of Udolpho*, which Madame Merle undoubtedly has in mind when she humorously questions Isabel about an ideal lover and his "castle in the Apennines" (3:287), at once suggest themselves. Another well-known Gothic work, J. S. Le Fanu's novel *Uncle Silas* (1864), bears even more marked resemblances in plot and relationship of characters to James's novel.

Like Maud Ruthyn, the narrator and heroine of *Uncle Silas*, Isabel inherits a fortune which exposes her to the designs and duplicity of adventurers. Just as Maud, after the death of her father, leaves a place of relative safety, Knowl, to enter upon her terror-stricken life at Bartram-Haugh, the house of her uncle and chief adversary, so Isabel, after the death of her uncle Daniel Touchett, leaves the safe and spacious Gardencourt to become, as Osmond's wife, a virtual prisoner in an Italian palace with a name that "smelt of historic deeds, of crime and craft and violence" (4:100). The role of Madame de la Rougierre, who insinuates herself at Knowl as Maud's governess and like an evil spirit turns up later at Bartram-Haugh in the service of the villainous Silas, is paralleled by the role of Madame Merle, who likewise appears shortly before the death of the heroine's benefactor, suddenly, without any advance warning, a total stranger to the heroine. Like Silas Ruthyn, Osmond is a villain of refined tastes and cruel wit. Each looks like a finely drawn portrait and has a voice that suggests the vibration of glass. Mrs. Touchett, Isabel's aunt, and Lady Knollys, Maud's cousin, both eccentric outspoken women, play similar parts. Even Isabel's devoted friend Henrietta Stackpole has a counterpart in *Uncle Silas*, in Maud's cousin and loyal companion Milly, whose boisterous spirits and untutored manners emphasize the more refined sensibilities of the heroine.

Admittedly such resemblances are superficial. If the characters within the two novels have similar relationships, they are not alike in their essential natures. Whereas the villains of Le Fanu are grotesque and unearthly creatures, death-marked and unnatural to a high degree, Osmond and Madame Merle, far from being unearthly, are so completely identified with the life of the world that Osmond declares himself to be not merely conventional but "convention itself" (4:21), and Madame Merle, in Ralph's words, is not worldly but is "the great round world itself" (3:362). Madame de la Rougierre connives with a man, Silas Ruthyn's son, who is as repulsive as she is; Madame Merle, also engaged in an attempt to draw the heroine into marriage, plots with a man as subtle and as attractive (to Isabel) as herself, a man who seems to Isabel as fine as a drawing in the Uffizi (3:356). Both women are ultimately rendered powerless, but whereas Madame de la Rougierre is murdered by her fellow conspirator, who thinks he is killing the heroine, Madame Merle is outdone in scenes of psychological, not physical, struggle.

The difference in the respective fates of Madame de la Rougierre and Madame Merle suggests the primary difference between *The Portrait of a Lady* and Gothic novels like *Uncle Silas*. In Maud Ruthyn's story the dominant emotion experienced by the heroine is the dread of physical harm; it is occasionally lulled, but at the end it rises to terror. In *The Portrait* the suffering and violence are of a mental and psychological, not a physical, nature. Isabel does not suffer bodily harm; Osmond does not cause her to fear for her life: "She was not afraid of him; she had no apprehension he would hurt her" (4:191). But she comes to feel that Osmond blights everything in her life that he looks upon. He not only strives to destroy Isabel's independence of mind and spirit; but he would force Isabel to accomplish the violation of herself when he presses her to procure Lord Warburton as a husband for Pansy.

In a novel in which the mind and spirit, not the body, of the heroine are threatened, it is appropriate that Gothic images of terror be converted into metaphors by which the heroine's consciousness of her plight is rendered. Isabel is not, like Walpole's Isabella, trapped in a subterranean vault with a guttering candle, but she comes to realize that her marriage to Osmond has led her "downward and earthward" to a "dark, narrow alley with a dead wall at the end." Three years of marriage have diminished and darkened her world, as if Osmond "had put the lights out one by one." She is not literally a prisoner—"She could come and go; she had her liberty"; but she feels the pressure of Osmond's mind as an imprisoning force: "She had lived *in* it almost—it appeared to have become her habitation." Like a gloating face at a cell grating Osmond's "beautiful mind . . . seemed to peep down from a small high window and mock at her." She is stifled by the "odour of mould and decay," trapped as she is in "the house of darkness, the house of dumbness, the house of suffocation" (4:189–196 passim).

The scene of Isabel's midnight vigil, from which these passages come—the scene James regarded as "a supreme illustration of the general plan" (3:xxi) of the novel—is the most sustained example in all James's fiction of his method of evoking a sense of violence and terror not through physical action but through image and metaphor. Outwardly nothing happens: Isabel merely sits and broods upon her life as the room grows darker and the hour later. Instead her consciousness becomes the stage of the action: "Her soul was haunted with terrors which crowded to the foreground of thought as quickly as a place was made for them" (4:188). This is the scene, the representation of Isabel's "motionlessly *seeing*," that James proposed to make as "'interesting' as the surprise of a caravan or the identification of a pirate" (3:xxi).

Given the fact that Isabel's consciousness is the source of most of the Gothic imagery in the novel, it is not surprising that her relation to the Gothic tradition is a complex one. Although unlike Catherine Morland in most respects, Isabel resembles Jane Austen's heroine in that she too lives with an awareness of a literary tradition and sees life in terms of the romantic novels she has read. She begs Ralph to show her the ghost at Gardencourt and delights in seeing Lord Warburton as a "hero of romance," his country house Lockleigh as a "castle in a legend." Later she pictures Osmond's life, "a lonely, studious life in a lovely land," in images of moss-grown terraces, gardens, and summer twilight that recall the opening scenes of *Udolpho* (3:91, 108, 399). She dwells upon his proposal, "drinking deep, in secret, of romance," telling no one because "it was more romantic to say nothing" (4:34).

Even deeper than her joy in seeing herself as the heroine of romance, however, is her pleasure in controverting the conventions, in acting as the heroines of Gothic romances do not act. She refuses not only Lord Warburton but also Caspar Goodwood, whose strength, expressed in images of armor, helmets, and warriors "plated and steeled," also gratifies her romantic nature. What Isabel most passionately affirms is her personal independence, her desire "to choose my fate" (3:220, 229). What she most emphatically rejects is the passive role which the conventional heroine plays and the conception of the woman's part which Hippolita of *The Castle of Otranto* expresses in extreme terms when she declares, "It is not ours to make election for ourselves; Heaven, our fathers, and our husbands, must decide for us."[36]

Isabel also has a strain of passivity absent from Ann Radcliffe's and Le Fanu's characters. Although the plot requires their heroines to be acted upon rather than to set action in motion, they exhibit an active unqualified resistance to evil which Isabel at the beginning does not show. It is true that the evil of Osmond is not so easily recognizable as that of Montoni or Silas Ruthyn. Isabel is betrayed into Osmond's hands, however, as much by her half-acknowledged desire to be formed and guided as by his readiness to exploit her. Her active desire to "choose my fate" coexists with the impulse to drift with the tide which the actions of other characters create around her. She is not altogether serious when she declares to Henrietta Stackpole that she does not wish to know where she is drifting, that she prefers " 'a swift carriage, of a dark night, rattling with four horses over roads that one can't see—that's my idea of happiness' " (3:235). But the picture of that fate to which the Gothic heroine is often literally subjected expresses one side of Isabel's nature that seeks its freedom in the abandonment to forces that relieve her of the burden of choice. And once she possesses the financial means to gratify her wishes, her freedom becomes a responsibility that she fears; she wonders whether "it's not a greater happiness to be powerless" (3:320). In time she wishes to transfer to Osmond the responsibility which her fortune has imposed upon her, and because she identifies the fortune with herself—it "became to her mind a part of her better self" (3:321–322)—her wish expresses also her half-conscious desire that she herself shall be fashioned by another for superior uses. If Osmond proposes to add Isabel to his "collection of choice objects," she herself is ready to be possessed in this way, as is clear when she rejoices that experience has enhanced her value to make her " 'worth more' . . . like some curious piece in an antiquary's collection" (4:9, 42).

Early in the action James says of Isabel that "sometimes she went so far as to wish that she might find herself some day in a difficult position, so that she should have the pleasure of being as heroic as the occasion demanded" (3:69). In marrying Osmond, Isabel is granted her wish. The fact that her unhappy life with him is pictured in imagery of the Gothic heroine's plight suggests that a part of Isabel desires such a fate and that her romantic view of life has not only clouded her perception of realities but has nourished a deeply rooted desire to suffer as the guiltless victim of another's cruelty.

The heroines of novels like *Uncle Silas* and *The Mysteries of Udolpho* do not act to bring suffering upon themselves, and they do not essentially change as a result of their terrible experiences. In contrast Isabel suffers as a consequence of her own choices, and her suffering effects inward change. Although denied the conventional reward of a happy marriage, Isabel achieves within the narrow limits of Osmond's world something of the kind of growth for which she had strived at the beginning and for which she had regarded her freedom as a necessary condition. It is the central irony of the novel that in the cold and selfish Osmond Isabel finds the person who of all the characters can best bring to maturity her potential strength and nobility. Only when another person holds her "vital principle" in contempt, as Osmond does, does this principle assert itself as the controlling force of her life. In resisting Osmond's ideals she creates a new basis for her own. It is Osmond's effort to create appearances which teaches her that freedom is maintained only if one asserts the importance of the substance of one's life over its "aspect and denomination." Just as Isabel gives Osmond the opportunity to pursue his system to the limit, so Osmond, more than any other character, enables Isabel to reveal and affirm herself. After their marriage, her personality as well as his, "touched as it never had been, stepped forth and stood erect" (4:189, 199).

Comparison of James's novel with the Gothic romance helps to illuminate the complex fate of Isabel and to show the extent to which James's strength and originality as a novelist are rooted in his power to assimilate the traditions of past literature. Certainly the much admired scene of Isabel's midnight vigil is a good illustration of T. S. Eliot's statement that no artist is to be valued alone, that often "not only the best, but the most individual parts of his work may be those in which the dead poets, his ancestors, assert their immortality most vigorously."[37]

Like *The American* but in a more subtle and delicate way, *The Portrait of a Lady* unites the wit and urbanity of the novel of manners with the emotional effects of the Gothic romances. In *The Portrait* James succeeded in investing the drama of a limited heroine's education (Jane Austen's subject in *Northanger Abbey*) with the sense of strangeness and mystery and perilous beauty that pervades *The Mysteries of Udolpho*. The result of this fusion of elements is a novel which is neither a comedy nor a romance with a happy ending but a drama in which tragedy and comedy inform each other, in which scenes potentially sentimental or melodramatic are controlled by the detached and comprehensive view of the author and ultimately by the maturing vision of the heroine herself.

5

Romance · II

Had James and Conrad produced the novelist's counterpart to *Lyrical Ballads*, James's part would have been to demonstrate the novelist's power to invest the inward life of normal characters in conventional society with the suspense of exciting adventure; Conrad's to render exotic scenes of perilous adventure in terms of familiar feelings, to express, in Coleridge's words, "the dramatic truth of such emotions, as would naturally accompany such situations."[1] For James the task was to "show what an 'exciting' inward life may do for the person leading it even while it remains perfectly normal" (3:xx); for Conrad the task was "to make unfamiliar things credible . . . to envelope them in their proper atmosphere of actuality" (14:viii). Romantic adventures—dangerous voyages, pirate attacks, shipwrecks—which appear as metaphors in James's depiction of the inner lives of his characters, remain an important part of the action in Conrad's fiction from first to last. Daring exploits in dangerous straits mark novels as different in spirit as *Heart of Darkness*, *Nostromo*, and *The Rover*. Describing their collaboration on *Romance*, Ford recalled Conrad's constant effort to "key up" the narrative, through the vivid rendering of exciting adventure.[2]

In his concern with the moral and psychological side of his characters' experience Conrad is closer to James than to Dumas or Scott. Like James, Conrad presents situations cast from romantic archetypes as they are reflected in the minds of characters whose own vision is romantic. Both novelists subject romantic ideals and illusions to the test of situations in which the falsity in romantic visions is exposed and the character's attempt to play a romantic hero's role invites disaster. Both James and Conrad portray the romantic temperament as a source of both strength and weakness, but the two novelists are preoccupied by different romantic prototypes, and their methods of rendering the psychology of their romantic protagonists are different.

Nearly all Conrad's novels could be contrasted to James's to illustrate these statements. But one may well begin with *The Rescue*, the novel which Paul Wiley judges "the most representative, if not the most popular, of Conrad's novels."[3] Begun early in 1896 and set aside in February 1899 to be completed in 1919, *The Rescue* (originally titled "The Rescuer") embraces almost the whole of Conrad's career as a writer.[4] In their studies of the manuscript and the completed novel, Thomas Moser and Bruce Johnson note that Lingard, presented in the 1896–1899 manuscript as a romantic egoist like Kurtz and Jim, emerges in the completed novel with qualities of the later protagonists, notably Heyst.[5]

To Conrad *The Rescue* also exemplified his practice of transforming a conventional romantic plot by making the feelings of the characters the focus of the narrative. Summarizing the action of the novel in a letter to William Blackwood, Conrad noted that the originality of the novel would lie not in the situation but in the treatment: "Of course the paraphernalia of the story are hackneyed. The yacht, the shipwreck, the pirates, the coast—all this has been used times out of number. . . . I think rightly or wrongly I can present it in a fresh way."[6] Conrad made essentially the same point years later in explaining to Pinker why a summary of the plot requested by *Cosmopolitan Magazine* would be useless: "Any sort of synopsis of events . . . would be of no help because the interest of that romance is all in the shades of the psychology of the people engaged. . . . Any tragedy there is in [the] 'denouement' will be all in the man's feelings; and whatever value there may be in that, must depend on the success of the romantic presentation."[7] Finally Conrad claimed for *The Rescue* the position of a culminating point in the development of a genre: "Novels of adventure will . . . be always written; but it may well be that 'Rescue' in its concentrated colouring and tone will remain the swan song of Romance as a form of literary art."[8]

If *The American* is judged the most romantic of James's novels, *The Rescue* may be said to hold a similar place in Conrad's work. Although *The American* is not, like *The Rescue*, a novel of passion, and *The Rescue* has none of the comedy of manners that distinguishes *The American*, the novels are alike in that both dramatize the abortive relation between a man of simple unstudied impulses and a woman of a sophisticated culture foreign to him. Like Newman the representative American who fills out "the national mould with an almost ideal completeness" (2:2), Lingard is introduced as an ideal figure of almost legendary strength, like his prototype Rajah James Brooke, "a true adventurer in his devotion to his impulse" (17:4).[9] Like Newman, Lingard undertakes to rescue the woman who has charmed him, although Lingard's chivalry to a greater extent than Newman's is grounded in egoistic confidence in the power of the will. Until Travers's stranded yacht threatens his plan to restore the exiled Malay prince Hassim and his sister Immada to their kingdom, and the presence of Edith Travers destroys his equilibrium, his world to his eyes lies "open in the sun to the conquering tread of an unfettered will" (17:210).

The vital difference between the two characters is that Newman's story culminates in victory over base impulses and futile longing, Lingard's in degeneration and defeat. Although Newman fails to win Madame de Cintré, he emerges from his ordeal unconquered: "One's last view of him would be that of a strong man indifferent to his strength" (2:vii). One's last view of Lingard is of a once-strong man sapped of power, who has not only failed to save his Malay friends but has lost even the will to act for them. Whereas James insists upon Newman's status as the victim of others' treachery, Conrad locates the source of conflict in *The Rescue* within the protagonist. Although the acts of other characters precipitate the disaster, the ultimate cause is Lingard's infatuation, which throughout the novel renders him, in Mrs. Travers's presence, bemused or stupefied when crises arise. Lingard himself perceives as much when he locates "the real cause of the disaster" within himself, "somewhere in the unexplained depths of his nature, something fatal and unavoidable" (17:329).

Whether or not Lingard is to be seen as the helpless victim of a fatal power depends on the way one sees Edith Travers, the chief agent in the destruction of Lingard. Like Lingard she is meant to be a representative figure: her statuesque beauty, her dazzling radiance and her power to induce in the man she charms indifference to everything but herself indicate that Conrad intended her to be an incarnation of the fatal woman, akin to Cleopatra, Salammbô, Delilah, or Helen of Troy (to whom Lingard's mate refers). Mrs. Travers is not a witch or a goddess, however, who would relieve Lingard of any responsibility for his surrender. Although like Lingard she creates the impression of having come into the world complete, without past, Conrad gives her a personal history and attempts to make her a complex figure whose meeting with Lingard is as momentous for her as for him. One wonders if Conrad had Isabel Archer in mind when he analyzes the youthful idealism which led Edith to marriage with a man who values her beauty but is "permanently grieved by her disloyalty to his respectable ideals" (17:152). But the character of James's whom Mrs. Travers most nearly resembles is the Princess Casamassima, who is also portrayed in images of radiance and who seems unique in her perfection at the same time that she represents the corrupting power of a decadent society. When Mrs. Travers, observing the quarrel between Lingard and her husband, breaks out that "this is truth—this is anger—something real at last" (17:132) she reminds one of the princess demanding of the revolution, "Then it *is* real, it *is* solid?" (6:48).

There is an important difference between James's and Conrad's portraits of the world-weary disillusioned woman of modern society—apart from the fact that the princess is one of James's memorable figures, Edith Travers one of Conrad's least effective. With her thirst for new sensations, the princess actively seeks "reality," in which pent-up ardor can be released. The salient trait of Edith Travers, on the other hand, is her detachment, her persistent habit of seeing the world as an artistic spectacle, herself as a figure in a work of art, a woman in a ballad or an actor "on a splendid stage in a scene from an opera, in a gorgeous show" (17:300).

The character Edith Travers most resembles is not one of James's heroines but Conrad's Felicia Moorsom ("The Planter of Malata"), another woman with a statuesque head, hair like a helmet, bred in a decadent society, and sexually inviolate.[10]

Lingard defines his mental state as "a conflict within himself" (17:329), and it is true that the two tasks he undertakes—to restore his Malay friends to their kingdom and to safeguard the lives of Edith Travers and her party—impose irreconcilable claims upon him. But there is little sense of inner struggle in Conrad's picture of Lingard, little sense of the "stress and exaltation" Conrad declared that he wanted to convey.[11] Not inner conflict or recklessness but an enervating sense of powerlessness and indifference is the principal effect of the fatal woman upon the hero. Although he is said to be "drunk with the deep draught of oblivion he had conquered for himself" he exhibits little of the passion of Tristan and other partakers of the enchanted potion. What infuses his "tense feeling of existence far superior to the mere consciousness of life" is not the burning ardor of a lover but the overwhelming desire for surrender—"the dreadful ease of slack limbs in the sweep of an enormous tide and in a divine emptiness of mind" (17:431, 432).

Such a state is of course very far from the resolution and self-possession of Newman at the end of *The American*, and indeed it is alien to all the protagonists whose minds James portrays. Even when James's protagonists succumb to visions of emptiness and peace and surrender, as do Isabel Archer, Strether, and George Dane ("The Great Good Place") the vision is temporary and succeeds to a return to the world of responsibility and struggle. Whereas certain of Conrad's characters, like Lingard, Jim, and Heyst may feel their mental faculties paralyzed in a crisis, James's characters while living a life devoid of perilous adventure engage in ardent mental acts. With Isabel, for instance, "suffering . . . was an active condition; it was not a chill, a stupor, a despair; it was a passion of thought, of speculation, of response to every pressure" (4:189). Passion of this kind makes the representation of Isabel "motionlessly seeing" a scene of intense activity. Without portraying directly the flow of Isabel's consciousness, James creates the illusion that her mind is the organizing force of the passage, that the growing momentum of the scene is sustained by the power of her thoughts.

As a number of readers have observed, Conrad rarely pictures the movements of his characters' minds as James does, preferring instead to symbolize inward states through depiction of objects, actions, and landscapes. *The Rescue* suggests one reason for Conrad's method: states of feeling in which the rational faculties are in abeyance are fittingly represented by natural forces which correspond to the emotions the character is powerless to control. The configuration of the Shore of Refuge with its creeks into which "the wreckage of many defeats unerringly drifts" and where islets "merge into a background that presents not a single landmark to point the way through the intricate channels" (17:63) is the visible counterpart of the mental world in which Lingard will lose himself. Lingard watches the eternal repulsion of waves and rocks as "he would have watched something going on within himself" (17:245). The impenetrable blackness of the night is the visible extension of the "mysterious obscurity that had descended upon [Lingard's] fortunes so that his eyes could no longer see the work of his hands" (17:202). Repeated images of immobility—the stranded yacht, the stagnant lagoon, and Lingard's brig, "a hopeless captive of the calm" (17:5)—correspond to the sense of paralysis both Lingard and Edith Travers experience. Images of sunsets and of sparks fading out in darkness portend Lingard's fall. The last vestige of the sun, a "red spark floating on the water," is an obvious symbol of Lingard, whose eyes "as if glowing with the light of a hidden fire, had a red glint in their greyness" (17:9–10).

Sunsets painted with the most splendid hues of romance—gold and crimson and "a trail of purple, like a smear of blood on a blue shield" (17:146)—presage a magnificent passage, through the "portals of the glorious death" to which the light, "dazzling and terrible," seems to lead (17:14). But the end Conrad envisages in later parts of the novel is not glory but annihilation. Darkness descends "like a destroying flood" (17:241). The ship with all Lingard's stores explodes "as if the life of the sun had been blown out of it in a crash" (17:447). Mrs. Travers's last view of Lingard, when in the distance his isolated figure appears immense, "the shape of a giant

outlined amongst the constellations," and then shrinks "to common
proportions" (17:463), reminds one of Leatherstocking's first appearance in *The Prairie*.[12] But there is no apotheosis of Lingard;
instead he awakens from his enchantment into a world cold and
barren. The empty sandbank where he stands with Mrs. Travers
and declares that "now the world is dead" (17:463) might suggest
the blank wall of the convent before which Newman stands. But for
Lingard there is no sense of satisfaction, no sense of a goal reached;
he knows not "release from ineffectual desire" which Newman is
granted (2:533), but the extinction of all vital feeling.

The scene on the sandbank is the daylight counterpart of Mrs.
Travers's dream, in which Lingard, like a crusader in chain-mail
armor, surrounded by a horde of barbarians, disappears in the
"flurry of a ghastly sand-storm" (17:458). As Paul Wiley observes,
the dream seems to symbolize not only the fall of Lingard but the
ending of a whole tradition of romantic chivalry.[13] But in various
ways in *The Rescue* Conrad not only implies that the light of
chivalry, of knight-errantry, has gone out of the world; he seems to
question the worth of the ideal, at least as Lingard embodies it.
D'Alcacer's identification of Lingard as a "descendant of the im-
mortal hidalgo errant upon the sea" (17:142) not only reflects the
irony which tinges nearly every statement of that speaker but also
associates with Lingard the ambiguity that attaches to Don Quixote, the victim of absurd illusions who in trying to live as a knight
of romance exposes the true baseness of the world and the hypocrisy of those who profess chivalric ideals. Even more telling is the
fact that the impression of Lingard as a noble man of "heroic quality" (17:162) is conveyed chiefly through the thoughts of Edith
Travers, who, as Bruce Johnson observes, romanticizes the primitive and untrammelled, idealizing the life of unrepressed passion
which she cannot and does not want to experience.[14] Her view of
Lingard reflects not only the power of the man but the desire gen-
erated by her sterile existence in a decadent society: "He had a
large simplicity that filled one's vision. She found herself slowly
invaded by this masterful figure. . . . The glamour of a lawless life
stretched over him like the sky over the sea down on all sides to an
unbroken horizon. Within, he moved very lonely, dangerous and

romantic. There was in him crime, sacrifice, tenderness, devotion, and the madness of a fixed idea" (17:215).

Undoubtedly Conrad too felt the charm in such a vision, but his affirmation of the value of the life "lonely, dangerous and romantic" is undercut by irony of a kind rare in James's novels. Both James and Conrad perceive their romantic protagonists on their weak or vulnerable sides but James protects his central characters against a purely skeptical view. Of Isabel Archer he observes: "She would be an easy victim of scientific criticism if she were not intended to awaken on the reader's part an impulse more tender and purely expectant" (3:69). How different is the tone when Conrad defines the romanticism of Lingard. Here the irony strikes to the root of the conception: "No doubt he, like most of us, would be uplifted at times by the awakened lyrism of his heart into regions charming, empty, and dangerous. But also, like most of us, he was unaware of his barren journeys above the interesting cares of this earth. Yet from these, no doubt absurd and wasted moments, there remained on the man's daily life a tinge as that of a glowing and serene half-light" (17:11).

The passage suggests that Conrad mistrusted the heart's lyrism because he felt its attractiveness only too keenly. Irony, which here struggles with sentimentality, seems to be a check on the impulses of the novelist's own nature. In any case James and Conrad not only create different kinds of romantic personalities; judging by *The American*, *The Portrait of a Lady*, and *The Rescue* Conrad is more equivocal than James in judging the ideals and impulses and goals of romantic protagonists. The differences between the two novelists are further illustrated when we turn to *Lord Jim*, the novel Conrad abandoned *The Rescue* to write, in which he placed at the very center the problem of how to judge romantic illusions and dreams.

II

As Conrad's fullest study of the romantic temperament *Lord Jim* occupies a place similar to that of *The Portrait of a Lady* in James's work. The two romantic protagonists, Jim and Isabel, have in common their egoism, their sense of superiority to others, their power to engage the interest of other characters, and their indulgence in self-glorifying fantasy. Like Isabel's, Jim's dreams of self and his ideas of the world have been shaped by romantic fiction: "After a course of light holiday literature his vocation for the sea had declared itself" (4:5). Neither character questions the truth of the picture of life the romances present;[15] at the beginning both characters assume that the world is governed by the providence that in books guarantees poetic justice and assures the fulfillment of romantic dreams. The settings of the novels initially seem to justify such faith; unlike the mean provincial society that imprisons Madame Bovary, Gardencourt, the Florentine villas, the ships on which Jim serves, and the isolated state of Patusan seem to be worlds in which, if anywhere, romantic visions can be realized.

The ideals that Isabel and Jim embrace are in themselves admirable, but they are expressed in different terms. Isabel's ideals appear to exist primarily as concepts: "She spent half her time in thinking of beauty and bravery and magnanimity" (3:68); Jim in his fantasy life engages in heroic actions:

He saw himself saving people from sinking ships, cutting away masts in a hurricane, swimming through a surf with a line; or as a lonely castaway, barefooted and half naked, walking on uncovered reefs in search of shellfish to stave off starvation. He confronted savages on tropical shores, quelled mutinies on the high seas, and in a small boat upon the ocean kept up the hearts of despairing men—always an example of devotion to duty, and as unflinching as a hero in a book. (4:6)

Because Jim seems to have a more precise idea of his desired destiny than Isabel has of hers, one might think that Jim is the more active character, better able to convert dreams into deeds. What Jim most profoundly desires, however, is not a life of action, such as Marlow in "Youth" embraces enthusiastically, but a world of ease and unthreatened serenity in which he can dream of heroic feats. In contrast Isabel's professed goal, "the free exploration of life" (3:155), implies the desire not simply to dream of action but to

act out her destiny in the world that surrounds her. Instead of indulging in a fantasy life of action, she regards new situations with
pleased expectation, wondering what possibilities for self-
development each experience holds for her. Jim, on the other
hand, not only does not seek opportunities for heroic action but is
rendered incapable of action by his indulgence in daydreams of
heroism. The enervating effect of such dreaming is twice
dramatized—when on the training ship Jim emerges from his fantasy world to find himself confounded by the realities of storm and
wind; and later, on the *Patna*, when a different set of circumstances
—ominous calm, a disabled ship, and eight hundred pilgrims seemingly doomed—finds Jim again unprepared.

Both fatal errors—Isabel's marriage to Osmond and Jim's jump
from the *Patna*—are irrevocable deeds which narrow the characters' field of action by permanently closing to them certain courses
they might have taken. The psychological consequences of their
acts are even more constricting. For both the fate is a fall to the
depths and an imprisonment: Jim's, a jump into "an everlasting
deep hole" (4:112); Isabel's, a journey "downward and earthward"
(4:189) to the prison house of darkness.

The ultimate consequences of their disastrous acts, however, are
in certain ways completely different. Although readers have argued
whether Isabel's marriage marks the end or the beginning of her
moral development, it is incontestable that she gains in knowledge;
her eyes are opened: she sees herself and Madame Merle and Osmond more clearly at the end of the novel than she does before her
marriage. In contrast Jim undergoes no process of enlightenment;
his dreams and his view of himself and of other people do not fundamentally change. Whereas Isabel comes to recognize certain of
her romantic ideas as false, Jim's romantic vision of himself is not
an idea he can judge true or false but a necessity of his nature. As
Marlow perceives, the *Patna* disgrace has not impaired Jim's power
to plunge deep into the "impossible world of romantic achievements" (4:83). But in one important respect Jim is different after
his desertion of the *Patna*. Reverie alone can no longer sustain him.
Failure which he cannot successfully rationalize compels him now

to act, if he is to continue to dream; and he embraces the chance to work as Stein's agent in Patusan with enthusiastic readiness such as he has never shown.

In one way Stein, the merchant, collector, connoisseur, and one-time adventurer who gives Jim his "chance to get it all back again" (4:179), plays a part similar to that of Ralph Touchett in *The Portrait*. Although Stein does not, like Ralph, seek his own fulfillment in watching the life of another—in fact Stein has already lived through experiences similar to those that await Jim in Patusan—he does enable the protagonist to enter into a new situation, which determines his ultimate fate. As Ralph by making Isabel an heiress effects Osmond's entrance into the novel, so Stein, in providing Jim "a totally new set of conditions for his imaginative faculty to work upon" (4:218), performs the act necessary to bring Jim to his most decisive test, his confrontation with Gentleman Brown. Whereas Ralph Touchett clearly exposes the falsity of Isabel's romantic idea of Osmond, however, Stein seems to affirm the worth of Jim's romantic dream. In his oracular utterances—that one must "in the destructive element immerse," and "follow the dream . . . *usque ad finem*" (4:214–215), Stein counsels not rejection of one's dream of perfection but submission to it in the search for the conditions in which it can be realized. Both the meaning and the value of Stein's words have been subjects of debate, but the words, placed as they are at the pivotal center of the novel, seem to sanction the continuation of Jim's struggle to realize his ideal of self; at the very least they dispose the reader to suspend judgment until Jim has met the test of a second chance in Patusan.

In Patusan, Conrad created a world which at first seems like a hermetic chamber sealed off from the outside. To Jim his friends Doramin and Dain Waris are "like people in a book"; to Marlow, Patusan is not merely an isolated place but a timeless realm like the world of the Grecian urn. "It remains in the memory motionless, unfaded, with its life arrested, in an unchanging light" (4:260, 330). Until the renegade Gentleman Brown threatens the order Jim has created in Patusan and subjects Jim himself to revolting insinuations of their hidden kinship, Jim's life in Patusan seems the fulfillment of every dream and the restoration of every loss. The defendant in the court of inquiry becomes the dispenser of justice; the outcast son of one father is welcomed as the son of another and "received . . . into the heart of the community" (4:258). In his own lifetime Jim becomes like the hero of an epic poem, a figure of legend, who arrives in Patusan like a "stranger-god," enjoys "heroic health," is credited with supernatural powers, and performs deeds which are "fit materials for a heroic tale" and are glorified in the "Jim-myth" (4:244, 226, 280).

No act in Conrad's fiction has provoked more debate than Jim's disastrous decision to spare Brown's life and give him "a clear road" (4:388) to safety. Whereas the triumphant end of "The Secret Sharer" seems to affirm the moral rightness of the captain's determination to give Leggatt "a clear road" (13:136), the destruction and death which follow upon Jim's decision call into question the motives and wisdom of his act. Several critics have defended it as a magnanimous Christian gesture, demanded by his code of honor, which by tragic irony of fate results in destruction and death. To others Jim's decision is evidence of crippling egoism which clouds his perception and compels him to judge Brown as he wants to judge himself, a victim of circumstances who must be given a second chance.

The ambiguity of Jim's act, which critics have persuasively interpreted in opposite ways, in itself distinguishes Conrad's treatment from the treatment of comparable situations in the romances of Hugo and Scott. At the end of *Ninety-Three*, for instance, the leader of the revolutionary forces, Gauvain, faces, like Jim, the choice of saving or destroying his enemy, who if spared will certainly continue the struggle and cause the deaths of more people. The irreconcilable claims of mercy and justice rend the hero: "His entire being was vacillating within him,"[16] and as Stevenson observed, the central question posed by the novel—"Can a good action be a bad action? Does not he who spares the wolf kill the sheep?"—is never conclusively answered.[17] But the ambiguity attaches only to the question, not to the motives of the hero. His noble impulses are untainted by self-regard, and no compulsion born of guilt obscures the central conflict, of which his mind is simply the battleground.

Unlike Hugo, Conrad does not portray his protagonist's thoughts as he wrestles with his impossible choice, and the fact that Jim remains opaque permits different interpretations of an act which, according to Marlow's analysis, Jim makes in the bitter consciousness of his past failure. Furthermore Gauvain, when he takes the place of his enemy in prison, acts with full knowledge of results; but Jim fails to foresee the consequences of his decision and is utterly confounded by them. Finally Gauvain's acts are approved by his soldiers, who as one man worship him as a martyr at his sacrificial death. In contrast to this hero of romance who embodies the ideals of his people, Jim exists in Patusan even before the catastrophe in "total and utter isolation." As Marlow several times emphasizes, Jim's devotion to the people of Patusan is rooted not in shared ideas but in his continuing need of their love and trust by which his faith in himself is sustained. Dependent upon their worship of him, he loves them "with a sort of fierce egoism, with a contemptuous tenderness" (4:272, 248).

Like his decision to let Brown escape, Jim's surrender of himself to Doramin has been seen both as noble idealism and as selfish folly. Comparison with *Ninety-Three* is again revealing. The contrived and simplified world of romance is nowhere more evident than at the end of Hugo's novel, when Gauvain, with the "heroic expression . . . of an archangel,"[18] achieves a glorious death which causes no devastation, no blasted lives, no collapse of the social order, a death which seems to be blessed by nature itself. If Jim at the end sees the "alluring shape" of success undreamed of in "the wildest days of his boyish vision," if in his last moments he "beheld the face of that opportunity, which, like an Eastern bride, had come veiled to his side," Conrad makes it clear that Jim has pursued his romantic dreams not in the world of romance but in the world of reality where blighted lives, the death of friends, and the ruin of a community may be the issue of a "pitiless wedding with a shadowy ideal of conduct" (4:416). Conrad's attitude toward Jim's sacrificial death may be inferred from his expressed conviction that "a man's duties are wide and complex; the balance should be held very even lest some evil should be done when nothing but good is contemplated."[19]

By inviting the reader to compare Jim with the unflawed heroes of romance, the novel moves him to ask whether Conrad's purpose was to expose the weakness inherent in Jim's character and in his idealism or to expose the falsity of romances which ignore the complexities of existence and exalt ideals unrealizable in the actual world. In so far as the novel shows "light holiday literature" responsible for encouraging in Jim false views of himself and the world, the novel is a criticism of such literature. But Conrad's primary purpose seems neither the criticism of a certain kind of fiction nor the expression of a particular attitude toward Jim. It is not easy to state the main theme or subject of the novel, but certainly one of Conrad's principal concerns is to analyze the sources of Jim's compelling interest to other characters. And for Marlow, who sees Jim as "one of us," a symbolic universal figure who stands for the "parentage of his race," analysis of Jim is a form of self-discovery. In asking questions about Jim, Marlow asks questions about human nature and about himself; his attitude toward Jim, who is above all romantic, indicates his judgment of all romantic dreams which men attempt to realize in a world where uncontrollable forces manifest themselves unceasingly, in the workings of chance, in natural perils, and in human emotions and actions.

Of all the characters in *Lord Jim* Marlow comes closest to expressing Conrad's ambivalence toward Jim. Marlow is at once sympathetic to Jim's dream of self and critical of his attitude and his actions. He is keenly sensitive to the idealism that separates Jim from Chester, Brown, and the *Patna* crew; he also realizes that Jim's romantic dreams which save him from degeneration render him forever incapable of "the perfect love of the work" (4:10). Marlow feels himself separated from Jim as he feels himself separated from his younger self in "Youth." But Marlow's very fear of betraying complicity in Jim's effort to rationalize his failure suggests that the romantic impulse is still strong within Marlow. His readiness to embrace Jim's romantic view of himself is especially evident in his narration of Jim's success in Patusan, in his insistence on Jim's likeness to epic heroes, and in his picturesque view of Jim and Jewel as "knight and maiden meeting to exchange vows amongst haunted ruins" (4:312). But Marlow's romantic tendencies are curbed by irony and skepticism. The incantatory power of Stein's words, enigmatic as Keats's "beauty is truth, truth beauty," does not obliterate Marlow's sense of life as a blind journey through a wasteland of error and death: "The great plain on which men wander amongst graves and pitfalls remained very desolate under the impalpable poesy of its crepuscular light, overshadowed in the centre, circled with a bright edge as if surrounded by an abyss full of flames" (4:215).

We see that Marlow's reluctance to accept Stein's words as the ultimate truth does not prevent Marlow from indulging in a different kind of romanticism, what G. S. Fraser has called "the romantic glamour of a kind of high pessimism, the romanticism of fate and destiny."[20] But Marlow's talk of "dark powers" and his vision of pain and death in a sublime landscape of flames and chasms do not destroy his sober regard for discipline and for "the hard facts of existence." In other words Marlow is neither in complete contrast to Jim nor a replica of him. His sympathetic response to Jim is always informed by awareness of Jim's weakness and by recognition of values above and beyond the ideals of the romantic individualist. Skepticism, however, does not preclude Marlow's readiness to exalt Jim in his success, to cast over Jim's story the "impalpable poesy" (4:215) of his (Marlow's) own kind of romanticism, and to imply that when Jim dies, man's last hope of realizing in life his dreams of perfection passes out of the world.

III

There is perhaps no single quality or attitude that links all the romantic protagonists of James and Conrad. But in most of them a strong sense of personal value and importance combines with confidence in their power to pursue their chosen course. Nearly all are committed to ideals of personal fulfillment, and they either see themselves as actors of romantic parts—the knightly rescuer, the persecuted victim, the earthly providence—or they see other characters in terms of romantic prototypes. While James's protagonists undergo a process of education and enlightenment during which romantic illusions are cast off or are modified by experience, most of Conrad's characters either struggle to the end to realize their romantic dreams, as do Jim and the Marlow of "Youth," or they degenerate under the pressure of outward circumstance and inward weakness as do Lingard and Kurtz. In only one novel, *Chance*, is it conclusively demonstrated to the protagonist that his perception of a situation is false.

The character who is thus enlightened, Roderick Anthony, goes farthest of all Conrad's romantic protagonists in attempting to live according to a romantic ideal. Moved by a sudden overpowering impulse similar to that which commits Lingard to Hassim and Immada, Anthony binds himself to Flora de Barral, the outcast daughter of a convict and "the most forlorn damsel of modern times" (13:238); marries her and takes her aboard his ship, where as captain he will presumably be master of their destinies. Pity, tenderness, and vanity, which drew him to the woman whose very life he has saved, compel him after the marriage to question the depth of Flora's feeling for him, to imagine that her desperate plight alone forced her into marriage, and to resolve that the marriage shall not be consummated. The spectacle of the lover who, convinced that he is not loved, represses his passion for his wife and so convinces her that *her* love is spurned is both tragic and comic in its implications. The suffering of Anthony and Flora, arising as it does from misunderstanding which at any moment could be ended, calls for the corrective power of comedy to expose error and restore health.

Although several characters sense the perversity of Anthony's course, the office of exposing folly belongs primarily to the main narrator Marlow. He is different from Marlow in *Lord Jim* in that he exhibits no uncertainty in his analysis of Anthony's motives and in his judgment of Anthony's conduct. Anthony's brand of heroism, that which "wears the aspect of sublime delicacy," Marlow pronounces not only "idiotic" but unnatural, a "transgression against nature" which exacts its price in suffering and in the wasting of vital energies. "The pain of his magnanimity . . . like all abnormal growths was gnawing at his healthy substance with cruel persistence." Anthony's error is twofold: he is deceived into believing that Flora does not love him, and he fails to recognize the power of erotic love until he becomes the "chafing captive" of a passion "profound, tyrannical and mortal" (13:328, 351, 416, 397).

Marlow not only pronounces on Anthony's psychological state; he unhesitatingly traces Anthony's motives to their origin, in the temperament and art of his father, "a delicate erotic poet of a markedly refined and autocratic temperament." Presumably the poetry of Carleon Anthony, which spiritualizes the passions and exalts "the most hopeless conventions of the so-called, refined existence," sanctions precisely the kind of perverse sacrifice that Roderick Anthony insists upon making. Marlow repeatedly insists upon the resemblances between father and son, explaining Roderick Anthony's conduct as his effort to embody in his life the "supremely refined delicacy" (13:309, 193, 332) of chivalrous love celebrated in his father's poetry. The fact that the refined poet was a domestic tyrant indicates that idealism and cruelty may spring from one root. The painful consequences of the poet's despotic acts, which worried his two wives into their graves and drove both son and daughter from home, portend the suffering to issue from Roderick Anthony's noble intentions.

The emphasis that Conrad places upon Carleon Anthony has led several critics to see *Chance* as a criticism of Victorian society, particularly its literary ideals of love and chivalry. Describing Carleon Anthony as a "composite Tennyson, Arnold, and Meredith," J. W. Johnson argues that in *Chance* Conrad deliberately parodies such Victorian novels as *Vanity Fair* and *The Ordeal of Richard Feverel* in order to expose the defects of Victorian culture.[21] Certainly in *Chance* Conrad makes his most explicit attack upon literary ideals which he sees as false and pernicious, but *Chance* is a strange mixture. If it contains Conrad's sharpest criticism of the conventions and sentiments of romantic chivalry, it is also the novel of Conrad which goes farthest in making the kind of idealizations it seems to reject. Anthony, who of all Conrad's characters most conclusively demonstrates the destructive effects of chivalric ideals, is at the same time the character who most nearly resembles the flawless heroes of chivalry like Gauvain. Anthony is guilty of the most egregious folly, but he seems immune from the corruption that infects

Lingard and Willems and Nostromo. He suffers but he does not degenerate, and his struggle for self-control augments the impression of his strength. With his strong haggard face and his "personal fascination" that never fails, he exerts a romantic charm that betrays even the sardonic and cynical Marlow into sentimental expressions of regard.[22]

Seeing Flora and Anthony as figures like Adam and Eve, "outside all conventions" (13:210), Marlow presents them as archetypal characters whose representative function is further emphasized by the titles of the two parts of the novel, "Maiden" and "Knight." To the narration of the archetypal love story Marlow brings a keen eye for the egoism that lurks in noble sentiments. But he does not tell the story of Flora and Anthony simply to display his irony in exposing the folly of Anthony's morbid chivalry. In the manuscript of the novel Conrad allows Marlow to declare himself "interested in the whole thing with its touches of romance and its possibility of being an idyll."[23] This statement and the passage following, also excised, suggest something of Conrad's intention. Reflecting on the nature of an idyll, Marlow commends its "mental serenity," and "a certain primitive fineness . . . unlike our modern notion of refinement which so often is but the grossest materialism turned inside out."[24] Through Marlow's analysis of Flora and Anthony's relationship, Conrad exposes an overrefined society's corruption of the chivalric ideal; Anthony's recognition of his error purifies the ideal of the infection, and triumph is celebrated by the time-honored happy ending that the world of romance permits. Marlow implies that young Powell suffers under an illusion in seeing the captain of a ship as "the prince of a fairy-tale," but the novel confirms Powell's romantic view of Flora's and Anthony's destiny. Anthony is rewarded not only by happiness in love but by a heroic death at sea; Flora by love which transformed "all the world, all life" (13:288, 444) and in the pages which Conrad added to the manuscript to make a "nicer" ending, by promise of marriage to her faithful suitor, Powell.[25]

Not only did Conrad rest on *Chance* his hopes of a popular success ("it is—as much as it lies with me—my bid for popularity"[26]), but he also wished to attain in this novel the highest artistic standard: "Rightly or wrongly, I ascribe a great importance to this novel and want to make it as perfect as possible from the literary point of view."[27] Conrad described *Chance* as "the biggest piece of work I've done since Lord Jim,"[28] and although few readers are likely to judge *Chance* the better of the two novels, it does tap some of *Lord Jim*'s sources of interest and appeal. In *Chance* Marlow does not so much probe and question as he constructs and fits together evidence, but the process affords the reader pleasure, even though it does not move him to ask the great unanswered questions about human destiny. *Chance* does not create between Marlow and Anthony the dynamic bond compounded of loyalty, affection, and self-doubt that makes the relation of Marlow and Jim so interesting, but the action aboard the *Ferndale* is more engrossing than the account of Jim's success in Patusan. And for readers who prefer that the narrator elucidate the truths his story reveals rather than declare the impossibility of affirming anything, Marlow's declaration of the power of passion—the most explicit defense of romantic love in Conrad's fiction—is no doubt satisfying:

Pairing off is the fate of mankind. And if two beings thrown together, mutually attracted, resist the necessity, fail in understanding and voluntarily stop short of the—the embrace, in the noblest meaning of the word, then they are committing a sin against life, the call of which is simple. Perhaps sacred. And the punishment of it is an invasion of complexity, a tormenting, forcibly tortuous involution of feelings, the deepest form of suffering from which indeed something significant may come at last, which may be criminal or heroic, may be madness or wisdom—or even a straight if despairing decision. (13:426–427)

Neither James nor Conrad would have rejected this statement but it hardly expresses the governing idea of their novels. It is true that neither writer pictures perverse sexual relationships as pleasurable; nor does either writer exploit the sensational aspects of abnormal sexuality. Olive's friendship with Verena in *The Bostonians* and Mr. Jones's abhorrence of women in *Victory* are about as far as James and Conrad overtly go in the depiction of the sexually morbid. But both novelists in almost every novel portray characters who either stop short of fulfillment or are destroyed by passion. For every character of James's who is united happily with the person that he loves (and most of these appear in the minor tales) there are more who profess love and are thwarted or betrayed (Roderick Hudson, Christopher Newman, Catherine Sloper, Isabel Archer, Milly Theale); sacrifice love and marriage to honor a principle of conduct (Fleda Vetch, Owen Wingrave); withhold themselves out of fear or pride (Marcher, Strether); or find their true romance in devotion to memory of the dead (Stransom, Marmaduke, and Merton Densher). *The Golden Bowl* seems to be an important exception, but Maggie endures anguish almost to the end, and the great act of her life seems to be not to love the prince but to devise and carry out the plan to save her marriage.

That James viewed sexual passion as destructive of the artist's powers is evident in *Roderick Hudson*, and it is strongly implied in *The Tragic Muse* and "The Lesson of the Master," in which the true artists forego romance to live for their art. In "The Middle Years," "The Death of the Lion," "The Figure in the Carpet," and "The Great Good Place" the successful artist has, instead of a wife or mistress, a young man who is his disciple. Roderick Hudson is the only character of James's ruined by passion, but other characters, such as May Server (*The Sacred Fount*), May Bartram (*The Beast in the Jungle*) and Madame de Vionnet, illustrate James's view of sexual love as a relationship in which one person drains the vital strength of the other. To James the vampire and the victim of the Gothic tales provided a compelling metaphor for the erotic relationship, inspiring not only the lurid action of "DeGray: A Romance" but also the symbolism of drinking and depletion in *The Sacred Fount*.[29]

Like James, Conrad portrays sexual passion as a destructive force, but while James pictures a dynamic relationship in which one person gains at the expense of the other, Conrad portrays relationships, like those of Lingard and Edith Travers, Willems and Aissa, Felicia Moorsom and Renouard, in which the man degenerates or wastes himself in passion, while the woman remains essentially unchanged, if not sexually inviolate. The fear of sexual passion has been observed in a number of James's and Conrad's characters. James's protagonists, like Isabel, Strether, and Rowland fear the capacities of their own natures; Conrad's characters generally fear the effects of the other person's power. Willems, Lingard (*The Rescue*), and Dain Maroola (*Almayer's Folly*) feel themselves depleted or menaced in the presence of the woman, who seems either a passionate temptress or a marblelike statue.[30] The man fares best when the woman he loves is a victim to be rescued and protected: Anthony, Heyst, Monsieur George, and Réal (*The Rover*) would seem to affirm the possibility of happiness and fulfillment, but Heyst's escape from his sterile detachment is only temporary and perhaps never complete; the very happiness of M. George and Rita seems to preclude the enduring of their relation beyond a few months; Réal's love of Arlette is overshadowed by Peyrol's sacrifice, upon which the epigraph, the words of Spenser's Despair, casts a somber light. Like *The Golden Bowl*, *Chance* portrays a relationship in which both characters are granted the best happiness their worlds can offer them; but even in these two novels reconciliation comes late, and the overriding theme of each novel is not the fulfillment, but the frustration, of desire.

It is clear then that one of the defining elements of romance is all but absent from James's and Conrad's novels: the fruitful, fulfilling love of man and woman, the resolution achieved in romances as different in form and mode as *The Faerie Queene*, *The Tempest*, and the novels of Ann Radcliffe. Nor does either James or Conrad portray lovers who fulfill their passion and achieve ultimate happiness in death, as is evident if one compares Roderick Hudson and Christina Light, Lena and Heyst, or Willems and Aissa with, say, Wagner's Tristan and Isolde. Nevertheless, many of James's and Conrad's characters attempt to live according to the conventions of romance, and the worlds in which they act bear certain resemblances to the worlds of the romances.

Perhaps we may best place James's and Conrad's novels if we consider them in relation to the opposing poles of nineteenth-century fiction. At one pole we may group novels like *Pride and Prejudice*, *The Newcomes*, and *Barchester Towers*, in which the characters arc members of an established society of a particular place and time depicted with realistic detail; and they are defined chiefly through their manners and engage in action dominated by questions of property, money, and social class. At the other pole we may group romantic novels like *The Mysteries of Udolpho, Jane Eyre*, and *Wuthering Heights*, in which, according to Robert Kiely, psychological rather than social and moral issues are uppermost, and characters live in isolation from established society, engaged in the drama of "the private life which communal rules cannot touch."[31] If we imagine nineteenth-century fiction as a continuum stretching between these two poles, then we may place the novels of James and Conrad, like those of Dickens and Balzac, somewhere in the middle, closer than *Salammbô* or *The Master of Ballantrae* to the novels of social realism but within the shadow of the heightened dream-like worlds of Udolpho and Wuthering Heights. On the one hand Conrad's ships and islands and James's country houses are worlds unto themselves which to some extent isolate characters from the press of society that shapes the lives of Thackeray's or Trollope's characters. But within these worlds, the acts of characters have moral as well as psychological importance; codes of manners and standards of conduct, grounded in the society from which the characters may be physically separated, are everpresent realities by which the feelings and acts of characters are to be judged.

In their carefully composed pictures of Americans on the grand tour, reformers in Boston, men on shipboard, traders intriguing in the East Indies, and exploiters in the Congo, James's and Conrad's novels are social documents no less than *Père Goriot* or *Little Dorrit*; but even more clearly than these novels such works as *The American, The Portrait of a Lady, Heart of Darkness*, and *Nostromo* reveal the outlines of the archetypal plots of romance, the myths and fables of search, conflict, and redemption which lie on the surface of works like *The Faerie Queene, Parsifal*, and *The Tempest*.[32] We have already noted James's and Conrad's association of characters with figures of myth and legend, by which the reader is invited to compare the action of the novel with the ar-

chetypal pattern. In the fiction of both novelists, images of labyrinths, serpents, blood, treasure, gardens, fruit, and enchanted potions reinforce plots which suggest mythic patterns of the fall from
innocence, sacrifice, descent into the underworld, and combat
with evil. Isabel Archer, for example, in marrying Osmond goes
"downward and earthward" (4:189) to a kind of hell—the house of
darkness, dumbness, and suffocation, ruled over by Osmond,
whose egotism lies hidden "like a serpent in a bank of flowers"
(4:196). The patterns of myth are even more apparent in James's
tales of the supernatural, which Earl Miner has termed "metaphysical romances."[33] The governess in *The Turn of the Screw*, ready to
see Bly as "a castle of romance" and to wonder if there is "a mystery
of Udolpho or an insane, an unmentionable relative kept in sus-
pected confinement" (12:163, 179), sees in the apparition of Peter
Quint the very figure of the devil, from whom she rescues Miles (if
she does) only at the cost of his life. In the unfinished *The Sense of
the Past*, according to Northrop Frye, the hero in entering the
world of the past, descends into a "labyrinthine underworld" from
which he is rescued, like Theseus, by the sacrifice of the heroine.[34]

Like James, Conrad unites fact and myth, making mythic patterns and documented pictures of particular conditions reinforce
each other. Marlow's journey up the Congo River, during which he
compares Kurtz to "an enchanted princess sleeping in a fabulous
castle," is also a journey into a kind of hell, where people are
"shades," the river is an "infernal stream," and the company station
is like a "gloomy circle in some Inferno" (5:106, 160, 66).[35] In
Heart of Darkness Conrad has crossed well over the line that separates the romance from the tale of grotesque horror; but in *Nostromo*, in which the horror of torture and murder is to some extent
offset by elements of conventional romance in the loves of Decoud
and Antonia and of Nostromo and Giselle, the motifs of a fairy tale,
introduced in the first chapter, reinforce the plot to the end. The
silver of the mine is not only the chief resource of a South American
country, but it is like the treasure of a fairy tale, baleful yet precious, subjecting Charles Gould's father to dreams of vampires,
and making Gould "the goose with the golden eggs" (7:314). As
several critics have observed, the treasure becomes the object of a

quest which subjects the central characters to ordeals by which their moral nature is tested—and found wanting.[36]

The fate of the characters in *Nostromo* and the fate of Isabel in *The Portrait of a Lady* clearly reflect what is perhaps the most important difference between Conrad's and James's use of the conventions, themes, and character types of romance. In James's fictions which owe the most to the romance—such novels as *The American*, *The Portrait of a Lady*, *The Ambassadors*, *The Wings of the Dove* and *The Golden Bowl*—the romance hero's adventure is internalized; that is, the traditional hero's ordeal and triumph become a drama of enlightenment and moral growth. The journey is inward, appropriately expressed through metaphors of voyages, descents, passages through labyrinths, and penetration from the outside of a temple or shrine to its inmost center. In all the novels just named the romantic illusions of the characters collide with the realities of their world, but the collision does not corrupt or destroy the protagonist. If there is outward failure there is inward growth. If Newman at the convent on the rue d'Enfer cannot harrow the hell that has imprisoned Claire, he can at least save himself. Although the treachery of others destroys Milly Theale's will to live, her sacrificial death transfigures at least one other person. If James's characters like Isabel, Newman, Hyacinth, and Strether lose the treasure that takes the form of wealth and earthly happiness they gain, in James's words, "the rich treasure itself of consciousness."[37]

Conrad in his fiction retains much more of the paraphernalia of romance than James does—the perils and adventures, the voyages actual as well as figurative, the confrontation with monstrous, almost supernatural beings, like Brown who resembles "some man-beast of folklore" (4:372); or the evil trio in *Victory*, suggestive of the gods or demons of Polynesian myth (15:228). But James's novels follow the *pattern* of romance—the plot of search, struggle, suffering and redemption more closely than Conrad's novels do If James internalizes the romance plot, Conrad inverts it, leading his characters not to inward victory but to failure and degeneration. Conrad's protagonists like Nostromo, Decoud, Heyst, Kurtz, and Lingard engage in the physical combats and the perilous adventures by which the heroes of romance are tested, but they fail to win the rewards—either of the world or of the spirit—that mark the hero's successful emergence from his struggle with evil. Charles Gould in *Nostromo* is the victim, not the hero, of his "moral romance" (7:218), as are Decoud and Nostromo also the victims of the roles that they have cast for themselves. The silver of the mine, far from symbolizing fertility as do the treasure hoards of romance, corrupts or dehumanizes the characters who seek it; the outcome of their efforts is not fruitfulness or redemption but barrenness and defeat: the sterility of the Goulds' marriage, the corruption and death of Nostromo, the suicide of Decoud. *Victory*, too, as Robert Secor has demonstrated, can be read as a parody or an inversion of romance, in which the protagonist Heyst not only fails to defeat the villains but partakes of their impotence and deathliness, renounces wealth and power instead of gaining it, and at the end is saved by instead of saving the heroine.[38] In *Lord Jim* the protagonist enjoys temporary success, but Jim's distance from the romance hero is indicated not only by the suffering and destruction that attend his sacrificial death but also by the fact that his ideal of self forces him to deny the traditional role as the defender of his lady. Marlow's journey in *Heart of Darkness* perhaps comes closest to fulfilling the traditional pattern of the quest romance, for Marlow overcomes Kurtz in their physical struggle and returns from the underworld with the treasure of knowledge. But here, too, the forces of inversion are at work. The ordeal which Marlow undergoes vicariously is not the sacrificial death of a savior but the "extremity" of one who had "taken a high seat amongst the devils of the land" (5:116). At the end knowledge compels the enlightened Marlow to speak not truth but falsehood.

Both James and Conrad depart from the pattern of a romance like *Quentin Durward*, in which the brave and virtuous hero not only preserves his integrity in the midst of false and licentious men but also triumphs over his enemies in combat to win his noble lady. In most of his novels James deprives his central characters of earthly rewards, but he endows them with intelligence and imagination which sustain them in their ordeal and, in Conrad's words, preserve for them "the robe of spiritual honour." In most of Conrad's novels, on the other hand, romantic adventure culminates either in the inward defeat of the protagonist or in an act of self-destruction by which the protagonist attempts to expiate past failure or to vindicate an ideal of conduct, the value of which is never conclusively affirmed.

6

Satire

In nearly all the novels of James and Conrad the comic is part of the strange alloy that James discerned in human experience. Comedy and romance inform each other in *The American*, *The Portrait of a Lady*, *Lord Jim*, and *Chance*. In the fiction of both writers characters of romantic temper are satirized or are identified with comic or grotesque figures. None of James's or Conrad's novels is satirical in all parts; nor is the fantastic confounded with the real as in the grotesque fiction of Gogol or Kafka. Most of James's and Conrad's novels, however, present characters whose deviation from an approved standard exposes them to the satirist's wit or subjects them, or the person who observes them, to the unsettling experience of the grotesque. Although satire and the grotesque are closely related, much that James satirizes is not grotesque, and a number of grotesque characters and situations in Conrad's fiction are not satirized. James satirizes characters—whether grotesque or not—to expose folly and to correct error. Conrad's satire expresses little hope that reform can be achieved through the offices of comedy.

I

A convenient way to approach James's satire is to note the different types of characters who are mocked or ridiculed in the novels and tales. We have already considered one type, the soft-headed sentimentalists like Mrs. Penniman who persist in romantic fantasies that reality belies. A second type, well-intentioned and foolish, includes characters like Mr. Leavenworth (*Roderick Hudson*) and Mr. Babcock (*The American*), who while asserting their intellectual and moral superiority utter sonorous banalities that make them appear pompous and inflexible. A third group, adventurers like the Moreens ("The Pupil") and Selah Tarrant (*The Bostonians*), persist in outrageous hypocrisy, living by their wits as they try to establish themselves in genteel society. Another group of characters, best represented by Mrs. Ruck and Sophy ("The Pension Beaurepas") and Mona Brigstock (*The Spoils of Poynton*), are distinguished only by their energetic vulgarity and dull-witted callousness that make them fit targets of satire. Related to this group but more attractive, powerful, and dangerous, are the aggressive worldly women of society, egoists who manipulate others and are blind to the nature of their own acts and to the best interest of others. Several of these characters—notably Mrs. Gereth (*The Spoils of Poynton*), the Princess Casamassima, Maud Lowder (*The Wings of the Dove*), and Gussy Bradham (*The Ivory Tower*)—play leading roles in the novels. Other important characters such as Olive Chancellor and Mrs. Burrage (*The Bostonians*), Lady Agnes (*The Tragic Muse*), and Madame de Bellegarde (*The American*) resemble the type, as do the intelligent and restless women like Mrs. Tristram (*The American*) and Mrs. Assingham (*The Golden Bowl*), who out of curiosity or unsatisfied energy meddle in the affairs of others. One last type should be given a place: the voracious journalist whose sin is a disregard for the private lives of others, a character whom James draws with benevolence and good humor in the portrayal of Henrietta Stackpole and with distaste and contempt in the portrayal of Matthias Pardon (*The Bostonians*) and Mr. Flack (*The Reverberator*).

The reader will recognize in some of these figures traits and impulses of several Jamesian protagonists, such as Rowland Mallet, Isabel Archer, Fleda Vetch, and Lambert Strether. But James sharply distinguishes the characters like Fleda and Strether, whom he terms "free spirits," from his "fools," the chief butts of his satire, who "have their subordinate, comparative, illustrative human value" (5:xii) and who "minister, at a particular crisis, to the intensity of the free spirit engaged with them" (10:xv) but cannot in themselves express the full value of the novelist's subject. Some of James's fools, like Mr. Leavenworth and Mr. Babcock, are harmless; others have the power, if not always the opportunity, to injure others. Some of the figures satirized are no more than types; several, like Olive Chancellor and Adela Gereth, are complex figures who are satirized by the novelist but are able to satirize others, who are blind to their own natures but are capable of intense suffering. Despite the differences among the various figures, however, all are fixed in their attitudes, incapable of growth, unable to see life from different perspectives or enter into another's point of view. James's statement that Mrs. Gereth "really had no perception of anybody's nature" (10:138) applies to most of the figures that he satirizes. All are blind or indifferent to the impression they make and to the effect of their behavior on others. The satirist views them with a sense of superiority and detachment which prevents the reader's sympathies from becoming deeply engaged.

The function of "fools" in James's fiction is well defined in his first long novel, *Roderick Hudson*, which presents a number of characters, notably Mrs. Light, Mrs. Hudson, Mr. Leavenworth, Mr. Striker, and Roderick himself, whose blindness, selfishness or narrowness of view engage the satirist's wit. Some of the qualities of James's satire are evident in the portrait, revised for the New York Edition, of Mr. Leavenworth observing the progress of his statue "Intellectual Refinement," which he has commissioned of the sculptor Roderick Hudson.

As a liberal customer, Mr. Leavenworth used to drop into Roderick's studio to see how things were getting on and give a friendly hint or exert an enlightened control. He would seat himself squarely, plant his gold-topped cane between his legs, which he held very much apart, rest his large white hands on the head, and enunciate the principles of spiritual art—a species of fluid wisdom which appeared to rise in bucketfuls, as he turned the crank, from the well-like depths of his moral consciousness. His benignant and imperturbable pomposity gave Roderick the sense of suffocating beneath an immense feather-bed, and the worst of the matter was that the good gentleman's placid vanity had a surface from which the satiric shaft rebounded. Roderick admitted that in thinking over the tribulations of struggling genius the danger of dying of too much attention had never occurred to him. (1:269)

The passage is characteristic in that it does not sustain the satire on one note but shifts in tone from one sentence to the next. The gathering force of Mr. Leavenworth as he confidently imposes himself is suggested by the progression of verbs *drop into, see, give,* and *exert.* The glint of sarcasm in the phrase *enlightened control* indicates the disparity between the way Mr. Leavenworth sees himself and the way others see him. The ponderous self-importance of the man, pictured in the deliberate way that he arranges himself and his cane, asserts itself in the pompous "enunciates the principles of spiritual art." At once, however, Mr. Leavenworth is diminished by the faintly sneering "species of fluid wisdom," followed by the lumbering homeliness of "rise in bucketfuls." The connotations of "crank" cast their shadow over "the well-like depths of his moral consciousness." The sentence is a good example of James's gift for uniting the abstract (*wisdom*) and the concrete (*bucketfuls*). The effect is of an incongruous mingling of elements comparable to the effect of burlesque when the lofty and trivial are confounded. The phrase *benignant and imperturbable pomposity* in itself has a suffocating effect, while the movement from metaphoric statement to the comparison of Mr. Leavenworth to a featherbed prepares the way for the direct statement that the surface of the man resists the "satiric shaft."

In his 1884 essay on the illustrator and satirist George du Maurier, James distinguishes between a caricature, in which a salient feature is exaggerated, and a portrait, in which intensity, not exaggeration, is the defining element.[1] In the light of this distinction the picture of Mr. Leavenworth is best described as a caricature. The author literally fixes him in position and exhibits one aspect of his character—his pompous self-assurance which is exaggerated and emphasized to the exclusion of other qualities. Beside Mr. Leavenworth other caricatures may be placed: Mr. Babcock, Mrs. Farrinder, Mr. Striker, and most of the correspondents in "A Bundle of Letters" and "The Point of View." A number of James's satirized figures, however, exhibit a complexity and variety that make them more than caricatures. For instance in "The Pupil" (1893) the picture of the Moreens, the Bohemian family that longs to be Philistine, has a depth and vivacity that make it one of James's most effective satiric portraits. The elements of James's mature style can be analyzed in the passage which introduces Mr. Moreen and his son as they are first seen by the tutor Pemberton.

Mr. Moreen had a white moustache, a confiding manner and, in his buttonhole, the ribbon of a foreign order—bestowed, as Pemberton eventually learned, for services. For what services he never clearly ascertained: this was a point—one of a large number—that Mr. Moreen's manner never confided. What it emphatically did confide was that he was even more a man of the world than you might at first make out. Ulick, the firstborn, was in visible training for the same profession—under the disadvantage as yet, however, of a buttonhole but feebly floral and a moustache with no pretensions to type. The girls had hair and figures and manners and small fat feet, but had never been out alone. As for Mrs. Moreen, Pemberton saw on a nearer view that her elegance was intermittent and her parts didn't always match. (11:517–18)

The tone of the passage is set by the fastidious refinement of language which often issues in periphrasis: a buttonhole is "feebly floral"; a moustache has "no pretensions to type"; elegance is "intermittent." The inflation of the trivial, which increases the distance between the narrator and the characters, both dignifies and makes comic the person satirized. The disparity between the inflated style and the trivialities and the vulgarities that it presents is also a way of characterizing people who inflate themselves, who have pretensions to social importance and assume positions the observer perceives to be false. The fact that being a "man of the world" is a "profession" for which Ulick is in "visible training" at once identifies father and son as poseurs.

Throughout, the narrator's view is that of an urbane, intelligent, sophisticated observer who is shocked by nothing, who rarely, if ever, descends to invective, and whose sense of security and superiority to what he sees is evident both in his circumlocutions and colloquialisms and also in the ease with which he shifts from one style to the other. Mrs. Moreen, faced with the prospect of "sudden dispersal—a frightened *sauve qui peut*"—is seen to be "closing the hatches for the storm." When the Moreens are evicted from their hotel, after a scene of the "last proprietary firmness," Pemberton perceives that "the storm had come . . . the hatches were down" (11:572, 574).

At the beginning Pemberton, who sees less than the author, is intrigued and beguiled by the gay chattering polyglot Moreens. Eventually he perceives what the author has implied from the beginning: he identifies the Moreens as a "band of adventurers" (11:533). To the bravely shameless pretensions of the Moreens, the urbanity of the narrator, and the growing distress which accompanies the enlightenment of Pemberton, James added yet another attitude and point of view essential to the satiric effect of the story. The precocious child Morgan Moreen, the pupil who teaches his tutor, lacks the narrator's detachment and sense of security, but he possesses all the other qualities and values which inform the narrator's satire. Witty and intelligent, Morgan is capable of a "whole range of refinement and perception"; a gentleman who knows when others are not, he has a "critical sense for the manners immediately surrounding him" and "a small loftiness which made him acute about betrayed meanness." Without malice or sentimentality he does for Pemberton what the narrator does for the reader: "He made the facts so vivid and so droll, and at the same time so bald and so ugly" (11:523, 546, 552).

"The Pupil" illustrates the salient feature of James's satire: the point of view and tone of an observer secure in his knowledge and position, knowing himself superior to what he ridicules, capable of taking a certain relish in what he observes, a relish sometimes tinged with good-humored contempt, sometimes with disgust. In a number of James's first-person narratives, such as " 'Europe' " and "The Death of the Lion," James bestows upon his narrator his own satiric powers. Other first-person narrators, notably those of "The Aspern Papers" and *The Sacred Fount*, take the detached critical ironic view but at the same time in their egotism and obsession with one idea expose themselves to a satirist's judgment. In a number of third-person narratives—*Roderick Hudson*, *The Spoils of Poynton*, and *The Ambassadors*, for instance—certain characters as well as the narrator satirize the deficiencies and excesses of the fools. In every case the satirist's detachment and sense of superiority are expressed chiefly through verbal wit, which in James's fiction exhibits itself in many ways.

We have already seen examples of one expression of the satirist's wit, in the sudden shifts from the elevated style to the colloquial, the ironic effect of which is often heightened by comparison of the person or his behavior to the undignified, ridiculous, or bizarre. Such comparisons range from the degrading and the reductive, as when Sarah Pocock's "thin lipped smile" acts as promptly "as the scrape of a safety match" (22:73) to the crass and showy, as when the aggressive editor in "John Delavoy" shows himself to be a "parti-coloured map, a great spotted social chart. He abounded in the names of things, and his mind was like a great staircase at a party—you heard them bawled at the top."[2] Especially in the late novels, vulgarity is caricatured in extravagant images which render the person at once formidable and preposterous. Maud Lowder, in *The Wings of the Dove*, waits in her cage like a lioness resplendent in "perpetual satin, twinkling bugles, and flashing gems" (19:30). Mr. Morrow, the brash interviewer in "The Death of the Lion," "glared, agreeably" through glasses that "suggested the electric headlights of some monstrous modern ship" (15:112). The ornate overheated hotel lobby in "A Round of Visits" resembles "some wondrous tropical forest, where vociferous, bright-eyed, and feathered creatures, of every variety of size and hue, were half smothered between undergrowths of velvet and tapestry and ramifications of marble and bronze."[3] In contrast to the narrators of early stories, the observers here—Kate Croy, the young disciple of Neil Paraday, and Mark Monteith—express in their impressions not only a sense of superiority but also a sense of helplessness before the force of assertive vulgarity which they can deplore but never defeat.

Often the observers in James's stories reveal the follies of other characters in ironic epigrams and paradoxes. The narrator of "Greville Fane," for instance, observes that the title character, the prolific author of sentimental novels, had "an unequaled gift of squeezing big mistakes into small opportunities" (16:122–123) and was "never so intensely British as when she was particularly foreign" (16:115). Sometimes observers reveal the deficiencies of their society through the placement of words in unexpected sequence. The provincial library in Blackport-on-Dwindle where Morris Gedge ("The Birthplace") languishes for a time, is "all granite, fog and female fiction" (17:133). The estate of Bigwood, to which Neal Paraday ("The Death of the Lion") is taken, is "very grand and frigid, all marble and precedence" (15:143). One notes, too, the satiric effect of James's names. His country houses where the vulgar and predatory gather include not only Bigwood but Prestidge, Doubleton, Matcham, and Mundham.

Like Thoreau, James had the gift of breathing life into a dead metaphor. Not only does the self-pitying Mrs. Saltram in "The Coxon Fund" "wash her hands" of her irresponsible husband, but she has "carefully preserved the water of this ablution, which she handed about for analysis" (15:301). Mrs. Penniman is left with "nothing but the memory of Mr. Penniman's flowers of speech, a certain vague aroma of which hovered about her own conversation."[4] Like the hyperbolic comparisons, and the epigrams and paradoxes, these amplifications of clichés achieve their effect through surprise. The reader is startled out of routine habits of thought and invited to look at a character from a new perspective. In participating in the exercise of the satirist's flexible wit, the reader stretches his own mind; he enjoys with the satirist the sense of superiority to all those characters like Mrs. Light, Sarah Pocock, and Mrs. Penniman, whose point of view is narrow and fixed.

From the outset of his career James satirized characters not only by his own comments but also through their speech. The technique is carefully analyzed by Richard Poirier, who shows how the egotism, shallowness, selfishness, and obsessive ambition that make characters like Mrs. Light, Roderick Hudson, and Mrs. Hudson, who are both ridiculous and harmful, betray themselves in the theatrical excesses of their speech [5] Comic in effect, the exaggerated pomposity of their language and the intensity with which they utter the clichés of melodrama turn the speakers, as Poirier points out, into caricatures and types. A second group of characters betrays its deficiencies through speech notable only for its flat banalities and crudities. Commenting on the assertive speech of such characters as Mrs. Ruck and Sophy, persons without imagination or feeling or taste, D. W. Jefferson observes the "stylistic value in flatness itself, combined with such assurance. Remarks without salt or savour, inadequacies beyond criticism or analysis, become the material of a dreadfully expressive dialogue."[6] The satiric effect is heightened when the banalities of the character and the circumlocutions of the narrator are brought together. In *Daisy Miller*, for instance, the contrast between the deplorable taste of Mrs. Miller's whining recital of her ailments during a morning call and the punctilious correctness of Winterbourne's polite engagement in "a good deal of pathological gossip" (18:49) with the sufferer makes the speaker seem even more vulgar, the listener more than ever stiff and pompous.

One aspect of James's satire evident particularly in the early and middle fiction is the avoidance of sarcasm or the tone of sneering contempt. Instances such as that in *The Spoils of Poynton* where Mrs. Brigstock is said to have ".a face of which it was impossible to say anything but that it was pink, and a mind it would be possible to describe only had one been able to mark it in a similar fashion" (10:172) are relatively rare. In several of James's last stories urbanity gives way to anger, and wit becomes an instrument of merciless ridicule. The narrator of "Julia Bride," "Crapy Cornelia," "A Round of Visits," and *The Ivory Tower* is moved to direct attack by the aggressions and vulgarities of a mercenary society in which "if people were but rich enough and furnished enough and fed enough, exercised and sanitated and manicured, and generally advised and advertised and made 'knowing' enough . . . all they had to do for civility was to take the amused ironic view of those who might be less initiated."[7]

In most of his stories and novels, however, James satirizes folly and vulgarity by paradox, ironic understatement, and circumlocution. His refusal to subject even the most venal and benighted of his fools to harsh scorn and invective is evident in *The Bostonians*, in his portrayal of the Tarrants, described by one critic as "the most appalling examples of vulgarity in James's fiction."[8] In the passage satirizing the hypocrisy of Selah Tarrant, who affects indifference when a rich woman takes up his daughter Verena, the irony mocks but does not lash or deride the mesmeric healer. It is left to other characters—Verena's patroness Olive Chancellor and Verena's suitor Basil Ransom—to denounce Tarrant as a charlatan and a scoundrel.

He committed himself to no precipitate elation at the idea of his daughter's being taken up by a patroness of movements who happened to have money; he looked at his child only from the point of view of the service she might render to humanity . . . Verena's initial appearance in Boston, as he called her performance at Miss Birdseye's, had been a great success; and this reflection added, as I say, to his habitually sacerdotal expression. He looked like the priest of a religion that was passing through the stage of miracles; he carried his responsibility in the general elongation of his person, of his gestures (his hands were now always in the air, as if he were being photographed in postures), of his words and sentences, as well as in his smile, as noiseless as a patent hinge, and in the folds of his eternal waterproof.[9]

The detachment of the narrator is highlighted by contrast with the wrathful denunciations of Ransom, the one outsider in Boston, who condemns his age as "talkative, querulous, hysterical, maudlin" (p. 189); the women's rights movement as the "wordy, windy iteration of inanities" (p. 237); and the public as "stupid, gregarious, gullible" (p. 319). In the violence of his outbursts Ransom himself becomes comic, but no one escapes the ironical view of the narrator, not the reformers, nor Ransom who denounces them, nor the editors of the periodicals whose rejection of his notions "was certainly not a matter for surprise" (p. 334).

The complexity of James's point of view is most fully shown in his portrayal of Olive Chancellor, whose possessiveness and self-deception expose her to some of his keenest satire but whose acute suffering at the end calls forth passages as eloquent as any he wrote. Like the Princess Casamassima, Olive is an educated woman of refined tastes, who detests the commonplace and vulgar, and yet is capable of uttering banal sentiments in the stock phrases of the day. James satirizes Olive when he records her long-time preoccupation with the "romance of the people" (p. 34); when he follows a statement of Olive's fervid longing to devote herself to the cause and die for it with the cool observation that "it was not clear to this interesting girl in what manner such a sacrifice (as this last) would be required of her" (p. 37); when he pictures her consoled by the "prospect of suffering" which was "always, spiritually speaking, so much cash in her pocket" (p. 160). The irony of Olive's belief that she "had never yet infringed on Verena's [liberty]" even as she seeks to gain "a more complete possession of the girl" (pp. 243, 129) is satirical in effect, if a more subtle form of satire than the narrator's exposure of Tarrant's lofty pretensions. Olive is a shuddering register of the Tarrants' vulgarity, but she no less than Selah exploits Verena for personal ends: his "grotesque manipulations" (p. 59) of Verena are only gross exaggerations of Olive's acts.

James's treatment of Olive is not, however, consistently ironic or derisive. Charles Samuels makes the acute observation that James presents Olive satirically so long as she simply embodies the reformers' fervor, but when her conflict with Ransom becomes intense, when she is "progressively besieged by [his] sexual power," she becomes an object of the author's sympathy.[10] In any case the scene in which Olive walks by the shore after the desertion of Verena, shedding slow tears of anguish and finding a "kind of tragic relief" (p. 408) in sparing "herself none of the inductions of a revery that seemed to dry up the mists and ambiguities of life" (p. 410), has all the intensity and passion of the "recognition" scenes of the late novels. More clearly than any other novel by James *The Bostonians*, which has been described as the most relentless of all his works, shows that the intelligence, flexibility, and self-possession of the narrator are revealed not only in his satirical wit but in his perception of the depths of suffering of which his subject may be capable.

II

Conrad's powers as a satirist are best seen in the political novels *Heart of Darkness*, *Nostromo*, *The Secret Agent*, and *Under Western Eyes*. In these works Conrad shows himself as capable as James of modulations of tone and shifts of perspective, but certain elements absent from James's satire are present in abundance in Conrad's. Most obvious are Conrad's pictures of squalor and brutality and the feelings of revulsion that they inspire in narrator and reader. How different the psychological state of Marlow is from that of James's narrators is felt at once in *Heart of Darkness*, in which the nature of Conrad's satire is first revealed fully.

Marlow is intelligent and observant, superior to the fools—or, as they are identified in *Heart of Darkness*, the hollow men—of whose rapacity, stupidity, and hypocrisy he is keenly aware. But whereas James's narrator usually knows himself unthreatened by what he satirizes, secure in his consciousness of his innate superiority, Marlow in *Heart of Darkness* is engaged in a constant struggle to keep himself from being overwhelmed by the dark forces that assail men in the solitude of a savage wilderness. During his journey Marlow confronts sights so shocking to his moral sensibilities, so far removed from the normal and the rational, that even before he reaches the Congo he feels himself caught "within the toil of a mournful and senseless delusion" (5:61).

What saved him during the journey itself, Marlow tells his listeners, was work, which riveted his attention to the "mere incidents of the surface" (5:93). What enables Marlow to live with the past and speak of it with any kind of composure is the adoption of a tone of grim and sardonic irony in the narration of his journey. The result is satire marked by bitter sarcasm completely foreign to James's satire. The quarrel over the black hens in which Fresleven dies is "this glorious affair" (5:54); the steamer passes towns on the African coast where "the merry dance of death and trade goes on" (5:62). Marlow meets the accountant whose starched collars are "achievements of character" and shakes hands with "this miracle" (5:67–68). He observes that the overseer of the natives in the chain gang "seemed to take me into partnership in his exalted trust. After all, I also was part of the great cause of these high and just proceedings" (5:65). He satirizes the agents by adopting their point of view and language: "Behind this raw matter [the natives] one of the reclaimed, the product of the new forces at work, strolled despondently . . ." (5:64). Often he satirizes the callousness and brutality of the Europeans simply by juxtaposing impressions. He watches the accountant make "correct entries of perfectly correct transactions" and sees fifty feet away "the still tree-tops of the grove of death" (5:70).

Suggestive of other forces which threaten the health and sanity of the observer are the scenes of disorder and confusion in which Marlow must live. Marlow's first sight of the company station reveals a mass of decaying machinery, smashed drainpipes, rusty nails, a boiler "wallowing" in the grass, a railroad car on its back, like a carcass. At the station itself the accountant's records are in order but "everything else . . . was in a muddle—heads, things, buildings" (5:68). Alvin P. Kernan has described the typical scene of satire as "disorderly and crowded, packed to the very point of bursting. The deformed faces of depravity, stupidity, greed, venality, ignorance, and maliciousness group closely together for a moment, stare boldly out at us, break up, and another tight knot of figures collects. . . . The scene is equally choked with things. . . . Pick up any major satiric work and open it at random and the immediate effect is one of disorderly profusion."[11]

Nothing in Conrad better illustrates the point than Marlow's picture of the arrival of the Eldorado expedition:

Instead of rivets there came an invasion, an infliction, a visitation. It came in sections during the next three weeks, each section headed by a donkey carrying a white man in new clothes and tan shoes, bowing from that elevation right and left to the impressed pilgrims. A quarrelsome band of footsore sulky niggers trod on the heels of the donkey; a lot of tents, camp-stools, tin boxes, white cases, brown bales would be shot down in the courtyard, and the air of mystery would deepen a little over the muddle of the station. Five such instalments came, with their absurd air of disorderly flight with the loot of innumerable outfit shops and provision stores, that, one would think, they were lugging, after a raid, into the wilderness for equitable division. It was an inextricable mess of things decent in themselves but that human folly made look like the spoils of thieving. (5:87)

Confronted by such scenes of disorder and degradation, Marlow decides not to attempt to reform the evil but simply to resist it. In the past, on occasion, Marlow was obliged to resort to physical violence, to "strike and fend off"; "I've had to resist and to attack sometimes—that's only one way of resisting" (5:65). To resist the human evil in the Congo Marlow attacks by means of satire. Through irony and sarcasm he asserts his superiority and at the same time struggles to protect the qualities of mind that distinguish him from those whom he satirizes. If the extravagant metaphors and fastidious refinements of James's satire reflect the narrator's unthreatened sense of superiority and security, the grim ironies and harsh sarcasms of Conrad's satire have their source in the narrator's sometimes desperate struggle to secure his powers in the face of the disorder and savagery that constantly threaten him.

A natural concomitant of the narrator's attitude in *Heart of Darkness* is the reduction of satirized figures to functionaries without identity save that as officials of the company. With the exception of Marlow, Kurtz, and the dead Fresleven, who have names, the other employees of the company are identified only by such titles as doctor, secretary, chief accountant, and manager, as if in the association with the company all other vestiges of humanity had been obliterated. The chief accountant with his starched appearance and perfect records is caricatured; the manager, who has no distinctive traits save the power to inspire uneasiness and survive in the tropics, is not caricatured; but both men are equally faceless, without past or future. There is a fundamental difference between James's satirized types like Mr. Leavenworth and these figures of Conrad, who are not so much personal or social types as embodied official functions. One notes, too, how much individualizing detail James includes in even his simplest caricatures; Mr. Leavenworth, for instance, not only has a name, an occupation (making borax), a place of residence (the banks of the Ohio), and the memory of his dead wife; he also has a future: he becomes engaged to Augusta Blanchard, the type of the genteel amateur painter. In contrast to James, whose figures are so vividly individualized that the satire does not seem directed against whole groups of people or against mankind, Conrad, in making the objects of his satire generic abstract figures, devoid of individuality, appears to direct his satire to an entire group or class. It is then but a step to ironic meditation on the follies of all mankind—on its capacity for self-deception, its willingness to believe what flatters its hopes, its readiness to clothe materialistic desire in noble sentiments. To a much greater extent than James, Conrad is moved to generalize on the basis of the particular experience, to reflect upon the nature of man, to place human beings into categories, as he does in *Heart of Darkness*, where Marlow divides people into saints and fools and those who are "neither one nor the other" (5:117). In *Chance* Marlow's propensity for generalization is such that the main function of the unnamed narrator, as is particularly evident in the manuscript of the novel, is time and again to halt Marlow's generalizing meditations and bring him back to the characters of the story.

That generalization does not require a first-person narrator is evident in *The Secret Agent*, in which the satire is based on an observation of the essential likeness of anarchists and police, and the reduction of characters is carried even further than in *Heart of Darkness*. Not only are certain figures like Heat, the professor, the assistant commissioner, and the patroness given generic names or no names at all; the repetition of epithets—Ossipon, the "robust anarchist"; Verloc, "the trusted agent"; the professor, "the perfect anarchist"—ridicules the characters through mock heroic inflation and reduces them to performers of single roles. Conrad draws certain characters in considerable detail. Michaelis, Yundt, and Ossipon, caricatures though they are, have names and physiognomies and pasts; Verloc is one of Conrad's most solid figures, his habits and thoughts rendered so vividly that his sluggish mind seems no less palpable than his piglike body. But there is an abstract quality about Verloc and the others, the effect of the narrator's consistent reduction of the passions, fears, desires, and anguish of the characters to the status of objects, to be scrutinized with detachment. The effect of detachment is heightened at moments of greatest tension when the character is analyzed like a specimen in an experiment. Just before Winnie kills Verloc, for instance, she moves in the grip of a rage which reveals itself in "an expression seldom observed by competent persons under the conditions of leisure and security demanded for thorough analysis" (8:260–261). Even characters like Stevie and Winnie's mother, whose infirmities cannot be satirized, are presented with almost sardonic detachment.

The sustained irony of *The Secret Agent* is the expression of a narrator in complete control of his subject, although here ironic detachment seems as much a means of maintaining control as the inevitable product of such control. But unlike Marlow the narrator has no apparent occasion to struggle for comprehension and for the means of expression. Nothing dislodges him from his position of detachment. He holds Verloc and the other characters at a distance, whether he mocks their folly in ironic inflation or analyzes it in dispassionate terms. The pleasure that even the basest of James's characters affords the narrator is absent from *The Secret Agent*. Nothing is a source of pleasure to the narrator, and no character's passion, however intense, causes him to drop his ironic mask.

As is evident in *Heart of Darkness* and *The Secret Agent*, Conrad's satire resists analysis in James's terms of "free spirits" and "fools." The fools abound in Conrad's novels; but even Marlow, the most enlightened of Conrad's characters, does not feel himself free in *Heart of Darkness*, haunted as he is by the memory of Kurtz. All the characters of *The Secret Agent*, even the "perfect anarchist" who prides himself on being "a force," are imprisoned by time. Stevie, Winnie's mother, Sir Ethelred, and most of the anarchists are incapacitated by physical abnormality; others like the assistant commissioner are confined by the bureaucratic system; nearly all are victims of the chain of events that destroys Stevie, Verloc, Winnie Verloc, and Ossipon.

The impossibility of applying James's term *free spirit* to Conrad's characters is demonstrated again in *Under Western Eyes*, which like *The Secret Agent* is based on the idea that two forces seemingly in opposition are in fact alike in nature. In *Under Western Eyes*, however, the two opposing forces—the Russian autocracy and the revolutionaries—are not in collusion as are the police and the anarchists in *The Secret Agent*, but are inseparable parts of a single process: a repressive autocracy based on power, not law, breeds lawless acts of violence which, whether or not they bring down the regime in power, will lead only to further acts of repression, tyranny, and violence. The basic opposition in this novel is thus not between representatives of the autocracy and the revolutionaries, for either group is the victim of the other. The basic opposition is between those characters who are ruled by a principle or an ideal—whether it is the principle of autocracy or of resistance to autocracy, and those who are ruled by their egoistic desires for personal glory, power, money, or sexual gratification. The first group, which includes such diverse figures as General T——, Haldin, and Sophia Antonovna, is not satirized, although General T——, the fanatical embodiment of autocracy, is portrayed as grotesque and inhumanly cruel, in contrast to the revolutionary Haldin, who is idealistic, self-sacrificing, and generous to a supreme degree. (Haldin under torture does not betray Razumov even when he is informed that Razumov has betrayed him.) The second group, the egotists and materialists, includes the two principal targets of Conrad's satire in this novel: Madame de S——, the most gruesome of all Conrad's satirized figures, and Peter Ivanovitch, the worshipper and exploiter of Madame de S—— and Conrad's chief portrait of the hypocrite.

Seen through the eyes of Nathalie Haldin and Razumov and the teacher of languages, Peter Ivanovitch emerges as a ludicrous yet sinister figure, fatuous when he mouths panegyrics on the nobility of women, ruthless in his brutal treatment of Tekla and in his talk of "filling up" the chasm between past and future. Like Ossipon and Yundt, Peter Ivanovitch is an adventurer who lives by his wits, off the bounty of women. He is distinguished from the anarchists in *The Secret Agent* by a kind of unassailable impudence which shields him no less than do the dark glasses perpetually hiding his eyes. Like the characters in *The Bostonians* and *The Secret Agent* he is satirized by epithets: "the heroic fugitive," "Europe's greatest feminist," and "the noble arch-priest of Revolution." As his autobiography indicates, he exploits everything, including his own suffering, to exalt himself. In his third-person summary of the revolutionist's escape from prison, the narrator satirizes the style of Peter Ivanovitch simply by adopting that style himself, and by shifting at exactly the right moment to direct quotation.

As if providentially appointed to be the newly wedded wife of the village blacksmith, the woman persuaded her husband to come out with her,

bringing some tools of his trade, a hammer, a chisel, a small anvil. . . .
"My fetters"—the book says—"were struck off on the banks of the stream,
in the starlight of a calm night by an athletic, taciturn young man of the
people, kneeling at my feet, while the woman like a liberating genius
stood by with clasped hands." Obviously a symbolic couple. (10:124)

The final sardonic comment, added to the manuscript, is but one
of the many changes which heighten the satiric effect of the portrait. In fact the portrayal of Peter Ivanovitch is a good example of
the way Conrad's revisions can change the picture of a character. In
contrast to James, who revised by amplifying and elaborating, Conrad usually revised by deleting sometimes whole paragraphs and
pages. Among the many passages deleted from the manuscript of
Under Western Eyes are a number which make Peter Ivanovitch
appear simply a fatuous egotist, a man of "blank, unshakeable infinite complacency" who seems foolish and vulnerable in his openly
pursued search for followers, "his hedgerow quest for . . . palpable
disciples" and in his undisguised longing for praise, "the atmosphere of respect scented with adulation" for which he "seemed to
be everlastingly sniffing even as he walked the republican streets
with an ostentatious large simplicity."[12] In the revised novel Peter
Ivanovitch's craving for homage and disciples is implied but never
directly stated. Other revisions help to create a sinister picture of a
man whose motives are never brought out in the open. In the
manuscript the narrator sees behind the glasses "the incessant
weak blinking of inflamed eyelids."[13] In the novel no one ever sees
the eyes behind the dark smoked glasses. In the manuscript Peter
Ivanovitch, on leaving Nathalie Haldin, "asserted his bulk" appearing a "mere mass" in a black coat.[14] In the novel, he is much more
formidable as he exhibits "bland curiosity," seizes his hat "with
great adroitness," and "towered before her, enormous, deferential,
cropped as close as a convict" (10:127–128).

If Peter Ivanovitch becomes more sinister in the revision, his
"mystic Egeria," the decaying Madame de S—— becomes even
more gruesome. Instead of merely looking "long-waisted and stiff,"
she becomes a "youthful figure of hieratic stiffness." Her "blazing
eyes" become "big gleaming eyes, rolling restlessly" (10:125); her

"lips [that] moved with an extraordinary rapidity"[15] become "carmine lips [that] vaticinated with an extraordinary rapidity" (10:223). The novel leaves unanswered the question of Peter Ivanovitch's motives: whether he feigns to worship even a "galvanized corpse" for her money, or whether he finds gratification in the ghastly presence. The reader is ready to believe that he does both.

In contrast to the figures James satirizes—psychological and social types defined by manners—most of Conrad's satirized figures are identified by their function in a political system. In addition to the company agents in *Heart of Darkness* and the police officers, secret agents, anarchists, and bureaucrats in *The Secret Agent* and *Under Western Eyes*, Conrad satirized in *Nostromo* a number of political types not represented in his other novels. The broadest in scope of all Conrad's novels in that it presents the history of a whole country over a period of some one hundred years, *Nostromo* portrays more than thirty characters who play different parts in the two main patterns of events that make the country's political history: the overthrow of a succession of governments within Costaguana and the foreign exploitation of the country's resources, chiefly by the railroad and the San Tomé Mine.

In *Nostromo* Conrad presents several of his most admirable and intelligent characters, but James's distinction between "free spirits" and "fools" does not apply to *Nostromo* any more than to Conrad's other novels. In Conrad's words the events of the novel flow "from the passions of men short-sighted in good and evil" (7:ix). All the characters, from the most to the least intelligent, suffer failures of perception or strength that make them victims of the tragic pattern of events which results in the corruption of the two central characters, Gould and Nostromo; the destruction of the spirit if not the form of the Goulds' marriage; and the deaths of Avellanos, Decoud, and Nostromo. The line between those characters who are the targets of Conrad's derisive satire and those who are not, however, is sharply drawn. In *Nostromo* a large group of characters is rarely if ever mocked: the Goulds and everyone connected with the mine except the American capitalist Holroyd; the representatives of the church and the old Spanish aristocratic families; the Violas and their protector Nostromo, who leads the Italian cargadores. The obsessions, vanities, delusions, and weaknesses of these characters are clearly revealed but they are not stripped of their dignity and humanness as are the "apes of a sinister jungle" (10:xi) in *The Secret Agent* and *Under Western Eyes*. An unnamed French capitalist paying court to Charles Gould is ludicrous as he "fell a prey to a screaming ecstasy, in the midst of sagely nodding heads" (7:199), but of all the important European and English characters, only Captain Mitchell, whose proprietary pride in Nostromo and self-important talk of "epochs" make him comic, is ridiculed. The satire, however, is relatively mild and genial, and the narrator concedes that "for all his pomposity in social intercourse, Captain Mitchell could meet the realities of life in a resolute and ready spirit (7:335).

It is the absence of such a spirit which marks most of the characters whom Conrad mocks in *Nostromo*. The largest group of these are the natives of Costaguana who make up the Monterist faction and foment the uprising which drives out the enlightened but ineffectual dictator Ribiera. Without exception the leading Monterists are rapacious men, adventurers and rabble-rousers without principles of any kind. Whereas the main targets of James's satire are the selfish exploiters of other people, the main targets of Conrad's satire are the plunderers, indolent, stupid, and cruel. Some, like Sotillo, who shifts his political allegiances for his own profit, and Pedro Montero, who aspires to be the Duke de Morny to his brother's Louis Napoleon, believe themselves enlightened men of the world, leaders of authority and wisdom. Others like Gamacho, whom even Pedro Montero calls a brute, lack the education to pose as men of culture. All are motivated by the basest self-interest and many by cowardice. The "flabby devil" which Marlow observes at work in *Heart of Darkness* has its counterpart in the craven spirit which inspires the ferocity of Guzman Bento's followers and drives Sotillo into agonies of fear before the most abject of his victims, Hirsch, the hide-merchant from Esmeralda.

In the career of General Montero, the leader of the rebel forces, Conrad represented a pattern which has repeated itself again and again in the history of South American dictatorships. Beginning as an obscure army captain at a time when one dictator is about to fall,

Montero attaches himself to the winning side, takes part in a decisive battle, becomes a popular hero, is named minister of war in
the new government, and six months later is leading a revolt
against it. In *Nostromo* every part of this typical career is satirized.
Montero joins the Ribierists at a moment when that "small adhe-
sion" had a "fortuitous importance"; he owes his reputation as a
great military hero mainly to the newspapers which inflated his
march into the "most heroic military exploit of modern times"
(7:38, 39). No less sharply than James, Conrad attacked modern
journalism—not for its invasions of privacy, however, but for its
sensationalism and distortion. At the ceremony marking the beginning of the railroad, Montero is set apart from all the others—the
Goulds, Sir John, Avellanos, and the foreign dignitaries—by his
crudities, his lack of European refinement, his childish desire for
attention, and his gorgeous barbaric uniform in which he suggests
"some military idol of Aztec conception and European bedecking."
Fixed by his "imbecile and domineering stare," he appears both
stupid and sinister (7:122).

Conrad satirizes two other important political types in *Nostromo*. In the figure of Don Juste Lopez, the Ribierist head of the
provincial assembly and author of a humble tribute to Montero,
Conrad ridicules the politician who, to save "parliamentary forms,"
is ready to hail as the legitimate ruler any man who seizes power.
The financier Holroyd, who endows churches to support "the
purer forms of Christianity," vaunts the power of "the greatest
country in the whole of God's universe," and proclaims that "we
shall be giving the word for everything" (7:77), is an obvious caricature of the American international capitalist.[16] Holroyd shows to an
extreme degree what can be observed in many of the European
characters: ignorance of or indifference to the plight of the Cos-
taguanan people and the disposition to view the country's struggles
as a game in which one gambles and hopes to find one's account.[17]
Without popular leaders except demagogues like Gamacho and
Pedro Montero, the people remain a mass, sunk in poverty and
apathy. The Monterist uprising creates a "mob," a "rabble," which
at the height of the conflict pours through the streets "like a torrent

of rubbish" (7:384); easily manipulated, diverted, lashed to fury and cowed, the mob reminds one of the Roman populace in *Antony and Cleopatra* who

> like to a vagabond flag upon the stream
> Goes to and back, lackeying the varying tide
> To rot itself with motion. (1.4.44–46)

The bias of the narrator is clear enough, but his relation to events is not always the same. Occasionally in the opening chapters the narrator assumes the character of a traveller recounting what he has seen and heard from old inhabitants like Captain Mitchell; he is one of those whom "business or curiosity" took to Sulaco in the early days, but he has not been back since the separation of Sulaco from Costaguana. Throughout most of the novel, however, the narrative voice is that of the omniscient author, who despite his clear perception of the Ribierists' weaknesses, shows his preference for them in their opposition to the savage leaders Bento and Montero. On occasion all the characters, Ribierists and Monterists, tortured and torturers, recede into the distance as the narrator steps back to view the scene as if from a great height. From this perspective the characters shrink to tiny figures on a remote stage; the motions of battling horsemen on the plain become the "passages of a violent game played . . . by dwarfs . . . yelling with tiny throats, under the mountain that seemed a colossal embodiment of silence" (7:27). Several of the characters, notably the Goulds and Decoud, have something of the narrator's double sense of involvement and detachment. They know that their hopes of happiness and security depend upon the outcome of the Monterist uprising, and yet the outbreaks in the country have to them an air of unreality; to Decoud they are part of *une farce macabre*, which he resolves to view with sardonic amusement; to both Charles Gould and his wife, the "grotesque extravagance" which attends the Monterist outbreak seems irremediably alien.

Nothing contributes more to the effect of macabre farce than the presence of the Monterists, who swagger, cringe, yell, loot, and sprawl in scene after scene of riot and disorder. The portrayal of Gamacho is a good example of the kind of irony, sarcasm, and invective which Conrad directs at such figures. Gamacho is introduced with fastidious irony by Decoud, as a self-styled "moderate," who as deputy to the Ribierist assembly "opposed every energetic measure with philanthropic pensiveness," until Montero's victory caused him and others to blossom into "convinced Liberals" (7:227). Gamacho is next seen at Pedro Montero's side, "big and hot, wiping his hairy wet face, [uncovering] a set of yellow fangs in a grin of stupid hilarity" (7:389). Left alone in the street, he bursts into an oration, "delectable to popular ears," which goes on "like the uncouth howlings of an inferior sort of devil cast into a white-hot furnace." He ends the day "lying drunk and asleep in the bosom of his family. His bare feet were upturned in the shadows repulsively, in the manner of a corpse. His eloquent mouth had dropped open. His youngest daughter, scratching her head with one hand, with the other waved a green bough over his scorched and peeling face" (7:392, 393).

No passage could better illustrate the qualities that distinguish Conrad's satire from James's. In none of his fiction does James subject any of his characters to such physically debasing states. Nor does one feel that James is revolted by his fools as Conrad is by his. The contempt which animates the picture of Gamacho is absent from James's satire, even from the most repellent of his pictures of that "cheapest kind of human product," Selah Tarrant, who at Miss Birdseye's can be observed "looking round him with a slow deliberate smile, which made his mouth enormous, developed two wrinkles, as long as the wings of a bat, on either side of it, and showed a set of big, even, carnivorous teeth" (pp. 59, 46). This is as far as James will go in the direction of the physically repulsive.

James expressed the view which governed his art when he complained to Violet Paget of a "certain ferocity," "a certain want of perspective and proportion" in her novel *Miss Brown* and went on to insist that "*life* is less criminal, less obnoxious, less objectionable, less crude, more *bon enfant*, more mixed and casual, and even in its most offensive more—, more *pardonable*, than the unholy circle with which you have surrounded your heroine."[18] Undoubtedly James's dislike of *Nostromo*, *The Secret Agent*, and *Under Western Eyes* sprang in part from his response to their savage irony. The "rich veins of dark and glittering satire and sarcasm"[19] which Arnold Bennett praised in Conrad's work, and the "sense of cruelty," "calculated mockery," and "sheer cold-bloodedness," that Arthur Symons noted in Conrad's "The Informer"[20] were never elements that appealed to James. He shared with his protagonist in "A Round of Visits" the desire "as with a desperate charity, to give some easier turn to the mere ugliness of the main facts."[21]

In his essay on Maupassant (1888) James contrasted the satire of the French with that of the English writers and identified himself with the English. "Even those of our novelists whose manner is most ironic pity life more and hate it less than M. de Maupassant and his great initiator Flaubert. . . . We have reserves about our shames and our sorrows, indulgences and tolerances about our Philistinism, forbearance about our blows, and a general friendliness of conception about our possibilities, which take the cruelty from our self-derision and operate in the last resort as a sort of tribute to our freedom."[22] In his criticism James never compared Conrad's satire to that of the French, but James's description of comedy in Maupassant as "for the most part the comedy of misery, of avidity, of ignorance, helplessness, and grossness,"[23] could be applied to passages in *Nostromo*, *The Secret Agent*, and *Under Western Eyes*.

Perhaps thinking of the difference between his art and James's, Conrad observed in his essay on James that "ugliness has but little place in this world of his creation." More sympathetic to James's bias than James was to his, however, Conrad praised James's art for its truthfulness, in which ugliness is "always felt," if not seen; "it is there, it surrounds the scene, it presses close upon it" (18:17–18). In Conrad's fiction, of course, ugliness does not simply "surround the scene"; it often occupies the center of it. In James ugliness of conduct can coexist with personal beauty and artistic power, as is proved by Roderick Hudson, Madame Merle, Osmond, and the Princess Casamassima; in Conrad ugliness appears in the countenances of the characters satirized, in the squalor and decay in which they live, in the disorder and destruction they perpetrate, and in scenes of brutal comedy which trap the noble and the base alike. The differences between the two novelists are even more strikingly illustrated by the different conceptions of the grotesque expressed in the novels and stories of James and Conrad.

7

The Grotesque

Even a cursory study of James's and Conrad's satire shows how important is the element of the grotesque in their portrayal of certain characters and situations. Often a physical characteristic or mannerism exists in such extreme form that the figure appears grotesque. To such targets of satire as Mrs. Light, Selah Tarrant, General Montero, the crew of the *Patna*, and Necator, the term *grotesque* is applied. In their portrayal of these and other grotesque figures, both James and Conrad are working within traditions well established in the nineteenth century. In their novels they stress the kinship of certain grotesque characters with figures in Balzac and Hoffmann and Dickens. They portray figures and scenes marked by characteristics by which Ruskin and Victor Hugo and their contemporaries identified the grotesque: the physical distortion like that of a caricature; action which calls to mind images of clowns and puppets; the impression of the unhuman or the outlandish confounding one's sense of reality; the fusion of incongruous elements inducing in the observer a sense of dislocation and insecurity. The broad range of effects which nineteenth-century novelists and critics have identified as grotesque, however, comprehends many different kinds of scenes and figures. To compare James's and Conrad's conceptions of the grotesque is to realize the truth of C. S. Lewis's observation that "the grotesque is a ridge from which one can descend into very different valleys."[1]

I

In his comments on caricaturists and painters of the grotesque, like Daumier, Gavarni, Jan Steen, and Isaac Van Ostade, James associates the grotesque with the ugly, the base, the sordid, and the licentious.[2] These qualities are not, however, the defining elements of his own grotesque figures. It is true that some of these characters are physically repellent. One recalls the nice combination of the false and the ravenous suggested by the "big, even, carnivorous teeth" of Selah Tarrant.[3] But what makes Tarrant grotesque is not so much his unattractive appearance as his actions, in particular his "grotesque manipulations" of Verena.[4] Olive Chancellor is grotesque not in appearance but in her behavior—in her fanatical devotion to the cause of women's rights, expressed in sudden uncontrollable outbursts that alarm or bewilder her listeners. Mrs. Wix, "in the eyes of the world a figure mainly to laugh at" (11:25), is grotesque not merely because her appearance suggests "the polished shell or corselet of a horrid beetle" (11:23), but because her infatuation for Sir Claude, given her age and position, is both ludicrous and pathetic. Gussy Bradham, the target of James's sharpest satire in *The Ivory Tower* or any novel, is not grotesque because she is ugly—in fact, Rosanna Gaw, her most unsparing critic, notes her "extraordinary perfections of neatness, of elegance, of arrangement" (25:50). She is grotesque because she has pressed the search for physical perfection so far that at the age of forty with her girl's figure she seems to have attained a state that "wasn't human . . . but might have been that of some shining humming insect, a thing of the long-constricted waist, the minimised yet caparisoned head, the fixed disproportionate eye and tough transparent wing, gossamer guaranteed" (25:50).

The mingling of human and nonhuman forms has long been a recognized characteristic of grotesque art. When carried to the extreme, as in the portrayal of the "countess" in *What Maisie Knew*, the confounding of human and animal produces an animated cartoon of the animal in human costume. "She literally struck the child more as an animal than as a 'real' lady; she might have been a clever frizzled poodle in a frill or a dreadful human monkey in a spangled petticoat. She had a nose that was far too big and eyes that were far too small and a moustache that was, well, not so happy a feature as Sir Claude's" (11:193).

The "countess" is one of the few figures in James who are identified as grotesque simply by the weirdness of their aspect. Nor does James make his characters grotesque by subjecting them to scenes of low comedy such as Conrad portrays in *Nostromo* and *The Secret Agent*. When violent uncontrolled motion occurs in James's novels it appears in metaphors. The effect of the grotesque arises from the incongruity of the outlandish image and the decorous conventional world in which the characters live. In *The Spoils of Poynton*, for instance, Mrs. Gereth does not strike observers as grotesque in appearance; but her obsession with the fate of Poynton's works of art, obsession which has "in a manner despoiled her of her humanity" (10:37), causes her to act with a violence expressed not directly but through grotesque images which register Fleda's sense of the older woman's excesses. In the intensity and blindness of her extravagant passion Mrs. Gereth evokes successively the images of an excited Don Quixote charging the windmills; a gorgeous tropical bird, "the creature of hot dense forests," helpless on a frozen wasteland; and a performer whose furious denunciation of Fleda affects the girl "as if it had been the shake of a tambourine borne toward her from a gipsy dance" (10:31, 146, 220). The fineness of Fleda's nature not only heightens by contrast the grotesque effects of Mrs. Gereth's passion but also intensifies that passion, driving Mrs. Gereth to even greater violence of statement.

Although James never uses the word *grotesque* to describe Mrs. Gereth, she illustrates the main characteristics of the figures in his novels whose extravagant behavior makes them appear grotesque. The perpetrator of excesses is usually one who, like Mrs. Gereth, ignores the feelings and violates the integrity of others. Several of the grotesque figures, including Abel Gaw, Olive Chancellor, and Mrs. Light as well as Mrs. Gereth, are driven by a single passion that has the all-consuming force of an obsession. Their grotesqueness is manifested not in monstrous physical deformity or in farcical action but in excesses of speech or in the extravagance of metaphor so incongruous in scenes of conventional decorum that the person who evokes the image seems outlandish or bizarre. Although the imagery may have frightening connotations, most of the grotesque figures in James are in some way comic; almost all his important grotesques, whether harmless like Miss Birdseye or baneful like Selah Tarrant, Mrs. Light, Abel Gaw, and Gussy Bradham, are satirized. They are brought under control by the satirist's wit; they do not create the impression of evil let loose, unchecked in the world, and one component of the reader's feeling toward them is always amusement.

To turn from James's grotesque figures to Conrad's is to perceive differences so marked as to make the word *grotesque* appear to be as elastic as any literary term. In contrast to James's figures Conrad's grotesques are notable above all for their physical abnormality, usually obesity or emaciation, which is sometimes so exaggerated as to seem monstrous. Many of Conrad's physically grotesque figures come in pairs, like the enormously fat captain of the *Patna* and his skeletonlike engineer, or the spectral Mr. Jones and the fleshy Ricardo in *Victory*, or the knitters in *Heart of Darkness*—one fat, one thin—as if the pair comprehends all fateful possibilities and negates any hope that contrast offers opposing forces of good and evil.

The qualities and effects Conrad was always to associate with the concept *grotesque* are indicated in his first novel *Almayer's Folly*. The protagonist Almayer is not himself a physical grotesque, but his inflated view of himself, so little in harmony with his ineffectual character, is shown to be grotesque when it is symbolized by the shadow which inflates his sleeping figure. "In the increasing light of the moon that had risen now above the night mist, the objects on the verandah came out strongly outlined in black splashes of shadow with all the uncompromising ugliness of their disorder, and a caricature of the sleeping Almayer appeared on the dirty whitewash of the wall behind him in a grotesquely exaggerated detail of attitude and feature enlarged to a heroic size" (1:158–159).

In its representation of the vanity of Almayer's dreams, the passage unites physical distortion with the theme of illusion so prominent in Conrad's later novels. This picture of disorder and distortion, rendered in sharp detail, also exemplifies Conrad's method of presenting grotesque figures. Most of them are caricatures of "uncompromising ugliness," often seen in humiliating or undignified positions or engaged in farcical action. Marlow's last sight of the skipper of the *Patna*, for instance, is of a grotesque whose cowardice is made comic by his effort to force his enormous bulk into a small gharry. "The little machine shook and rocked tumultuously, and the crimson nape of that lowered neck, the size of those straining thighs, the immense heaving of that dingy, striped green-and-orange back, the whole burrowing effect of that gaudy and sordid mass troubled one's sense of probability with a droll and fearsome effect, like one of those grotesque and distinct visions that scare and fascinate one in a fever" (4:46–47).

Many of Conrad's grotesques are diseased or moribund, as are James Wait and Donkin (*The Nigger of the Narcissus*), Kurtz (*Heart of Darkness*), the chief engineer of the *Patna* and Gentleman Brown (*Lord Jim*), Michaelis and Yundt (*The Secret Agent*), Madame de S—— (*Under Western Eyes*), Mr. Jones (*Victory*), and Ortega (*The Arrow of Gold*). In all these figures the physical distortion and the diseased condition are the outward signs either of spiritual emptiness or of moral depravity. Impotent grotesques like the engineers on the *Patna* and Michaelis are ludicrous by virtue of the enormous disparity between their aims and pretensions and their mental and physical capacities. Others like Mr. Jones, Gentleman Brown, and Ortega are acknowledged outlaws—renegades and murderers.

Like Almayer sleeping on the veranda, these physically grotesque figures are presented in precise detail (we recall the conjunction of "grotesque" and "distinct" in the passage from *Lord Jim*). Often they appear close-up, in glaring sunlight which renders visible the stripes on their clothes and the hairs on their faces. There is nothing vague or shadowy about Conrad's grotesque figures, nor are they divorced from the everyday world. In their physical abnormality, however, they appear devoid of humanity. Madame de S—— actually affects Razumov as would "a wooden or plaster figure of a repulsive kind" (10:225). His impression of Nikita

Necator, the police spy masquerading as a revolutionary, who maims Razumov at the end, also suggests, despite the sharp delineation of detail, a creature scarcely human.

The squeaky stress put on the name "Razumov—Mr. Razumov" pierced the ear ridiculously, like the falsetto of a circus clown beginning an elaborate joke. . . . The stolidity of his attitude, the big feet, the lifeless, hanging hands, the enormous bloodless cheek, the thin wisps of hair straggling down the fat nape of the neck, fascinated Razumov into a stare on the verge of horror and laughter. . . . How could that creature, so grotesque as to set town dogs barking at its mere sight, go about on those deadly errands and slip through the meshes of the police? (10:266–267)

To those who observe them, grotesque figures like Nikita, Kurtz, Wait, and Mr. Jones seem to be apparitions or phantoms, fantastic beings, many of whom are further dehumanized in their resemblance to animals of a repulsive or predatory character. Again the contrast to James is striking. On occasion James's grotesques call to mind images of rapacious beings: Abel Gaw waits like a "ruffled hawk" (25:6) for his one-time partner to die; Mrs. Rimmle (" 'Europe' ") hovers over her children like a vulture; Beale Farange (*What Maisie Knew*) has glittering teeth like fangs. Such imagery is rare, however, when compared to the many images of toads, bats, beetles, ravens, spiders, and vermin which fill the pages of *Lord Jim* or *Victory*. Often Conrad compounds the effect of the grotesque by identifying his characters with nonhuman forms which in themselves are physically abnormal. Mr. Jones is not simply a specter; he is a "starved spectre" (15:118), just as General Montero is not simply a caricature but "the exaggeration of the cruel caricature" (7:122); the Carlist agent, Baron H., in *The Arrow of Gold* (a figure "somewhat grotesque"), resembles an "obese raven" (16:260); Donkin, the archetypal shirker and fomenter of violence, is like a "sick vulture" with shoulders that "drooped like the broken wings of a bird" (3:128, 10).

Far more often than James, Conrad in his creation of grotesque figures explicitly calls attention to the presence of contradictory elements, comic and terrifying, which inspire in the observers of these characters complex feelings of revulsion, fascination, contempt, and dread. The *Patna* skipper, who produces a "droll and fearsome effect"; Nikita, who brings Razumov to the "verge of horror and laughter"; the satanic sisters in "The Inn of the Two Witches," "grotesque in their decrepitude," who would have "been laughable if the sight of their dreadful physical degradation had not been appalling to one's eyes" (14:148)—all illustrate Ruskin's definition of the grotesque as "in almost all cases compounded of two elements, one ludicrous, the other fearful."[5] Often the grotesque incongruity is suggested by the yoking of incompatibles, as when Mr. Jones produces a smile of "ghastly amiability" (15:235); Therese, the sister of the heroine of *The Arrow of Gold*, is "piously ghoulish" (16:246); Azzolati, one of the suitors of Doña Rita, shows himself "the ruthless, the ridiculous financier" (16:119); and Karl Yundt, a "moribund murderer," displays his "impotent fierceness" (8:42–43). Incongruous images make the fearful seem ludicrous, as when the murderous Mr. Jones is seen to resemble a "grotesque toy"; and Schomberg, soon to send his evil guests to Heyst, asserts himself as "one inflates a collapsing toy balloon with a great effort of breath" (15:389, 130). On occasion characters are deflated when compared to diminutive forms of mighty beings: the *Patna* skipper is like a baby elephant (4:37); Ortega is like a "little Prometheus" at whose liver sparrows peck (16:111).

Perhaps the chief source of the contempt and fear inspired by Conrad's grotesque figures lies in the impression that they create of persons not in control of themselves—an impression reinforced particularly in the later novels by comparison of characters to mechanisms or automata: Mr. Jones twitches like a puppet on a string (15:389); Madame de S—— talks compulsively like a "galvanized corpse" (10:215); Ortega's performance before the locked room seems "almost inconceivable . . . like the effect of a trick or of a mechanism" (16:318–319). In Ortega and others the machinelike motion is the sign of obsession, almost to madness, by a fixed idea or passion. When the narrator of *The Arrow of Gold* understands Ortega's insane passion for Rita de Lastaola he grasps the key to that "grotesque and sombre personality" (16:309); the key to the "grotesque psychology" of Schomberg (15:viii) is his mad hatred of Heyst. Not only Ortega and Schomberg, but Kurtz, Gentleman

Brown, Mr. Jones, de Barral, and Scevola (*The Rover*) illustrate the observation of Wolfgang Kayser that "the encounter with madness is one of the basic experiences of the grotesque which life forces upon us."[6]

James also portrays grotesques who are obsessed by one idea (although not to the point of actual madness) and whose behavior suggests the mechanism that can make only one response. In his fiction the grotesque appearance is sometimes the sign of moral blindness or baseness: Selah Tarrant, Abel Gaw, and Mrs. Rimmle are all physically ugly and spiritually repulsive. On the other hand the appearance described as grotesque—whether physically ugly or not—is not necessarily a sign of evil nature. The word *grotesque* may indicate simply that which is to an extreme degree ineffectual or unconventional or incongruous. Colonel Gifford, the exploited partner of the mesmerist in "Dr. Fargo," is "grotesquely sad."[7] To Ransom, Verena Tarrant speaking at Miss Birdseye's is a figure of "sweet grotesqueness."[8] Miss Birdseye was created to "embody in a sympathetic, pathetic, picturesque, and at the same time grotesque way, the humanitary and ci-devant tendencies."[9] The chief note of Mrs. Wix's vain plea to Sir Claude is its "grotesque pathos."[10] Lady Aurora (*The Princess Casamassima*), in her embarrassed benevolences is "the poor devoted, grotesque lady" (5:136). With such words as *devoted*, *sad*, *sweet*, *pathos*, and *sympathetic* compare the words Conrad used in conjunction with *grotesque: appalling* (Wait), *vile* (Cornelius in *Lord Jim*), *atrocious* (Montero), *murderous* (the politicians of Costaguana), *terrible* (General T——), *shocking* (de Barral), *horrible* and *monstrous* (the two witches).

Not only do James's grotesque figures differ from Conrad's, but the relation of the grotesque figure to the protagonist differs in the fiction of the two novelists. One of the most important functions of James's comic or grotesque figures is to caricature traits or attitudes of the protagonist. Richard Poirier was the first critic to stress this relationship of characters, when he pointed out the resemblances between Isabel Archer and Henrietta Stackpole in their longing to see "specimens" and gain the "inner view" of European life.[11] The effort of Rowland Mallet to assist the development of the sculptor

Roderick Hudson has its distorted parallel in the struggle of Mrs. Light, who is likened to "some extravagant old woman in a novel—in something of Hofmann or Balzac" (1:164), to fashion her daughter for a great marriage. Strether's deeply felt exhortation to "live all you can" is comically exaggerated when Jim Pocock on arriving in Paris declares that "I want to come right out and live here myself. And I want to live while I *am* here too" (22:84). In each instance a resemblance is established, but the effect is not to degrade the protagonist, to suggest that Strether is essentially like Pocock, or Rowland like Mrs. Light, or Isabel like Henrietta. Instead the comparisons make one aware of the depth and complexity of the protagonists which set them apart from the fools. As Poirier observes, Isabel grows beyond her Henrietta-like pronouncements, leaving "Henrietta alone to absorb James's satire on provincial Americanism."[12] What the presence of Jim Pocock points up is not Strether's likeness to him but the fate of the man completely submerged in a society ruled by women, the fate that Strether manages to escape.

On occasion Conrad by presenting the grotesque figure as an exaggeration or distortion of the protagonist reveals the differences between them. Peter Ivanovitch's worship of women as the saviors of mankind is a travesty and perversion of Razumov's surrender to the saving power of Nathalie Haldin's idealism and trust. The excited claim of the Russian in *Heart of Darkness* that Kurtz has "enlarged my mind" (5:125) helps to reveal, by its very shallowness, the depth and transforming effect upon Marlow of *his* experience of Kurtz. A more important function of the grotesque figures, however, is to project in distorted form, as the shadow of Almayer is a distortion of the body, qualities and impulses present in the protagonist but repressed and often unrecognized by him. The skipper of the *Patna*, "the incarnation of everything vile and base that lurks in the world we love" (4:21), symbolizes potentialities in all men, including Jim, although Jim can never acknowledge this. The resemblances between Heyst and Mr. Jones, both of whom have rejected sanctions for action and have detached themselves from society, have often been noted.[13] Schomberg, too, with his "low-spirited stoicism," his conviction that "life was a hollow sham" and his disposition to "let things take their course" (15:119,109) also emerges as a gross caricature of the man that he hates.

The arrival of Mr. Jones only intensifies Heyst's sense of power-lessness and futility, which has called forth its grotesque embodi-ment in the spectral presence of his enemy. When Heyst's opportunity comes to kill Mr. Jones, "his very will seemed dead of weariness" (15:390). Several of Conrad's protagonists, however, notably Marlow and M. George (the narrator of *The Arrow of Gold*) are able to resist and gain ascendancy over their grotesque adversaries. M. George in recognizing "a most horrible fellowship" (16:274) with Ortega and Marlow in accepting his bond with the appalling Kurtz both gain a measure of control not only over their opponents but over the irrational impulses within themselves. In contrast Jim, who can admit his guilt but never accept his imper-fection, is defenseless against all his grotesque counterparts, from the engineer whose blubbering "I am one of them fearless fellows" (4:26) is a travesty of Jim's self-confidence, to the satanic Gentle-man Brown with his Iago-like gift of divining his victim's weakness.

The difference in the way James and Conrad portray the relation of protagonist and grotesque figures can be clearly seen if one com-pares their grotesques which most closely resemble each other: the two evil financiers, Abel Gaw in *The Ivory Tower*, for which James made preliminary notes in 1910, and de Barral in *Chance*, pub-lished serially in 1912. Both characters are obsessed with one sub-ject, the making of money; both have been swindlers, but looking back, at the end of their lives, both are convinced that they have been cheated and betrayed; and they brood incessantly upon their fate. Each looks to his one child, a daughter, as his sole companion and source of comfort. Both exhibit an unexpressive mildness which in de Barral, no less than in Gaw, "so far from suggesting any positive tradition of civility was somehow that of a commonness instantly and peculiarly exposed" (*The Ivory Tower*, 25:12–13). Both are small faded shrunken men; the image suggested by the yellowish pallor of Gaw's face, an empty glass once filled with wine (25:12), recalls the ultimate fate of de Barral, who dies by drinking the glass of poison intended for Roderick Anthony. Both Gaw and de Barral stand in marked contrast to the heroes of the novels, Graham Fielder and Anthony. Fielder, without "any sort of faint germ of the money-sense whatever," is the opposite of Gaw in every way—in his notes for the novel James stressed "the utterness of his difference" (25:212, 339); but Anthony, while he is enduring the anguish of his false position, is twice seen as the double of the grotesque, as if de Barral were a shadow cast by the cruel idealism to which Anthony has subjected himself and Flora.

As is evident, grotesque figures in general play a more important part in Conrad's novels than they do in James's. James's novels would be impoverished without their Henrietta Stackpoles, Selah Tarrants, Abel Gaws, and countesses, genuine and spurious; but most of the grotesque figures, to use James's image, are merely wheels to the coach; they do not ride within (3:xix). Grotesque figures embody in exaggerated form qualities or attitudes of the protagonist; some help to create the pain and misery which engulf central characters. Seldom, however, do James's grotesque figures minister directly to the fate of the main figures.

In most of Conrad's novels, on the other hand, grotesque figures play a direct part in the central experience of the main character. Although observers like Jim, Razumov, and Heyst consistently view their grotesque adversaries as being of a nature different from their own, these antagonists body forth in distorted form the dark irrational side of the protagonist's nature. At the same time they assist in the destruction of those illusions of the self and the world in which he once found security, and thus they help create the situation by which the integrity and strength of the protagonist are tested.

The effects of the grotesques in Conrad's fiction differ from novel to novel. The "flabby devil" which in *Heart of Darkness* produces conditions that Marlow calls grotesque inspires in him feelings of contempt and revulsion that make the folly and cruelty of European imperialism a "sordid farce" (5:72, 61). Grotesque characters and situations help to create the impression of the "cruel futility of things" in *Nostromo*, but in the novel the value to the characters of what is sacrificed—the marriage of the Goulds, and the lives of

Decoud, Nostromo, and Avellanos—turns a vain struggle into a "tragic farce" (7:364). In contrast the outcome of *Chance* is fortunate; the grotesque villain de Barral—grotesque in appearance and in his morbid obsession with one idea—is an antagonist fit not for tragedy but for the "sinister farce" of the courtroom where the "grotesque details" of his swindles, when revealed, excite laughter verging on hysteria (13:84). Ortega pounding at the locked door at the climax of *The Arrow of Gold* also releases rather than intensifies the repressed emotions of his hearers; and because, unlike de Barral, he is powerless to do more evil, he is a comic, not a sinister, figure in a "ferocious farce" (16:322). In each novel, however, the narrators and protagonists view a world in which elements of the ludicrous, the pathetic, and the tragic are mixed; in which ignoble characters reveal the flaws of the potentially noble; in which hopes and aspirations, both generous and base, are defeated by human weakness and folly and by the operation of what Conrad's characters see as blind destiny or chance. The elements may be weighted differently in James's and Conrad's novels, but Conrad like James sought those themes James celebrated in the preface to *What Maisie Knew*, the themes that "reflect for us, out of the confusion of life, the close connexion of bliss and bale" (11:viii).

II

The grotesque is most easily analyzed when it manifests itself in the appearance and actions of individual characters. The grotesque may also manifest itself as a sinister or dreamlike quality which the world assumes when a character's sense of security has been destroyed. Wolfgang Kayser has analyzed in detail this experience in what he terms the "alienated" or "estranged" world. The defining element is the sudden transformation of a world familiar and seemingly secure into a place nightmarish and sinister, inspiring not the fear of death but the fear of life. Elements in our world "which are familiar and natural to us . . . suddenly turn out to be strange and ominous . . . the categories which apply to our world view become inapplicable."[14] The experience of alienation or estrangement may be traceable to the mind's activity—to a morbid heightening of the imagination or to a sudden intuition of horrifying realities hitherto concealed below the surface of life. In a number of the works Kayser analyzes, such as Büchner's *Woyzeck*, Hoffmann's *Der Sandmann*, and Poe's "The Masque of the Red Death," the disrupting force is external; or internal malaise is externalized in the form of figures, often demonic, who seem to intrude from the outside. In any case the grotesque world—unstable, often dreamlike, and on the verge of dissolution or collapse—induces in its victim feelings of oppression, bewilderment, and fear.

Kayser mentions neither James nor Conrad, but several of James's novels and almost all of Conrad's can be studied in terms of the concept of the grotesque or "estranged" world. In the novels of both writers elements of the grotesque are reflected by the consciousness of characters who make distinctions between sanity and madness and who resist what they feel to be the unnatural and the bizarre. Both writers portray the struggle of characters to maintain themselves against the forces that menace them. It is in the nature of the disruptive force and in the outcome of the struggle that the important differences lie.

In nearly all James's novels the main characters enter a world baffling to them; they confront people whose motives are not easily fathomed and whose manners are signs that may easily be misread. Feelings like those of Lambert Strether, when he is conscious that "he was moving verily in a strange air and on ground not of the firmest" (21:266), are shared by many of James's characters: by Christopher Newman when he sits in the Bellegardes' drawing room and feels as if he were at a performance in the theater; by Isabel Archer when she pays her first visit to Osmond's villa, from which she senses it would take "an act of energy" to escape (3:364); by Hyacinth Robinson when with the princess at Medley he feels himself "quite at sea and could recognise no shores" (6:27). In none of the novels in which these scenes appear is the feeling of disorientation or malaise sustained long enough to render the world of the novel grotesque. The situation is otherwise, however, in two of James's novels: *What Maisie Knew*, in which grotesque characters

and situations are reflected by the mind of a child, who from beginning to end must struggle to understand the action taking place
around her; and *The Golden Bowl*, in which the prolonged suffering of the heroine fills her mental world with images of the bizarre
and terrifying.

Undoubtedly for many readers what is most grotesque about the
world of *What Maisie Knew* is the central situation itself: the rapid
succession of disintegrating marriages and liaisons of parents, step-
parents, and lovers, an ever-shifting pattern which is all Maisie has
ever known. No one surpasses James in the portrayal of perverted
family relationships, and nothing in James surpasses the picture of
Maisie's profligate parents, who prey upon everyone, including
their own child.

James gives the key to his method of representing the child's
vision of her world when in the first chapter he declares it "the fate
of this patient little girl to see much more than she at first understood" (11:9). Every scene in the novel is reflected in Maisie's consciousness; nothing is portrayed which she is not there to observe;
but the child, without an understanding of the passions and appe-
tites which rule the adults around her and govern the meaning of
such words as *bad*, *propriety*, and *immoral*, lacks the means to
interpret the surfaces her world presents to her. Seen from the
child's perspective, Maisie's world, as Tony Tanner points out in
his excellent study of the novel, is a place unstable and delusive,
where the day-to-day life of the adults is a constant source of anxiety
and mystification. People fade in and out of Maisie's life; they suddenly appear without warning and stay away without explanation.
Adults are capricious in their expressions of anger and affection for
Maisie and change in their feelings for each other.[15] What Maisie
sees is constantly shifting—disappearing, reappearing, looming
large, vanishing. "She was taken into the confidence of passions on
which she fixed just the stare she might have had for images bound-
ing across the wall in the slide of a magic-lantern. Her little world
was phantasmagoric—strange shadows dancing on a sheet" (11:9).

Nothing contributes more to the effect of the phantasmagoric
than the sudden intrusions in Maisie's field of vision of figures
which to the child seem enormous, their faces dominated by one

feature. Seen by the narrator, Beale and Ida, who "made up together . . . some twelve feet three of stature" and carry clothes "as
a train carries passengers" (11:7–8), are comic grotesques. To
Maisie her parents are looming presences who provoke sudden
shocks and fearful speculation. Her father's laugh is "like some
trick in a frightening game" (11:31). Her mother, "concrete, immense and awful" (11:xii), is an even more frightening figure—her
desperation, passion, and hatred seemingly distilled into her
enormous eyes, which as her marriage to Sir Claude disintegrates,
grow thicker in their circumference as the color of her lips and hair
becomes more violent. In the Kensington Gardens, where Maisie
and her stepfather Sir Claude unexpectedly come upon Ida and
one of her lovers, "Maisie received in petrification the full force of
her mother's huge painted eyes—they were like Japanese lanterns
swung under festal arches." That Maisie is not inured to the grotesqueness of her world is made clear not only by her sensations of
fright but even more poignantly by her plea to the "captain" that he
be different from the others, that he love her mother "always"
(11 : 143, 155).

The parallel scene in which Mrs. Beale and Maisie encounter
Beale and his mistress—a scene which, with the other, forbids any
choice between parents and shows that selfishness and betrayal are
the only constants in Maisie's world—is in some ways even more
shocking to Maisie than her confrontation with her mother. In the
second scene there is no kind and sympathetic figure like the captain to mitigate the horror of the situation; and the meeting takes
place not in a green glade in the Kensington Gardens but at an
exhibition filled with grotesque sights: "a collection of extraordinary foreign things in tremendous gardens, with illuminations,
bands, elephants, switch-backs, and sideshows" (11:166). Beale
and his "countess" emerge from a booth as if they were themselves
figures of the sideshow; and in fact, to Maisie, the countess is as
frightening as a circus grotesque. The scene which follows, in the
luxuriously furnished rooms of the countess, is of all the scenes in
the novel the most disturbing in its mingling of elements—
beautiful, frightening, and vile. The room itself, filled with
brocaded nooks, silver boxes, velvet screens, pictures and mirrors,

charms Maisie as no place has ever charmed her. To this room, in which Maisie feels that "the Arabian Nights had quite closed round her" (11:175), her father has brought her to cast her off—or rather, as Maisie perceives, to place her in the position in which she will cast him off. The entrance of the countess, whom James in the preface described as "deplorable" (11:xii) and who to Maisie is scarcely human, transforms the room into a frightening place, its beautiful objects blighted by the look on the countess's face: "All in a moment . . . that queer expression had leaped into the lovely things. . . . There was something in the countess that falsified everything" (11:196).

Throughout the action James evokes the tension between what he calls "the *constant* force that makes for muddlement" (11:xiii) and the effort of the child to interpret and clarify, to make order and sense of what she sees. Early in the action she begins to reason by analogy, sometimes unwittingly exposing the hypocrisy and double standard of her society, as when she wonders why if Miss Overmore can live in Beale's house as Maisie's governess, her mother's companion cannot live at her mother's house as Maisie's tutor (11:40). Shortly after the first of Ida's lovers, Mr. Perriam, is introduced—proof that her marriage with Sir Claude has spoiled— James notes the "high quickening of Maisie's direct perceptions, of her sense of freedom to make things out for herself" (11:99). In the preface James referred to "the particular kind of truth of resistance" which he identified with his heroine. The powers of "resistance" are to be found in Maisie's active intelligence, in her capacity for feeling, in her "perceptions easily and almost infinitely quickened" (11:xi, viii).

During Maisie's last conversation with her mother, the child in an extraordinary moment of illumination suddenly glimpses, as if through a rent in the surface, the full horror of her mother's probable future. "There was literally an instant in which Maisie fully saw—saw madness and desolation, saw ruin and darkness and death" (11:225). The reader is reminded of *The Secret Agent*, of the words "madness and despair," which, although they sound only in the final chapter, might well be the leitmotif of the whole novel.

The dark vision does not, however, govern the tone and mood of *What Maisie Knew*. The tone of the novel is created as much by the wit and clear-eyed compassion of the narrator and by the spirit of hope and capacity for enjoyment that never desert Maisie as by the neglect, cruelty, and betrayal to which she is subjected. James refers to Maisie as living with "all intensity and perplexity and felicity" in her "terribly mixed little world." The end of the novel is not "happy"; Maisie must give up Sir Claude, the person she loves most and who best appreciates her; she is paired at the end with Mrs. Wix, who from the beginning has been shown to be unfit to educate a child. But what abides with the reader of *What Maisie Knew* is the vigor of the child's powers of intelligence and feeling, which not only oppose themselves to the force that "makes for muddlement" but also, in James's words, create for the other characters, however grotesque, "a precious element of dignity" (11:viii, xi).

In James's third-person narratives at least two points of view are established: that of the omniscient author and that of the character who functions as the register or center of consciousness. In *The Golden Bowl* the narrator's view embraces the consciousness of the four principal characters. Two of them, however—Adam Verver and Charlotte Stant—function as registers in only eight of the forty-two chapters of the novel; their sense of the situation is thus subordinated to that of Amerigo the prince, whose point of view dominates the first half of the novel, and that of Maggie, the princess, the only character whose mind is dramatized in the second half. The two principal characters are alike in that each offers a consciousness "highly susceptible of registration" (23:vii); both in marrying sacrifice their old security for a new life in which they confront elements bewildering, unfathomable or frightening. Both must discover the capacities within themselves and others for betrayal, suffering, and resistance; both must endure isolation and the torment of uncertainty before they are united at the end. Their situations are essentially different, however, as are the feelings of bewilderment they suffer. The experience of both characters contains elements of the grotesque but what to the prince is grotesque is of a radically different nature from the images of the sinister, bizarre, and droll which Maggie's consciousness reflects.

Throughout the first half of the action the prince confesses to feelings of uneasiness and anxiety. At the same time he reposes in an unshaken confidence in his judgments, opinions, and personal power—confidence which rests on his awareness of himself as a highly bred man of the world, a *galantuomo* whose first desire is to charm and accommodate those in whom he looks to find his own personal gratification. On the eve of his marriage, he imagines himself drifting, like another Gordon Pym, toward a dazzling white curtain, behind which are concealed the as yet undiscovered expectations of Maggie and her father. The dominant note of the opening chapters is not, however, the prince's fear but his sense of superiority to the innocent and romantic Ververs. What he does not know about them seems less a deficiency and a source of danger than what they do not know about him.

Before and after his marriage he insists to the confidante, Mrs. Assingham, that she must "see him through," must support and counsel him in his new relation. Once Charlotte becomes Adam Verver's wife and the dominant figure in his world, he yields to her insistences, until Maggie shows the force of her will and power to act, and then he turns to her. Always the prince looks to another person to give the direction to his life, but despite his passivity—or perhaps because of it—he seems essentially secure within himself. The equivocations of English society confront the prince with "a mere dead wall, a lapse of logic, a confirmed bewilderment" (23:354–355), but the word *confirmed* suggests an attitude to which the prince is habituated, and the novel does not imply that the prince feels himself in any way inferior to the society which bewilders him. He has his "private subtlety," and during his country-house visits he has recourse to "the trick of a certain detached, the amusement of a certain inward critical, life" (23:327).

The attitude of critical detachment determines the prince's perception of the grotesque, which he experiences not in the form of a terrifying situation that threatens mental equilibrium but as an anomaly appearing to his sophisticated and critical sense ludicrous and absurd, utterly at odds with what wisdom and knowledge of the world and human nature would dictate. What is grotesque above all to the prince is the blindness and innocence of the Ververs and the position in which their failure of imagination has placed himself and Charlotte, encouraged as they are to appear together without their *sposi* but trusted to feel no attraction for each other.

It had taken poor Maggie to invent a way so extremely unusual—yet to which none the less it would be too absurd that he should merely lend himself. Being thrust, systematically, with another woman, and a woman one happened, by the same token, exceedingly to like, and being so thrust that the theory of it seemed to publish one as idiotic or incapable —this was a predicament of which the dignity depended all on one's own handling. What was supremely grotesque in fact was the essential opposition of theories—as if a galantuomo, as *he* at least constitutionally conceived galantuomini, could do anything *but* blush to "go about" at such a rate with such a person as Mrs. Verver in a state of childlike innocence, the state of our primitive parents before the Fall. (23:334–335)

The prince's sense of his situation as grotesque is heightened by the scene of these reflections, the great country house of Matcham where "every voice . . . was a call to the ingenuities and impunities of pleasure" (23:332), making the assumptions on which Maggie acts seem more than ever ludicrous.

The differences between Maggie and the prince are suggested throughout the first half of the novel. Unlike the prince, who rests on his confidence that "by instinct" he will always perceive the crack in what is flawed (23:120), Maggie defers to others in matters of form and appearance, ready to "accept with modest gratitude any better description of a felt truth than her little limits . . . enabled her to make" (23:163). Once married to the prince, she is only too glad to retreat to the security of her childhood relationship with her father, leaving the prince and Charlotte to shine alone at Matcham. In the conscious exaggeration of her confession to her father, "I live in terror. . . . I'm a small creeping thing" (23:181) there is a measure of truth. When the point of view shifts from the prince to Maggie the nature of the reflected life undergoes a profound change. Instead of situations pronounced grotesque by the prince, who views his world with irony and detachment if not with complete comprehension, there are scenes of outward decorum pregnant with violence, inducing in Maggie feelings of oppression and fear which find their expression in mental images exotic and sinister beyond anything hitherto seen in James's novels.

In these images that fill Maggie's mind, the strangeness and terror and sinister beauty of the Gothic romances enter the world of *The Golden Bowl*. Maggie feels herself imprisoned as by a heavy vault that arches over the "solid chamber of her helplessness"; the crisis at Fawns hovers like a ghost in the deserted passages of the great house (24:44, 211). The hidden evil in Maggie's life meets her "like some bad-faced stranger surprised in one of the thick-carpeted corridors of a house of quiet on a Sunday afternoon." By the end the characters take refuge in the perfunctory as in "some spacious central chamber in a haunted house, a great overarched and overglazed rotunda where gaiety might reign, but the doors of which opened into sinister circular passages" (24:237, 288).

What creates the distinctive atmosphere of *The Golden Bowl*, however, is not the imagery of the sinister by itself but the commingling of the bizarre and the droll, the sinister and the comic. Repeatedly Maggie sees her situation, which is not comic, in images of the homely and the undignified. She is like the wheel of a carriage, a housemaid picking diamonds out of a dustbin, a dressed doll who talks when its "firmly stuffed middle" is pressed, and a box labelled and shoved into a van for transit. In contrast to the prince with all his traditions and ancestors, Maggie is like a trader on the frontier who figures "in the likeness even of some Indian squaw with a papoose on her back and barbarous beadwork to sell" (24:323–324). As D. W. Jefferson observes, these images of "the grotesque and the droll" reveal Maggie's humility and modesty, her inability to think of herself as a tragic victim: "Her plight has for her an element of the absurd as well as the agonizing."[16]

Grotesque effects of a different kind are created when Maggie at the end experiences vicariously Charlotte's anxiety and torment, when "she absolutely looked with Charlotte's grave eyes" at Adam Verver, moving slowly back and forth "with his indescribable air of weaving his spell." The "prolonged futility" of Charlotte's action, James observes, "might have been grotesque to a more ironic eye"

(24:283, 284). What the reader is likely to feel as grotesque, however, is not the futility of Charlotte's efforts but the enormity of the contrast of beauty and cruelty in the scenes at Fawns, where amidst priceless treasures Charlotte moves as if led by Adam Verver on a silken leash (24:287). The sinister splendors of *The Golden Bowl* are at some distance from the jeweled horrors of Poe's tomblike bridal chambers and decaying mansions, but in this novel, with its images of opium smokers, rococo chamberlains, circus performers, pagodas, mosques, incense, and eastern caravans, James goes as far as he was ever to go in the direction of the *grotesqueries* of "Ligeia." Scenes like that in which Charlotte, displaying the priceless *vieux Saxe*, is stricken with a voiceless shriek of anguish that only Maggie hears suggest the description in *Roderick Hudson* of the sculptor Gloriani's art, in which "the graceful and the grotesque" are mingled; in which "hideousness grimaces at you suddenly from out of the very bosom of loveliness, and beauty blooms before your eyes in the lap of vileness" (1:107).

Throughout the second half of *The Golden Bowl* Maggie feels her world as unstable and delusive; behind surfaces lurk reasons "kept uncertain for the eyes by their wavering and shifting" (24:52). Repeated experience of moments that are "vertiginous" and sensations as of being drowned in the "dizzying smothering welter" of "submarine depths" and of whirling aloft through space (24:43, 73) belie the placid appearance that she strives to maintain. At the same time, however, Maggie's sense of control steadily increases. To an even greater extent than in *What Maisie Knew*, *The Golden Bowl* shows the powers that make for harmony, decorum, and order dominant over the forces that make for disorder and disintegration. Maggie constantly sees her situation in terms of a problem she must solve, a price she must pay, a game in which certain cards must never be played, a labyrinth from which she must guide herself and the prince. Of all James's characters Maggie suffers the keenest and most prolonged sense of unrest and anguish, but she exhibits as does no other character in James the power to conceive a plan, manipulate appearances, foresee consequences, and effect the desired result. Her effort to preserve the marriages of the prince and herself and of Charlotte and Adam Verver—effort which requires her to exercise "the constructive, the creative hand" (24:145)—comes as close as any act in James's novels to being analogous to the creation of a work of art. Even as she feels herself menaced by Charlotte, her head upon the block, Maggie is conscious of "all the possibilities she controlled." She sees herself as a creator, the others as "figures rehearsing some play of which she herself was the author" (24:236, 235). She imagines herself as a scapegoat who takes from the others "the whole complexity of their peril" but unlike the "scapegoat of old," a passive victim "charged with the sins of the people," she will take the burden voluntarily, will "charge herself with it." The final scene, "crystallised . . . to the right quiet lustre" (24:234, 358), is the result of the control exercised by all four characters.

More powerfully than any of James's other novels *The Golden Bowl* shows that the greater the threat to order and decorum the greater are the forces of control brought into play. Indeed the force may be so great that it will itself come to seem unnatural or grotesque. For a time Charlotte and the prince exercise the controlling power, which induces in Maggie a sense of helplessness and oppressive wonder. It is against Charlotte, however, that forces of control exert themselves most powerfully and frighteningly. Indeed the worker of the remedy may appear more sinister than the wrongdoer when control evokes the image of a silken noose around the victim's neck. The arrangement which virtually forces the prince and Charlotte together is, to the prince, grotesque; Maggie's awakening to the reality of evil, to "the harsh bewildering brush, the daily chilling breath of it" (23:384–385), subjects her imagination to a world of grotesque forms and prowling dangers. In the end, however, the picture of Adam Verver, playing out his leash, weaving his spell, always quiet and self-effacing, admired by Maggie, gazing with his daughter in satisfaction upon his acquisitions, the prince and Charlotte, magnificent "human furniture" (24:360) may for many readers be the most disturbing reality in the novel.

For the reverse of this pattern, for the situation in which characters instead of exerting control struggle helplessly against the forces that threaten them, one has only to turn to Conrad's fiction.

With the one exception of *Chance* the novels picture a struggle which is at best inconclusive in its outcome and which in its most extreme form results not in extraordinary shows of power and control on the part of the characters but in their total subjection to a coil of events that like an infernal machine unwinds inexorably.

III

The bond between Conrad's protagonists and their grotesque counterparts indicates that Conrad shared Victor Hugo's belief that the portrayal of the grotesque is essential to a complete picture of life.[17] This belief finds expression in one of the most notable elements of Conrad's fiction: the creation of scenes tragic in their consequences but farcical in effect. One of the most memorable examples of the episode grotesque in its incongruities is the scene of "low comedy" on the *Patna*, which culminates in Jim's desertion of the ship and his jump into an "everlasting deep hole" (4:101, 111). During the twenty-seven minutes upon which Jim's future life depends, the captain and his two engineers, in vain efforts to launch their lifeboat, engage in struggles "fit for knockabout clowns in a farce" (4:104). Utterly at odds with all Jim's dreams of heroic action, the scene confounds him as much by its "burlesque meanness" (4:121) as by the images of disaster it evokes. To Jim the situation is like a grotesque being with features and facial expression, animated, as Gentleman Brown will later appear to be, by "a directing spirit of perdition that dwelt within, like a malevolent soul in a detestable body" (4:31).

The scene on the *Patna* indicates that Conrad's concern is not with grotesque characters in themselves but with their effect upon the protagonist who undergoes—as a result of the intrusion of grotesque figures—the sudden transformation of a world, familiar and secure, into a place of disorder and terror. Whether or not the protagonist triumphs over his adversaries, the effect of grotesque characters and situations is to rob him of his mental equilibrium and to threaten his power to choose and act. Sensations like those suffered by Heyst when "everything round him had become unreasonable, unsettled, and vaguely urgent" (15:258) are experienced by most of Conrad's central characters.

In his discussion of the grotesque in French and German literature, Kayser analyzes a number of themes, motifs, and devices which are also important in Conrad's portrayal of the estranged or alienated world: scenes of ruin and decay; remote exotic settings like jungles and tropical islands; social groups disrupted by such forces as storms, pestilence, famine, and war; mechanical objects which assume a life of their own; human beings reduced to mechanisms, as if they were "agents of something strange and inhuman";[18] the apparently illogical sequence of events, triggered by an irrational or a trivial act, which makes the whole world appear to be a demonic mechanism. Although Conrad, unlike Poe or Hoffmann or Dostoevsky, never makes an insane mind the reflector of his action, he does evoke in most of his novels the impression of a world menaced or on the verge of chaos. Pictures of corruption or disintegration are created by many of Conrad's settings: the ruinous houses of sinister quiet in *Under Western Eyes* and *The Arrow of Gold*; the rotting structures of the defunct coal company on Heyst's island; the nightmare landscape of Patusan, fecund and spectral, where white coral shines like bleached skulls, and graves are garlanded by flowers of shapes "foreign to one's memory" (4:322). The terrifying sensation of tottering at the edge of an abyss, beyond which lies unimagined horror, overwhelms a number of Conrad's characters—from Nina Almayer to Marlow and Razumov.

Almayer's dream, in which his next step, into nothingness, will bring the "crashing fall" of his universe and the "anguish of perishing creation" (1 : 158, 159), foreshadows Conrad's later evocation of dreamlike worlds of impending collapse. Not until *Heart of Darkness*, however, does Conrad sustain through a whole work a protagonist's consciousness of moving through the fantastic landscape of a dream. Repeatedly Marlow stresses the unnerving effects of the nightmare journey through a "strange world of plants, and water, and silence" (5:93). What most oppresses him is not the constant struggle against physical obstacles—terrible though these are—but the sense of being cut off from normal life, of losing one's own reality in a world of insane distortion: "We were cut off from the comprehension of our surroundings; we glided past like phantoms, wondering and secretly appalled, as sane men would be before an enthusiastic outbreak in a madhouse." Grotesque sights— the natives with faces like "grotesque masks"; the emaciated body of Kurtz, "pitiful and appalling," animated by "grotesque jerks"; the fabulous harlequin figure, grotesque because his very presence in the jungle is a fantastic incongruity—all work to create what Marlow calls the "dream-sensation" of the experience, "that commingling of absurdity, surprise, and bewilderment in a tremor of struggling revolt" (5:96, 61, 134, 82).

Of Conrad's characters Marlow is the most accessible to sudden glimpses into infernal regions, to sudden visions of a universe drained of light and bereft of order. It is of the essence of Marlow's character, however, that he will not lose himself in "the chaos of dark thoughts," and such visions last only a moment. Without exception Conrad's protagonists—even the weakest like Almayer and Willems—struggle like Marlow to keep their hold on what he calls "the sheltering conception of light and order which is our refuge" (4:313). In *The Secret Agent* and *Under Western Eyes* the protagonist, in maintaining a false identity, is engaged in conscious deception and as a result is especially vulnerable to the power of grotesque characters and situations and is inclined to feel the world as hostile and alien.[19] As if to reflect the malaise of the protagonist, the world in which he moves wears permanently the "vast and dismal aspect of disorder" (4:313), which Marlow glimpses only for a moment. It is in these two novels, then, that Conrad's methods of creating an estranged world in which characters are confounded, trapped, and destroyed can be most fully studied.

The Secret Agent is unique among Conrad's novels in its picture of characters at the mercy of a chain of events initiated by human acts but seemingly beyond human control. To a greater degree than elsewhere in Conrad's fiction, the characters' sense of their world as grotesque or estranged is owing to their plight as victims of what appears to be an infernal mechanism, empowered by the irrational fears it produces, working to no logical or foreseeable end. The very act which sets the mechanism in motion—Mr. Vla-

dimir's command that Verloc bomb the Greenwich Observatory—
is, as Mr. Vladimir states, intended to result in a deed of insane
ferocity "so absurd as to be incomprehensible, inexplicable, almost
unthinkable." The act of "shocking senselessness" (8:33) confounds
all the characters and ultimately subjects three of them—Verloc,
Winnie, and Ossipon—to the terrifying experience of feeling the
supports of their existence suddenly collapse and life become a
nightmare.

The impression of the city as unhuman and hostile to man is
evoked for the reader in the opening scene as Verloc begins his
walk toward death through a "town without shadows" under the
corrosive light of a "bloodshot" sun (8:11). The effect of Mr. Vladimir's instructions is to waken the somnolent Verloc to the horror
of such a world, to induce in him a powerful sense of alienation and
estrangement. His obsessive dread of the act he must perform renders the city to his haunted eyes an "inhospitable accumulation"
of mud and bricks and stones, an "enormity" so unfriendly to
human life that he apprehends it with a force "approaching to positive bodily anguish." Eventually the fear that produces the ghastly
hallucination of Mr. Vladimir's face, pressed like a luminous seal on
the "fatal darkness" (8:56, 57), infects every part of Verloc's being.
The "black care" that becomes his "fatal attendant" (8:186) not only
isolates him from his wife and from every other human being; it
imposes itself like a wall or a veil between himself and the universe, cutting him off from the world apprehended by the senses
and transforming the world of his "mental vision" into the "solitude
of a vast and hopeless desert" (8 : 154, 174, 179).

No less than her husband Winnie Verloc suffers the disintegration of her world, but whereas Verloc experiences slow mounting
dread that paralyzes him, Winnie, when she learns of her brother's
death at Verloc's hands, receives a shock that instantly destroys her
mental equilibrium. Estrangement, which in Verloc takes the form
of isolation from the outer world of appearances, in Winnie is registered as violent disjunction within the self: "Her personality
seemed to have been torn into two pieces, whose mental operations did not adjust themselves very well to each other." For her,
as for Verloc, shock alters "even the aspect of inanimate things,"

but unlike Verloc, who shrinks from action, Winnie is impelled to action, by grief and rage. Once her murderous passion has spent itself in the killing of Verloc, however, she too succumbs to an overpowering sense of the city as an alien world, a black abyss from which she is powerless to escape (8:254, 249, 271).

When Ossipon appears in the final scenes, Conrad introduces the last link in the chain created by the impact of one character's acts upon the mind of another. As Mr. Vladimir's command destroys the mental balance of Verloc and as Verloc's act shatters the moral nature of Winnie, she in turn destroys the equilibrium of Ossipon, who comes upon her as she leaves the house after the murder of Verloc. Like a number of Conrad's characters Ossipon, when confounded by a situation that defies comprehension, has the sensation of sinking into depths where he struggles to keep his footing (8:279). When the truth of the situation finally flashes upon him, he like Winnie suffers an overwhelming shock, which in him registers itself as an insane terror, recalling the delirium of the *Patna* engineer: Ossipon "positively saw snakes now. He saw the woman twined round him like a snake, not to be shaken off" (8:291). Ossipon is successful in shaking off Winnie, as Winnie is successful in killing Verloc; but Ossipon too is a victim of the "madness and despair" that destroys the others: "He was menaced by this thing in the very sources of his existence" (8:307). The impending degeneration of Ossipon is merely stated, not vividly rendered as are the mental states of Verloc and Winnie; but his fate is clearly meant to be another piece in the pattern created by the successive acts of Mr. Vladimir, Verloc, and Winnie.

Throughout the novel the impression of characters powerless to control a mechanism they have set in motion is reinforced when they themselves seem like machines.[20] Verloc answering the shop bell not only moves like an automaton but has "an automaton's absurd air of being aware of the machinery inside of him" (8:197). Terror reduces Ossipon to a mechanism whose words come "as though he had released a catch in order to speak" (8:294). The news of Winnie's suicide transforms his brain into a machine which he cannot control but can only observe as if it were "suspended in the air before him . . . pulsating to the rhythm of an impenetrable mystery" (8:310). Conversely machines assume a terrifying life of their own: the speaking tubes with "gaping mouths" (8:97) menace the assistant commissioner; the broken-down cab subjects Winnie and her mother to such violent motion that the world outside seems to collapse behind them; the explosive mechanism of the bomb blows up Stevie. The sinister life of all the mechanisms beyond human control is perfectly represented by the player piano in the Silenus bar which twice executes a tune without human agency—when the death of Stevie and, later, of Winnie are announced.

The violence of the incongruity of the trivial music and the ghastly deaths indicates the chief source of the grotesque in *The Secret Agent*. Indeed in no other novel does Conrad exploit incongruities so extreme and so numerous to produce a world and characters which confound the reader's sense of what is normal and rational. Not only are the physically monstrous figures like Michaelis and Yundt absurd beyond Conrad's other grotesques in their espousal of changes that they are utterly powerless to effect; but the grotesque situations such as that of Winnie and Ossipon struggling on the shop floor surpass scenes in the earlier novels in the enormity of the contrast of those ghastly and farcical elements which are yoked to produce effects of grisly comedy. Finally in no other novel does Conrad so consistently create grotesque effects through the resources of the mock-heroic style. The extreme disparity between the squalid lives of the characters and the epic world evoked by references to Ulysses, Penelope, and Virgil's Silenus not only intensifies the desolate horror of the situation, but at the same time it makes the horror bearable. The violent incongruities in scenes such as the cab ride, "a perfection of grotesque misery" (8:170), in which the grandiloquent style is shockingly at odds with the pitiful miseries that it inflates, intensify the reader's sense of a world out of joint, in which nothing fits, with everyone at cross purposes; and the whole chain of events confounds the reason.

As in *The Secret Agent*, Conrad places his protagonist in *Under Western Eyes* in the midst of physically grotesque persons and subjects him to a sequence of events set in motion by a violent act and leading to consequences that reason could not foresee. The tone of this novel, however, is different from that created by the sustained irony of *The Secret Agent*. In *Under Western Eyes* the picture of an estranged world is created not primarily by the physically grotesque characters and situations nor by mock-heroic style but by the protagonist's awareness of distortion and incongruity. Of all Conrad's novels *Under Western Eyes* gives the fullest, most sustained picture of grotesque realities as they are reflected by a tormented consciousness.

The protagonist Razumov, whose mind is the stage of the action in three of the four parts of the novel, is admirably conceived to serve as the mirror of the estranged world of the novel. Like Jim he is at the mercy of a powerful imagination which, when his life is menaced, subjects him to intense visions of ruin; like Marlow he struggles to resist the power of the irrational and the bizarre: he is one of those men who keeps "an instinctive hold on normal, practical, everyday life" (10:10), and his very horror of the grotesque strengthens its hold on him. Thus, when Haldin suddenly appears like an apparition in Razumov's rooms, confesses that he is the assassin of the minister-president, Mr. De P——, and seeks Razumov's aid, Razumov succumbs to an overpowering sense that his very existence has been undermined, that he is at the mercy of any "destructive horror" that might suddenly walk in upon him (10:78). His sense of a world suddenly become unstable and sinister is expressed in familiar terms—in sensations of falling to the bottom of an abyss, of feeling the moral supports of his life collapse, of living through the disconnected sequences of a dream (10:23, 76, 315).

What transforms Razumov's world of sober realities into a nightmare realm peopled by phantoms and demons is not simply the presence of Haldin but his betrayal of Haldin. It is not Haldin himself but Razumov's decision to give Haldin up to the police that inspires in Razumov a "suspicious uneasiness, such as we may experience when we enter an unlighted strange place" (10:35). Even the trivialities of everyday existence become strange and menacing: "When he had got back into the middle of things they were all changed, subtly and provokingly in their nature: inanimate objects, human faces, the landlady, the rustic servant-girl, the staircase, the streets, the very air" (10:298). Far from easing his tortured state, his interviews with General T—— and Mikulin only intensify his torment, subjecting him to the gnawing anguish of knowing himself suspect and forcing him to sustain a false identity—as a revolutionary in the pay of the imperial police. Naturally given to viewing his own thoughts with detachment, he suffers as a result of the betrayal the sense of being split into two persons: a frenzied actor and a dispassionate sardonic observer of the self whose sudden compulsions to speak he can sometimes but not always control. This double consciousness makes Razumov appear to the narrator at one point as though "he were turning the knife in the wound and watching the effect" (10:351).

Razumov is the victim of unenlightened egoism which impels him to seek his own security at any cost. At the same time, however, he is the victim of external forces: the revolutionary ardor embodied in Haldin, and the power of the autocracy, equally destructive and irrational, incarnate in General T——, "the embodied power of autocracy, grotesque and terrible" (10:84). The deathlike nature of the forces which have claimed Razumov is expressed most obviously by the physical distortion which marks the revolutionaries no less than the goggle-eyed General T——. In Razumov's fevered vision the abnormality of the grotesque is heightened, but figures like Peter Ivanovitch and Madame de S—— seem macabre and bizarre to Nathalie Haldin and the teacher of languages as well as to Razumov.

What emerges, then, in parts 2, 3, and 4, in which Razumov, the teacher of languages, and Nathalie Haldin all serve as reflectors, is a composite vision of a world which seems in its distortion to mirror the tormented mind of Razumov but which is in its nature unstable and sinister, rendered grotesque by certain effects more pervasive in *Under Western Eyes* than in any of Conrad's other novels. Razumov's sense of the world as sinister and strange is intensified when ordinary acts of speaking and listening appear to be distorted: when Peter Ivanovitch's voice seems to issue from beneath his spectacles, not from his lips, when the squeaks of Nikita's voice seem to come from his distended stomach, when Razumov's voice appears to reach Sophia Antonovna through the pupils of her eyes (10:216, 266, 257). Scenes in the novel, notable for their sharp contrasts of black and white, their distortion, their effects of silence and immobility, repeatedly suggest the dreamlike effects of surrealist painting. The descriptions of the Château Borel, for instance, achieve effects remarkably similar to those of Chirico's early metaphysical paintings. The sense of eerie silence and of empty space that seems ominous is evoked by the appearance of the Château Borel as a place deserted yet guarded, with its windows shuttered, its door wide open. The emptiness of the abandoned place is haunted by the sound of a voice which seems to Nathalie "as though . . . left behind by the departed inhabitants to talk to the bare walls" (10:144). Here, as in Chirico's paintings of towers and streets and squares, the intensity of lines and shapes, rendered with supernatural clarity, enhances the strangeness of the world:

The landing was prolonged into a bare corridor, right and left, desolate perspectives of white and gold decoration without a strip of carpet. The very light, pouring through a large window at the end, seemed dusty; and a solitary speck reposing on the balustrade of white marble—the silk top-hat of the great feminist—asserted itself extremely, black and glossy in all that crude whiteness. . . . [Razumov] stepped on the first step and leaned his back against the wall. Below him the great hall with its chequered floor of black and white seemed absurdly large and like some public place where a great power of resonance awaits the provocation of footfalls and voices. (10:226)

Scenes like these and those in which Razumov sees the phantom of Haldin come as close as anything in Conrad to the fantastic and the supernatural. *Under Western Eyes* is realistic in the sense that action is always to be explained in natural terms; in none of Conrad's works are natural laws suspended. Characters do not awaken to find themselves turned into insects or their noses detached from their faces. Whereas Kafka's Gregor Samsa and Gogol's Major Kovalyov are grotesques in worlds in which normal reality has been displaced, Conrad's protagonists inhabit a world in which pink toads exist only in the visions of delirium and the distinction between sanity and madness is always made. All Conrad's novels are informed by a point of view which distinguishes between the normal and the abnormal, whether the narrator is the omniscient author or a character like Marlow, who declares in *Chance* that "the normal alone can overcome the abnormal" (13:429).

Given the stress on the powers of the mind in such novels as *What Maisie Knew* and *The Golden Bowl*, one might suppose that James makes as clear a distinction as Conrad makes between the normal and the abnormal, between sanity and madness, between what is grotesque and what is not grotesque. In a number of James's novels—*The Bostonians*, *What Maisie Knew*, and *The Ambassadors*, for instance—such distinctions can be easily made. In certain works, however, the line between the normal and the abnormal is not easy to draw. The discrepancy between what James or his characters designate as grotesque and what seems grotesque to many readers raises fundamental questions about James's intentions. *The Turn of the Screw*, for instance, presents in the person of the main narrator, the governess, a character who to some readers is a figure of devotion and courage engaged in a struggle with the forces of evil; to others she is herself the chief source of evil and the prime embodiment of the grotesque.

In itself the governess's tale, which James called an "excursion into chaos" (12:xvii), illustrates a number of elements that Kayser has identified in the grotesque literature of the nineteenth century: the intrusion of the demonic in a peaceful world, the confrontation of the hideous and the beautiful, the sense of a struggle with inexplicable forces. The sudden transformation of a world seemingly secure and beautiful into a place of strange and sinister portent is precisely the effect for the governess of the first appearance of the apparition of Peter Quint on the tower.

There came to me thus a bewilderment of vision of which, after these years, there is no living view that I can hope to give. . . . The place . . . in the strangest way in the world, had on the instant and by the very fact of its appearance become a solitude. . . . It was as if, while I took in, what I did take in, all the rest of the scene had been stricken with death. I can hear again, as I write, the intense hush in which the sounds of evening dropped. The rooks stopped cawing in the golden sky and the friendly hour lost for the unspeakable minute all its voice. (12:176)

Except for one appalling moment, "confounding and bottomless" (12:307), when she wonders if perhaps the child Miles is innocent, the governess does not doubt that she struggles with a situation "revoltingly against nature" and that she confronts figures of "unmistakeable horror and evil" (12:295, 203). Her description of Peter Quint, with his red hair, sharp eyes, arched eyebrows, and "white face of damnation" (12:308), is clearly a picture of the devil, whose grotesqueness is heightened by contrast with the angelic beauty and seeming goodness of the children.

In the opinion of many readers, however, the terms the governess applies to her adversaries are best applied to herself. It is she, many argue, who is unnatural and even monstrous; she who imagines the existence of the ghosts; or granting their existence, she is nonetheless the most frightening figure in the children's world. J. A. Ward expresses the view of a number of critics of the story: the governess "is, if not a malignant force like the demons, a grotesque person who would seem satanic to any child."[21] To James the main problem in the tale was "to add, organically, the element of beauty to a thing so foully ugly,"[22] but readers do not agree which are the elements of beauty, which are those of foul ugliness.

In a letter to H. G. Wells, James, in referring to the governess, alluded to "the grotesque business I had to make her picture."[23] This together with his discussion in the preface of the properties of his ghostly presences suggests that Quint and Miss Jessel have an existence independent of the governess's romantic fancy. But even if one grants the existence of the ghosts, questions remain: have the ghosts the motives the governess imputes to them? Do the children see them? Are the children possessed and also corrupted? Does Miles at the end address the cry of "you devil" to Quint or to the governess? Conrad, in praising *The Turn of the Screw* for the "intellectual thrill" which James drew from his subject,[24] was perhaps referring to apparently deliberate ambiguities. Unless one denies that this is a tale of the supernatural, one grants the presence of the ghosts; but the disquieting traits of the governess—her possessiveness, her craving to be a sacrificial victim, and her habit of jumping convulsively from speculation to assertion—reveal her as a figure of disturbing tendencies, hitherto latent, which are brought to the surface and intensified by the evil presences, who acting not only on the children but on their protector, give another turn of the screw.

The governess, a first-person narrator, is a character whose reliability as a witness we are invited to question, as we are not moved to question the narrator of, say, "The Secret Sharer" or Marlow in *Heart of Darkness*, who repeatedly declares himself unable to pronounce conclusively on the meaning of his experience. The very certainty with which the governess declares the motives of her ghostly adversaries provokes doubts. Even James's third-person narratives, however, raise questions about the fundamental nature of the characters. No character of Conrad, even the problematical hero of *Lord Jim*, has elicited such a variety of responses as Adam Verver, for instance, who has been pronounced by one critic "cold, inhuman and inadequate" as well as "obscenely cruel"; celebrated by a second as the embodiment of godlike wisdom and Christian *caritas*; dismissed by a third as essentially simple, of "a primal innocence of intention"; and analyzed by a fourth as the type of Yankee trader, "far more shrewd and deep and powerful than he seems."[25]

Whereas the direction of James's later work is toward increasing ambiguity, toward the portrayal of situations in which characters affect different readers in diametrically opposite ways, the direction of Conrad's later work is toward the portrayal of clearcut conflicts between figures embodying the forces of good and evil as distinctly as figures in allegory. But in all Conrad's fiction—in *Nostromo* and *Lord Jim* as well as in *Chance* and *Victory*—one distinguishes without uncertainty between the noble and the base, the predators and the victims. Oddly enough Conrad's world, felt by the characters to be treacherous, unfathomable, and dreamlike, is less ambiguous than James's world, in which characters formulate hypotheses and deduce conclusions, solve mysteries and exult in their knowledge. As we have seen, the excessive development of the rational faculties, or the excessive confidence in one's powers of divination, causes characters like Adam Verver and the narrators of *The Turn of the Screw* and *The Sacred Fount* to appear to some readers unnatural, grotesque, and even evil. Conrad's repeated stress on the limits of human intelligence and the dangers of the imagination, coupled with the characters' sense of uncertainty, shock, and helplessness in the presence of the grotesque, tends to sharpen the distinctions between the normal and the abnormal.

The mental energies of James's characters are proved by every manifestation of the grotesque in the novels: the situation judged grotesque by a sophisticated observer, the experience of the grotesque as a sinister or terrifying situation which calls forth powers of resistance and control, and the excessive development of the rational or imaginative faculties to the point that the possessor himself becomes grotesque. The power of the mind to control the forces that make for disorder and confusion marks James's satire as well as his portrayal of the grotesque. It is also the power with which the artist, as depicted in James's prefaces, undertakes to shape the rich but formless substance of life into art. The experience of Conrad's protagonists who engage in vain or inconclusive struggles against the power of the grotesque is likewise consistent with other aspects of Conrad's work: the momentary glimpses of realities too terrifying to be endured for long; the grim and bitter satire which the perception of the intolerable calls forth; the insistence of the novelist and his characters upon the impossibility of knowing any other person; and finally the picture of the artist as one who, like the characters he creates, engages in a perilous struggle with forces which he but dimly understands and imperfectly controls.

8

Tragedy

To consider the grotesque in such novels as *What Maisie Knew*, *Lord Jim*, and *The Secret Agent* is to see the truth of Conrad's observation that "in human affairs the comic and the tragic jostle each other at every step."[1] Unlike Conrad, James did not mingle tragedy and farce; he did not introduce low comedy into scenes of crisis. But James was fully aware of the coexistence of tragedy and comedy in human experience. In a review of Howells's *Foregone Conclusion* he noted "the way human levity hovers about the edge of all painful occurrences."[2] He frequently mentioned the tragic as one in a mixture of several elements: Rowland Mallet's relation to the action of *Roderick Hudson*, for instance, had to be "a sufficiently limited, a sufficiently pathetic, tragic, comic, ironic, personal state to be thoroughly natural" (1:xvii). In the fiction of both James and Conrad the tragic is intermingled with romantic, satiric, and grotesque elements. The fear experienced by characters to whom the world seems grotesque or estranged may be tragic in its intensity. Romantic illusions may lead to fatal consequences. Two of the works discussed under the heading of *Romance—The Portrait of a Lady* and *Lord Jim*—have often been called tragic novels. Several of the novels to be considered in this chapter—*Roderick Hudson, The Princess Casamassima, The Wings of the Dove*, and *Nostromo*—also exemplify the novelists' use of the conventions of romance.

In their fiction, essays, and letters both James and Conrad used the words *tragedy* and *tragic* in a general sense to refer to human suffering, loss, disillusionment, and defeat.[3] The most important differences in their ideas of the tragic are illustrated by the four statements quoted below. James's fullest statement appears in the preface to *What Maisie Knew:* "No themes are so human as those that reflect for us, out of the confusion of life, the close connexion of bliss and bale, of the things that help with the things that hurt, so dangling before us for ever that bright hard medal, of so strange an alloy, one face of which is somebody's right and ease and the other somebody's pain and wrong" (11:viii).

In citing Shakespeare's Hamlet and Lear to illustrate the powers all protagonists should possess, James indicated what he deemed most important in the tragic hero: "Their being finely aware—as Hamlet and Lear, say, are finely aware—*makes* absolutely the intensity of their adventure, gives the maximum of sense to what befalls them" (5:viii).

Conrad comes closest to defining the tragic in his letter of January 31, 1898, to R. B. Cunninghame Graham:

What makes mankind tragic is not that they are victims of nature, it is that they are conscious of it. To be part of the animal kingdom under the conditions of this earth is very well—but as soon as you know of your slavery, the pain, the anger, the strife—the tragedy begins. . . . There is no morality, no knowledge and no hope; there is only the consciousness of ourselves which drives us about a world that, whether seen in a convex or a concave mirror, is always but a vain and fleeting appearance.[4]

The word *tragic* might be added to the list of adjectives describing life in Conrad's letter of August 24, 1901, to the *New York Times Saturday Review:* "The only legitimate basis of creative work lies in the courageous recognition of all the irreconcilable antagonisms that make our life so enigmatic, so burdensome, so fascinating, so dangerous—so full of hope."[5]

Two related points of differences are apparent. Both novelists refer to opposites, but James's "close connexion of bliss and bale" suggests a fusion or a balance, whereas Conrad's "irreconcilable antagonisms" implies forces eternally in conflict. James and Conrad define tragic awareness in different ways. For James the awareness exemplified by Hamlet and Lear lifts a character above the ordinary, gives him dignity, and makes his adventure a matter of importance and deep human meaning. The consciousness which to Conrad makes men tragic is their awareness of helplessness in a world without purpose save what men themselves conceive. In a word James defines consciousness as a constructive force, Conrad as the cause of suffering.

The novelists' ideas of the tragic are clearly illustrated in their treatment of three themes: degeneration, irreconcilable conflict, and sacrificial love.

I

The theme of degeneration is much more prominent in Conrad's fiction than in James's. At least five of Conrad's important characters—Almayer, Willems, Lingard (in *The Rescue*), Kurtz, and Nostromo—are victims of inward corruption. This testifies to Conrad's belief that "morbid psychology . . . is a perfectly legitimate subject for an artist's genius."[6] The psychology of a number of James's characters, such as Olive Chancellor, Marcher, Stransom, ("The Altar of the Dead"), and Marmaduke ("Maud-Evelyn"), can be described as morbid; but these victims of obsessions do not undergo a process of degeneration. In fact *Roderick Hudson* is the only novel in which James portrays the disintegration of a main character. Because it illustrates the basic elements of tragedy in James's fiction it may be compared with *An Outcast of the Islands*, Conrad's most detailed study of degeneration, to illustrate the different sources of tragic effects in the fiction of the two writers.

James did not describe the title character of *Roderick Hudson* as a tragic hero, but in a number of ways, the central action to which James refers in the preface (1:xvi), the disintegration of the sculptor, follows a pattern customarily identified as tragic. An artist of remarkable gifts Roderick achieves a supreme success, the highest point of which his genius is capable; he then morally and psychologically degenerates and dies. Although Roderick denies any responsibility for his fall, in the very act of asserting that he is "the last circumstance" (1:231) upon which his success or failure depends, he induces in himself a sense of powerlessness and so creates one of the circumstances responsible for his fate. That his degeneration is a fall from greatness to ruin is repeatedly emphasized: by Roderick's first statues, of Adam and Eve in their prelapsarian innocence; by such statements as Roderick's "If I hadn't risen I shouldn't have fallen"; by Rowland's image of Roderick "plunging like a diver into a misty gulf"; and finally by Roderick's actual fall in the Alps "from a great height" (1:436, 314, 523) to death. In the first chapter of the novel his statue of a youth draining the cup of life portends his fate;[7] and his death sends shock waves registered in the anguish of those who gather by his body at the end.

In the preface James refers to only one action, the fall of Roderick; but in making Rowland's view of that action the subject of the novel, James created a second action of tragic possibility— the rise and fall of Rowland's hopes for Roderick. Because Rowland grounds his own expectation of happiness in his plan to promote the success of another person, his self-interest and his generosity perpetually reinforce each other, placing him always at the mercy of what others do, and making renunciation of his effort psychologically impossible.[8] If Roderick has the tragic hero's disposition to embrace extremes and reject moderation, Rowland, the "most rational of men" (1:525), has the tragic capacity to commit himself utterly to one course and hold to it even when he perceives the folly of his effort. The ruin of Roderick makes Rowland a scapegoat who must bear a double burden of blame which is imposed by himself and by Roderick's family.[9] At the end he must swallow his "daily dose of bitterness," and he at last feels the "cup of his own ordeal full to overflowing" (1:434, 506).

The egoism, blindness, and perversity that convert romantic dreams into tragedy are evident in all three main characters: Roderick, Rowland, and Christina Light. But the reader has valid grounds for agreeing with the first, if not the second, part of Roderick's declaration, that his failure "won't be a tragedy, simply because I sha'n't assist at it" (1:231). Clearly Roderick by his very passivity does assist at his fall, but in failing to show any sign of inner struggle he seems (in James's words) "to place himself beyond our understanding and our sympathy" (1:xiv). Rowland exhibits complexities of feeling and motive which render him, more so than Roderick, a potentially tragic figure. Because he is a man of conscience and sympathy, he has a capacity for suffering far greater than Roderick's. But the situation is such that Rowland's ordeal, like Christina Light's vain struggle, is inevitably over-shadowed by the disintegration of Roderick and thus lacks the con-centrated force of a tragic action.

If none of the characters is the protagonist in an action that we believe to be tragic, the novel has moments of revelation and rec-ognition in which characters suffer with an intensity that becomes tragic. As well as any novel, in fact, *Roderick Hudson* illustrates Ellen Leyburn's observation that characters of James whom the "strict theorist" would judge pathetic, not tragic, may evoke the tragic emotions of pity and fear."[10] Certainly Roderick's anguish in the midst of beauty to which his spirit is dead has the force of despair. The tremendous words exchanged at the end by Rowland and Roderick are ultimate and irrevocable like the act in tragedy which precipitates catastrophe. But the word *tragic* belongs above all to the scene in which Rowland, watching by the body of Roderick, confronts the irreducible fact of death, suffers the full-ness of his loss, and in anguish inflicts upon himself mentally the mutilation to which the tragic hero may be driven:

He watched in the flesh for seven long hours, but the vigil of his spirit was a thing that would never cease. The most rational of men wandered and lost himself in the dark places of passion, lashed his "conduct" with a scourge of steel, accusing it of cruelty and injustice: he would have lain down there in Roderick's place to unsay the words that had yesterday driven him forth on his ramble of despair. Roderick had been fond of saying that there are such things as necessary follies, and he, of all men, was now proving it. The great gaunt wicked cliff above them became al-most company to him, as the chance-saved photograph of a murderer might become for a shipwrecked castaway a link with civilisation: it had but done *its* part too, and what were they both, in their stupidity, he and it, but dumb agents of fate? (1:525)

Like *Roderick Hudson* nearly all James's novels in which the element of romance is strong reach their climax in scenes wherein characters experience reality with a force that the reader feels to be tragic. We have already noted several of such scenes: Newman standing before the convent wall, Isabel comprehending the full misery of her life as she sits by the dying fire, Olive Chancellor suffering the pain of loss which dries up "the mists and ambiguities of life" and affords her at last "a kind of tragic relief," Madame de Vionnet amidst her elegance prophesying her doom as Strether apprehends "the fine free range of bliss and bale" (22:286). All these scenes illustrate the "strange alloy" in human experience. All attest to James's conviction that good and evil are inextricably mixed; that enlightenment exacts a price in suffering, which becomes in turn the "downright consecration of knowledge."[11] Characters like Isabel, Hyacinth, Strether and Maggie Verver, who grow through suffering, illustrate the equivalence or balance of opposites, held to be essential to tragedy, whereby the source of joy is also a source of pain, and inward victory follows outward defeat.[12]

It may seem that suffering and loss are overemphasized when *Roderick Hudson* ends: Roderick is dead; Mary's life is blighted; Christina, who seems to Rowland in her last appearance "almost tragic" (1:492), has vowed that her marriage shall put her beyond redemption and prepares to act accordingly; Rowland will live with the eternal burden of remorse and guilt. At the same time the principle of equivalence is repeatedly emphasized in *Roderick Hudson*, as if James were setting forth the ideas that he was to dramatize in his later works. Rowland in analyzing Roderick marvels at "so much power . . . going with so much weakness" and sees genius as a "double-edged instrument," "priceless, beneficent, divine," but also "capricious, sinister, cruel" (1:294, 222). Rome itself is a source of pleasure and pain, the city where one's serenity is most mellow, one's depression most unbearable. In answer to Mary Garland, who wonders that so much beauty should surround Roderick in his ruin and fill their "sad strange summer" Rowland argues James's essential principle—that joy and pain are equivalent and inseparable: "We shouldn't be able to enjoy, I suppose, unless we could suffer, and in anything that's worthy of the name of experience—that experience which is the real *taste* of life, isn't it?—the mixture is of the finest and subtlest" (1:457).

If *Roderick Hudson* fails to dramatize the idea of equivalence as fully as do the late novels, if the sense of loss and life wasted is dominant at the end, by the same measure we perceive how much of value once existed. Suffering is great when the good lost is precious. Roderick's pose is theatrical, but his words sound James's theme of lost value: "I'm bidding farewell to Italy, to beauty, to honour, to life. I only want to assure you that I know what I lose" (1:467). To illuminate James's idea of tragedy as the sacrifice of good we have only to place *Roderick Hudson* beside *An Outcast of the Islands*, in which we see not great gifts wasted and chances for fulfillment lost but the terrified consciousness of alienation and degradation to which a man utterly lacking in nobility may be brought.

The differences between James's and Conrad's portrayal of degeneration are put in relief by the superficial similarities between Roderick Hudson and Willems, the protagonist of *An Outcast of the Islands*. Each wastes himself in passion for a woman whose force of will is superior to his own, and each sinks into apathy and despair. Willems is an egoist like Roderick who holds himself superior to rules of conduct, in all matters making himself the point of reference, his pleasure and advancement the justification for any act: "His clear duty was to make himself happy" (2:142). Unlike Roderick, Willems derives satisfaction from ruling over others and initially cherishes illusions that he can control events and escape unpleasant consequences. But Willems, no less than Roderick, is a hollow man, whose degeneration is rendered in images of depletion and exhaustion. Unlike Roderick, who sheds his misdeeds like an unwanted skin and apparently never feels guilt or remorse or shame, Willems struggles vainly against a passion that he can only condemn as evil. But, like Roderick, Willems refuses to accept responsibility for his deeds, viewing them as the work of forces independent of his will. Both protagonists owe their initial success to patrons who out of benevolent egoism place their protégés in the settings where the degeneration begins, and who then watch as their protégés, whose capacity for ruin their patrons had failed to measure, betray them and their hopes for them.

Despite these parallels, however, the two protagonists are radically different in nature. Roderick not only sees himself in romantic terms but is conceived romantically by James as the artist of genius who burns himself out as if he craved destruction and who dies consumed but unmarred, so that Singleton may say at his death, "He was the most beautiful of men!" (1:524). Willems in contrast is utterly without great gifts such as James imputed to his protagonist. Until his theft of his employer's money is discovered, Willems enjoys power and sway; but his pride in his cleverness is ignoble; his pleasure in his half-caste family's worship of him debases him; and because his authority and sense of worth are grounded in his feeling of racial superiority, once he has surrendered to a native woman he feels robbed of his very self. What Conrad represents through Willems is not a fall from a height, such as James pictures, but the repetition of acts of betrayal on ever lower planes. As Willems stole money from Hudig, his employer, believing that he could soon pay it back and return to the "monotonous but safe stride of virtue," so he goes to Aissa telling himself that "he could return at any moment" (2:3, 79). In his enslavement to Aissa he betrays Lingard, his protector and patron, as he betrayed Hudig; then by offering to abandon Aissa, he tries to regain Lingard's favor.

In depicting Willems in his outcast state Conrad, like James, shows "the close connexion between bliss and bale"; but in *An Outcast* the evil overshadows the good and the emphasis falls on the negative. The wilderness is fecund and deadly, redolent of the "acrid smell of decaying life"; the sun that "dazzles and withers" is "beneficent and wicked—the giver of light, perfume, and pestilence"; the river, "ready to help or to hinder, to save life or give death," is "a deliverance, a prison, a refuge or a grave" (2:74, 248, 214). In the inner lives of the characters there is no sense of reconciliation or balance such as Rowland's words on the value of suffering imply. Aissa's is the "incomplete soul that knows pain but knows not hope" (2:334). Because Willems abhors his passion, he experiences not resolution but ambivalence, either the "shock of warring impulses" (2:129), or the alternation of hatred and desire for the woman he blames for his degradation.

That Willems understands what is happening to him, even as he clings to illusions that he is guiltless, makes him worthy of study. Although his degeneration is accompanied by violent physical action—blows given, murder attempted, settlements raided—the critical points in Willem's history are moments of perception and recognition. His degeneration is essentially a drama of self-discovery, discovery of "sensations he had never experienced before in the slightest degree" (2:80). At the turning point in the novel, as Willems totters on the brink of ultimate surrender to Aissa, he suddenly sees, with absolute clarity, the truth of his inner world: "There was no safety outside of himself—and in himself there was no refuge; there was only the image of that woman. He had a sudden moment of lucidity—of that cruel lucidity that comes once in life to the most benighted. He seemed to see what went on within him, and was horrified at the strange sight" (2:80).

Such moments of "cruel lucidity" in Conrad's novels, however, rarely afford the tragic relief that comes to James's characters. Whereas in James's novels recognition comes usually at the culmination of the action and either releases characters from vain longing or strengthens them to endure their fate, in Conrad's novels the illuminating moment often comes *before* a decisive act is performed, as the character poises on the verge of action that his rational self mistrusts or condemns. The prospect of a second betrayal yields Willems another moment of cruel lucidity, when he resolves to betray Lingard for Aissa's sake, "measured dismally the depth of his degradation," and perceives as never before the "hopeless diversity" between himself and Aissa: "It struck him suddenly that they had nothing in common—not a thought, not a feeling" (2:126, 128).

Such perceptions do not keep Willems from taking the next step downward; they merely intensify his "despairing wonder at his own nature" (2:274) and strengthen the hold on him of the passion for which he has sacrificed everything. At the same time it is by such moments of recognition that the protagonist achieves what tragic dignity he has. If James's characters attain their greatest good through their greatest suffering, Conrad's characters like Willems are lifted above their insignificance and mediocrity by their very perception of the degradation of which they are capable. Willems comes closest to arousing the tragic emotions of pity and fear, not when he agonizes over the life he has lost, for this seems mean enough, but when he knows himself exposed in a strange un- sounded world of horror, separated, utterly, from his former self and his old life: "He felt as if he was the outcast of all mankind . . . it seemed to him that the world was bigger, the night more vast and more black" (2:30). In such a moment Willems is more than the contemptible victim of his venality. In the completeness of his iso- lation he becomes a powerful symbol of what might be the fate of any man who is cast out of his world.

The outcast is not only isolated from civilized society: in vain he seeks support from a nature indifferent and alien to him. At several points Conrad emphasizes the absolute separateness of nature and human suffering, marking that "aspect of cold unconcern" in nonhuman things that he would render most powerfully in *The Secret Agent*. Twice in moments of crisis Willems longs to cry out for help to the wilderness, and both times he is overwhelmed by its silence, its immobility, and its "cruel unconcern" (2:242, 80).

Willems's subjective experience can be seen at times as magni- fying to an intolerable degree that consciousness of alienation and separateness which in Conrad's view made men tragic. But tragic perceptions and gestures do not make a tragic hero, as *An Outcast of the Islands* proves. In his climactic scene with Lingard, Willems is grotesque, not tragic: "a being absurd, repulsive, pathetic, and droll" (2:271). Like James in *Roderick Hudson* Conrad at the end compares his protagonist to a shipwrecked castaway, but he de- prives Willems of the dignity of anguish such as Rowland suffers. If at the end Willems's haunted state seems awesome in its ghastly horror, if Willems is impressive in the finality of his recognition "I am a lost man" and his gesture "careless and tragic" (2:340), his self-pity robs his plight of any grandeur it might have; and when his wife comes to vie with Aissa for his love, he acts toward both women with a brutality and a selfishness that reveal his character essentially unchanged. Willems's obsessive fears have prompted his being compared to Macbeth in his extremity.[13] Given the mediocrity of Conrad's protagonist, however, the last chapter with its Gothic horrors—the death-filled sunlight, the visions of bleaching bones, decay, and yawning graves—seems more like melodrama—like *The Monk* or *McTeague*—than tragedy. The end of the novel, in which Almayer and a drunken guest take the part of chorus to pronounce the final words, is a travesty of tragedy. The profound questions that tragedy raises seem empty and idle when shouted by the befuddled Almayer: "Where's the sense of all this? Where's your Providence? Where's the good for anybody in all this? . . . Why should I suffer? What have I done to be treated so?" Any force that may reside in the words of Almayer, whom gin has induced "to assume a rebellious attitude towards the scheme of the universe" (2:367, 368), is dissipated by the craven impudence of the maledictions he shouts into the night.

Probably most readers of Conrad's first four narratives which portray the degeneration of a leading character—*Almayer's Folly*, *An Outcast of the Islands*, *The Rescue*, and *Heart of Darkness*—would agree that the fall of Kurtz comes closest to the classic pattern of tragedy. Like Willems, Kurtz degenerates when he is isolated in the wilderness where savage lusts are unrestrained by the pressures of civilized society. Willems is a commonplace man with no gifts but his talent for billiards and shady business deals, but Kurtz is extolled by everyone who speaks of him, whether in reverence or in grudging envy, as a man of extraordinary powers. During Marlow's journey up the river Kurtz is described in increasingly extravagant terms by agents successively more spiteful, as "very remarkable," "exceptional," a "prodigy" and a "universal genius" (5:69, 75, 79, 83). Various characters remark his gifts as painter, musician, poet, journalist, and orator. Unlike Willems he is an

idealist as well as an egoist; he falls not from the plane of routi..
mediocrity but from the height of his aspiration to be a bearer of
light into darkness, to make each company station a beacon "on the
road towards better things" (5:91).

The irony of his fate is powerful if obvious: the man who aspired
to raise the savages from darkness becomes himself the god of their
worship in "unspeakable rites." That Kurtz's professed aspirations
are not mere hypocrisy is indicated by Marlow's identification of
himself with Kurtz when confronted by his "choice of nightmares."
As Walter Wright observes, if Kurtz were an ordinary hypocrite,
Marlow's office would be simply to expose Kurtz through satire.[14]
To Marlow, Kurtz's eloquence, by which his idealism is expressed,
is not simply an instrument of deception but a double-edged gift
to be defined in opposites, "the bewildering, the illuminating, the
most exalted and the most contemptible"—a gift by which Kurtz
has inspired others but also seduced himself: as a minor character
says of him, "He could get himself to believe anything" (5:118,
138, 113, 154).

In the complete corruption of his altruism Kurtz is "exalted" only
in his "incredible degradation" (5:144). If this were his final state,
he would be merely horrifying, but in his last moments he seems to
undergo what to Marlow is a moment of supreme revelation, the
anagnorisis or enlightenment which one scholar has termed
"tragedy's basic, and minimal, affirmation."[15]

Anything approaching the change that came over his features I have never
seen before, and hope never to see again. Oh, I wasn't touched. I was
fascinated. It was as though a veil had been rent. I saw on that ivory face
the expression of sombre pride, of ruthless power, of craven terror—of an
intense and hopeless despair. Did he live his life again in every detail of
desire, temptation, and surrender during that supreme moment of complete knowledge? He cried in a whisper at some image, at some vision—
he cried out twice, a cry that was no more than a breath—"The horror!
The horror!" (5:149)

What vision or image is part of Kurtz's "supreme moment of
complete knowledge" is never revealed. Given Kurtz's dying obsession with his "immense plans" (5:143), his last words perhaps

express the appalled recognition that he is to be obliterated utterly. Perhaps his words register horror of the world of death into which he is about to pass. Marlow interprets Kurtz's last words as "a judgment upon the adventures of his soul on this earth" and detects in his words the "vibrating note of revolt" (5:150, 151). Some readers have interpreted Kurtz's "complete knowledge" as his recognition of nothingness, within and without, to which the term *tragic* can be applied.[16] And yet Kurtz's "incredible degradation" and the "colossal scale of his vile desires" (5:156) give one good grounds for agreeing with Northrop Frye that such a figure goes beyond accepted human limits and seems melodramatic rather than tragic, "a study of obsession presented in terms of fear instead of pity."[17] But if one hesitates to apply the term *tragic* to Kurtz, there is no question that Marlow believes he witnesses in Kurtz's last moments a victory such as tragedy represents, a victory which exacts its full price in suffering: to Marlow, Kurtz's dying cry is "an affirmation, a moral victory paid for by innumerable defeats, by abominable terrors, by abominable satisfactions" (5:151). Like Roderick Hudson, Kurtz owes what tragic significance he has chiefly to the observer, who sees the victim as tragic, insists upon his exceptional powers and responds to him with the profound emotions we expect the tragic hero to evoke.

In the final scene Marlow through his "true" lie unwittingly enables another character, Kurtz's intended, to experience the tragic fusion of joy and grief and so to sustain *her* vision of Kurtz. Unable to speak the truth when asked to repeat Kurtz's dying words, Marlow replies with the words which wring from her "an exulting and terrible cry . . . the cry of inconceivable triumph and of unspeakable pain" (5:161–162). The faith of the intended, of course, rests on a delusion. Possibly Marlow's view of Kurtz is no less illusory, but he speaks out of knowledge, not ignorance, and in so doing he exemplifies the artist's power to impose form and meaning on experience. If *Heart of Darkness* is tragic it is so not because Kurtz lives and dies as he does but because Marlow narrates the story as he does. Not only do the experiences as he interprets them attest both to the powers that work destruction and to the "inborn strength" (5:97) that resists evil; in the act of narrating, of giving form to experience from which the horror has yet to be purged, Marlow brings into a balance the forces that make for order and disorder.

II

Marlow's vision of Kurtz in his moment of supreme knowledge illustrates one of the fundamental experiences that James and Conrad deemed tragic: the revelation of truth, overwhelming and irresistible, like an initiation, a passing of boundaries to which one can never return. The works of the two novelists illustrate another kind of experience often tragic in its intensity, from which tragic consequences may flow: the guilt and anguish suffered by characters forced to choose between irreconcilable desires or obligations. One thinks of Rowland's struggle with the temptation to seek profit in Roderick's collapse; Strether's effort to "save" Madame de Vionnet without betraying Mrs. Newsome. a struggle which induces such a burden of guilt that he welcomes the role of scapegoat; Jim's bitter struggle when faced with the alternatives of sparing or killing Gentleman Brown.

The tragedy inherent in acts of choice is intensified when the protagonist reaches an impasse, when he is compelled to make a choice of some kind yet finds himself unable to act for either side that claims his allegiance. The plight of a character so trapped is most fully portrayed by James in *The Princess Casamassima* (1886) and by Conrad in *Under Western Eyes* (1911), novels in which the protagonists are caught between forces which cannot be reconciled and between which they cannot choose. In both novels the plight of the protagonist is made more acute by the fact that the forces acting upon him are political in nature and threaten his destruction despite the choice that he makes.

The resemblances between *Under Western Eyes* and Dostoevsky's *Crime and Punishment* are so striking that little attention has been given to the relation of Conrad's novel to *The Princess*

Casamassima or to *Virgin Soil*, Turgenev's study of a Russian student, intelligent and introspective, destroyed by his participation in revolutionary politics. Like Turgenev's Neshdanoff, both James's and Conrad's protagonists are the illegitimate unacknowledged sons of noblemen, condemned by their birth to poverty and obscurity. Seeking recognition in a society in which they have no inherited place, both Hyacinth Robinson and Razumov commit themselves to a course of action which they soon discover to be intolerable but from which they can escape only by becoming sacrificial victims. In pledging himself to the anarchists, Hyacinth forfeits his freedom and puts himself on the road to impasse as completely as Razumov does when he betrays Haldin and is forced to become a police spy. In the end Hyacinth can escape only by suicide; Razumov, by confession to the revolutionaries, which like Jim's surrender to Doramin, is a virtual suicide. The vital difference is that Hyacinth embodies, and is subject to, conflicting forces which claim his allegiance and represent values he is loath to sacrifice; Razumov is the victim of conflicting forces similar in nature, which he rejects and condemns as evil. Hyacinth is trapped because he is bound to both sides; Razumov, because he can accept neither alternative.

By his very nature Hyacinth is committed to irreconcilables. The son of a French shopwoman who murdered her lover, an English lord, Hyacinth is the victim of inherited impulses perpetually in conflict, of the "extraordinarily mingled current in his blood" through which the plebian mother and the aristocratic father continue to array themselves in "intolerable defiances" and come once again, within Hyacinth, to their "death-grapple." Thus Hyacinth feels himself fated "to be divided to the point of torture, to be split open by sympathies that pulled him in different ways" (5:171). That the forces acting on Hyacinth in the first half of the novel are equal in strength is indicated as Hyacinth, through his relationships with Paul Muniment and the Princess Casamassima, moves simultaneously to his pledge to the arch-anarchist Hoffendahl and to his recognition at the princess's country estate that his deepest sympathies commit him, not to the murderous art of Hoffendahl, but to the art which preserves beauty and creates tradition, symbolized in "the favoured resistance" of Medley (6:7).[18] In contrast Razumov, once he is aligned with the regime, knows only intense revulsion for the aims and leaders of both sides—autocracy and revolutionaries. That existence is a choice between destructive alternatives is emphasized repeatedly—in Sophia Antonovna's conviction that "in life . . . there is not much choice. You have either to rot or to burn"; in the misery of Mrs. Haldin, "a victim of tyranny and revolution"; in Razumov's sense of himself at the mercy of "lawless forces," trapped by the "lawlessness of autocracy . . . and the lawlessness of revolution" (10:250, 335, 77).

The difference between James's hero, rent by opposing sympathies, and Conrad's hero, trapped by intolerable alternatives, is reflected in every aspect of the two novels—character, setting, and structure. In *The Princess Casamassima* scenes of misery and squalor are balanced throughout by scenes of splendor and beauty. In *Under Western Eyes* the contrast is of settings both bleak—of Russia pictured as immense and formless covered by a winding sheet of snow, "like a monstrous blank page awaiting the record of an inconceivable history" (10:33), and of Geneva, banal, graceless, and sterile, like an ugly tinted photograph or a piece of mechanism. Hyacinth is nourished and educated by a city which on the last day of his life "had never appeared to him to wear more proudly and publicly the stamp of her imperial history" (6:420), but Razumov moves between two worlds, one yet to be formed, the other closed and dead.

As the quoted passages suggest, the essential difference between the two novels is reflected in the fact that the element of romance is completely absent from *Under Western Eyes*, whereas it infuses every part of *The Princess Casamassima*. The princess, whose beauty here, as in *Roderick Hudson*, has "an air of perfection" (5:207), is a consistently romantic figure. Hyacinth not only delights in romantic stories of noble characters; he himself is conceived in romantic terms, as the image of the beautiful youth, like Hyacinthus, doomed to an early death. His childhood friend, the shopgirl Millicent Henning, perceives something "romantic, almost theatrical, in his whole little person" (5:79). His longing to commit himself to both sides invests with the glamor of romance his relations with both the anarchists and the princess. As a result of his closer association with Muniment, "the whole complexion of his life seemed changed; it was pervaded by an element of romance" (5:161). At Medley he drinks from "the cup of an exquisite experience," a potion fatal yet "purple with the wine of romance, of reality, of civilisation" (6:41). Romance has no place in a novel like *Under Western Eyes*, in which tragedy arises from the absence of any cause to which the hero can commit himself; but it is a natural element when the hero suffers "an intense admiration for what he missed" (5:170), when he is above all conscious of the good he is doomed to lose.

As its name suggests, the enchanted world of Medley into which Hyacinth awakens in a scene immediately following the ride through darkness to Hoffendahl illustrates the balancing of loss and gain which informs the novel throughout. Indeed *The Princess Casamassima* is James's most complete expression of the principle of equivalence first developed in *Roderick Hudson*. Given Hyacinth's inherited duality, every act, every impression and encounter, is inevitably a source of pleasure and pain since everything that gratifies one side of his nature denies the other. The recurrent metaphors of creditors, debts, payments, bankruptcy, liquidation, and accounts to be settled underline the principle of compensation illustrated at every point in Hyacinth's career. He for whom "nothing in life had such an interest or such a price . . . as his impressions and reflexions" must ultimately make the full payment, of his life. At the same time, his awareness yields him rewards which Muniment, who is certain to be "one of the first to be paid" (5:159, 113), will never know. For the money Hyacinth spends in Paris he receives "a rich experience," thus becoming "master of a precious equivalent" (6:151). Nearly all the characters symbolize the conflicting impulses which Hyacinth embodies; thus all augment the mingled pain and pleasure to which his dual nature subjects him. The two characters to whom he owes his intensest happiness, Muniment and the princess, are the two who in their indifference and failure of sympathy, inflict on Hyacinth his keenest suffering.

Ultimately Hyacinth comes to see equivalence as the very principle of existence. In Paris, where he marvels that "the most brilliant city in the world was also the most blood-stained," he concludes that he can support one value only at the expense of the other, that everything has its price. To work for social justice is to sacrifice "the treasures, the felicities, the splendours, the successes of the world." To work for the preservation of European culture is to accept all the "despotisms, the cruelties, the exclusions, the monopolies and the rapacities of the past" on which that culture is based (6:121, 217, 145).

Razumov is trapped too but his drama unfolds not as a sequence of experiences in which gain and loss are balanced but as a series of reversals so painful in their effects that they seem not merely ironic but tragic. By betraying Haldin, Razumov has hoped to preserve his freedom, but his betrayal destroys his mental equilibrium and forces him into the service of the autocracy. In his confrontations with Peter Ivanovitch, in which each man tries to sound the mind of the other while keeping his own thoughts hidden, Razumov is victorious in that he successfully maintains his disguise; but his success in deception intensifies the stifling sense of falseness which finally drives him to confession. His love for Nathalie Haldin impels him at last to reveal the truth, but by the act of confession he forfeits her love and severs himself from her forever.

The final acts of James's and Conrad's heroes are therefore completely different in meaning. Hyacinth's suicide can be seen as his refusal to deny the claims represented by both of his parents: "To desert one of these presences for the other—that idea was the source of shame, as an act of treachery would have been" (6:264). When Razumov confesses to the revolutionaries, he acknowledges the falsity of his commitments and repudiates his service to both sides. So concerned was Conrad that Razumov's confession not be mistaken for a change of heart, a conversion to revolutionist ideas, that he added to the passage in the manuscript in which Razumov declares his betrayal of himself the statement which concludes:

"Only don't be deceived, Natalia Victorovna, I am not converted. Have I then the soul of a slave? No! I am independent—and therefore perdition is my lot" (10:361–362).[19]

Because Conrad identifies Razumov with Russia, of necessity he must picture the Russian scene—the operations of the bureaucracy, the tactics of the revolutionaries, the attitudes of the exiles in Geneva—with a certain precision and fullness. Whereas the relationships James portrays are private and personal, not political in nature—he does not even picture Hyacinth's meeting with the archconspirator Hoffendahl—Conrad brings his hero into direct contact with political institutions, government officials, and revolutionary leaders. A revolutionary act of violence, such as Hyacinth cannot perform, sets in motion the action of *Under Western Eyes*. But Conrad, like James, is chiefly concerned with the subjective experience of his protagonist. Indeed the first part of *Under Western Eyes* is the most sustained portrayal in all Conrad's fiction of the drama of mental conflict enacted upon the inner stage of the character's mind.

In their emphasis upon the moral and psychological sides of their heroes' experience, both James and Conrad took the path of Turgenev, whose wisdom, James declared in his review of *Virgin Soil*, was shown in his recognition that a secret revolutionary movement is "particularly fertile in revelations of character—that it contains inevitably the seeds of an interesting psychological drama."[20] Neither Hyacinth nor Razumov, however, shares the weakness of Turgenev's heroes, whose function, according to James, was to be "conspicuous as failures, interesting but impotent persons who are losers at the game of life."[21] It is true that by their own acts Hyacinth and Razumov deprive themselves of their freedom and enter into what Northrop Frye calls "the process of causation,"[22] but in neither novel do flaws of character seem the spring of tragic action. Hyacinth is guiltless of betrayal, and Razumov's suffering is portrayed not so much as punishment for his betrayal of Haldin as illustration of the anguish to which political conflict in Russia subjects its representative figure. Rather than "losers at the game of life," Hyacinth and Razumov are victims of social and political processes and conditions. Hyacinth is the victim of opposing claims which society, symbolized by his duality, cannot reconcile; Razumov is the victim of an infernal dynamics, whereby "senseless tyranny" provokes "senseless desperation" (10:viii).

By any standard *Under Western Eyes* is a dark picture, darker than *The Princess Casamassima*. It is true that Hyacinth, who begins his life under the care of a devoted woman, dies isolated from all his surrogate parents and friends, whereas Razumov moves from isolation to a place in the Russian community, where he is cared for by Tekla and visited by the revolutionaries. In James's world, however, the political action which Hyacinth is unable to perform is not essential to his fulfillment; Hyacinth's history dramatizes James's lifelong belief that observation and appreciation can yield benefits surpassing those gained through political involvement, that political action requires "the sacrifice [of] all sorts of blest freedoms and immunities, treasures of detachment and perception."[23] In Conrad's world, on the other hand, political commitment is destructive of personal identity and human life; but without commitment Razumov's life is sterile. While Hyacinth from the beginning exhibits the capacity James most valued—"No one could . . . cultivate with more art the intimate personal relation" (5:228)—Conrad, by making Razumov betray another, suggests the deficiencies of the existence for the sake of which Razumov could betray both himself and Haldin. The presence of the main narrator, the teacher of languages, might suggest that the role of the observer is a satisfactory alternative to political commitment; but even the narrator dwells on the poverty of a life in which one is only the witness of others' acts. The obvious alternative to Razumov's isolation is participation in the life of a community, but no community exists in Russia in which Razumov can act without destroying himself. Thus, to his tortured sense, "perdition" is his fate.

In *The Princess Casamassima* the splendors of the world do not obscure its miseries or blind Hyacinth to the indifference of an alien universe. The street in which he waits alone to receive his message from the anarchists offers him only "the vista of the low black houses, the dim interspaced street-lamps, the prowling cats who darted occasionally across the road and the terrible mysterious far-off stars, which appeared to him more than ever to see everything of our helplessness and tell nothing of help" (6:374–375). In their extremity James's characters, like Conrad's, look in vain for support or strength outside themselves. But at the end of *The Princess Casamassima* one feels above all how much that is precious the hero has been forced to sacrifice. At the end of *Under Western Eyes* one feels above all how little Razumov's world has ever offered him, how desolate and barren of happiness and beauty his life has been from the beginning. In James's novel the sense of tragedy arises from awareness of values lost; in Conrad's novel, from the anguish of existence that must somehow be endured.

III

In *Modern Tragedy* Raymond Williams identifies two contrasting ideas of tragedy, expressed by Hegel and Schopenhauer, which became dominant in the nineteenth century.[24] For Hegel and his followers the central concerns of tragedy were the conflict and reconciliation of principles which have divided the ethical substance against itself. Tragic conflict between characters or within the mind of one character arises when competing claims are made, rightful in themselves but incompatible with each other. The resolution of the conflict may require the death of the actors who in upholding one principle to the exclusion of others have disrupted the balance in which all legitimate claims are recognized. The outcome of tragedy, however, is to restore order—to reveal the interior harmony of the conflicting forces and to affirm the harmony as a divinely ordained principle. "The true course of dramatic development consists in the annulment of *contradictions* viewed as such, in the reconciliation of the forces of human action, which alternately strive to negate each other in their conflict."[25]

In *The World as Will and Idea* Schopenhauer denies the premises of Hegel's definition and sets forth a radically different idea of tragedy. What tragedy represents is not the restoration of order

and the reconciliation of forces in conflict but rather the terrible
side of life, inevitable and unalterable: "the unspeakable pain, the
wail of humanity, the triumph of evil, the scornful mastery of
chance, and the irretrievable fall of the just and the innocent."[26]
No divine principle of order exists, suffering is the inevitable condition of all men, and the end to which the tragic hero moves is not
reconciliation, but resignation, the surrender of the will to live: "In
tragedies the noblest men, after long conflict and suffering, at last
renounce the ends they have so keenly followed, and all the pleas-
ures of life forever, or else freely and joyfully surrender life itself."[27]

Considering the novels already discussed, one might be tempted
to say that James's fiction exemplifies the Hegelian concept of balance, Conrad's the pessimism of Schopenhauer. The fiction of both
novelists, however, illustrates ideas of both Hegel and Schopenhauer and expresses convictions opposed to statements of both
philosophers. The plight of Hyacinth, rent by his bond to both
parents who symbolize his inner duality, seems to illustrate
Hegel's idea of tragedy as a conflict of "powers and individuals
equally entitled to the ethical claim,"[28] but the point of James's
novel is that the "essential accord" or "inner harmony" Hegel
posits can never exist between the competing claims. Hyacinth
dies not because he has disrupted a divinely ordered harmony but
because he embodies forces that are by nature irreconcilable. One
might also see Razumov's dilemma in Hegelian terms: as the
conflict suffered when competing obligations—to one's self, to
one's fellow student, to one's country—make incompatible demands. But "inner harmony" exists only in the abstract and cannot
be realized in the world of "irreconcilable antagonisms" which
Conrad's characters inhabit.

As several critics have shown, the fiction of both James and Conrad suggests Schopenhauer's ideas.[29] The ego of characters such as
the Princess Casamassima, Kurtz, and Jim can be compared to
Schopenhauer's "Will." Characters who strive to realize their
ideals through action in the world are thwarted or corrupted in
their effort. But both James and Conrad reject the kind of resignation and withdrawal from the world which Schopenhauer advo-

cates. Neither Hyacinth nor Razumov, whose situations are as intolerable as those of any of the novelists' characters, surrenders his will to live, renounces the world, or denies the value of his aspirations. Thus neither character exemplifies Schopenhauer's idea of suffering as a sanctifying force which purifies men of the will to live and strive in a world of evil. Suffering impels Conrad's characters like Jim and Razumov to try to regain what they have lost. For James's protagonists like Isabel, Strether, and Maggie Verver suffering leads not to surrender of the will to live but to a fuller sense of life; it is chiefly through suffering that James's characters engage in the reality that surrounds them and know the sense of "having lived."

What we observe in the novels of both James and Conrad is the drama of characters impelled by the need to engage in relationships with others and to strive to realize certain ideals or aims, however skeptically they view the efficacy of action. At the same time they struggle in a world where no divine harmony exists in which all opposing claims can be reconciled, a world in which the defeat or the destruction of the protagonist effects no redeeming change in the life of the society. In other words James's and Conrad's protagonists recognize the claims of those forces which, according to Hegel, "carry in themselves their own justification" and which inspire the acts constituting the "ethical life of true tragic characters."[30] They confront the irremediable evil, the unresolvable conflicts which for Schopenhauer made suffering, not resolution, the essential tragic fact. The main difference revealed by the novels considered thus far is that in James's works the principle of equivalence, of loss balanced by gain, is dominant; in Conrad's works what is dominant is the suffering which attends not only defeat but apparent success. We may test this generalization by comparison of the novels which many regard as the greatest works of the two novelists: *The Wings of the Dove* and *Nostromo*, in which the different kinds of tragic action arising from relations between men and women are most fully developed.

The Wings of the Dove was the second of two novels which James traced to the idea of a person deprived of the experiences that he most desires and from which he could most profit. The first novel, *The Princess Casamassima*, grew from the idea of "some individual sensitive nature or fine mind . . . capable of profiting by all the civilisation, all the accumulations to which [London streets] testify, yet condemned to see things only from outside" (5:vi). *The Wings of the Dove* originated in a similar conception of deprived capacity. "The idea, reduced to its essence, is that of a young person conscious of a great capacity for life, but early stricken and doomed, condemned to die under short respite, while also enamoured of the world; aware moreover of the condemnation and passionately desiring to 'put in' before extinction as many of the finer vibrations as possible, and so achieve, however briefly and brokenly, the sense of having lived" (19:v).

Mortal illness, which is equivalent in *The Wings of the Dove* to Hyacinth's fatal duality, makes Milly Theale, the orphaned girl of fabulous wealth, a figure both romantic and tragic, in whom the power of the mythic is felt. Her immense fortune isolates her in the glamor that envelops a royal personage. Her fatal illness, untainted by the odor of medicines, enhances the glamor; and the beauty and inaccessibility of the Venetian palace in which she dies assure that her death shall have the mystery and the fatal beauty of romantic tragedy. It is the representatives of the Old World—Kate Croy, Merton Densher, and Maud Lowder—who have the health and power of survival associated with the New World, whereas the representative American is the "final flower" and "the mere last broken link" of a doomed family "wrecked in a high extravagance of speculation and dissipation" (19:111).

Like Hyacinth, Milly Theale is a sacrificial figure, but unlike him she is the victim of a calculated plot; she is betrayed by people who deceive as well as exploit her. As the victim of those who plot for her money Milly resembles Isabel Archer, but unlike Isabel's betrayal Milly's results not from errors of judgment but from the potent effect upon others of her wealth, her craving for life, and her fatal illness. If Milly does not fathom Kate's scheme, it is not surprising, for Densher himself does not fully understand it until Kate, on the occasion of Milly's last appearance at the great reception in Venice, draws his attention to the wealth symbolized by Milly's pearls and compels his recognition of Kate's intent: that Densher shall marry the dying girl with the expectation of receiving her fortune at her death. Milly's death, precipitated by Lord Mark's revelation to her of Kate and Densher's engagement, is presented not as the result of flaws of character or errors of perception but as the means by which the spiritual and moral principle that the character embodies can be best revealed, the tragedy inherent in the situation be made most poignant. The plot of Densher and Kate is not a means of testing Milly, but, as John O'Neill points out, a way of investing the heroine with the personal dignity which formidable opposition confers and of giving substance to her intense but unfocused desire "to live."[31]

Betrayal and early death do not of themselves, in James's eyes, make Milly a tragic figure. What makes her tragic is the principle she embodies of "passionate, of inspired resistance" to death (19:vi). Milly's intense response to social occasions such as Maud Lowder's dinner party and the day at Matcham, her quickness to feel her situation as romantic, and her tireless analysis of her impressions of others and their impressions of her are all expressive of her "inspired resistance." At Matcham where Milly, having felt most keenly "all the freshness of response of her young life" (19:209), is shown, as the image of herself, the Bronzino portrait of the woman long dead, the opposing forces—the energy of resistance and the inescapable fate—are clearly joined. The turning point comes soon afterward, when Milly, walking alone in London after her interview with the great doctor Sir Luke Strett, realizes that she is passing from one stage of her life to another. The counsel of the doctor, that her life depends upon her will to live, that she can live if she wills, acts as a challenge, as

the final push, as well as the touch that most made a mixture of her consciousness—a strange mixture that tasted at one and the same time of what she had lost and what had been given her. It was wonderful to her, while she took her random course, that these quantities felt so equal:

she had been treated—hadn't she?—as if it were in her power to live; and yet one wasn't treated so—was one?—unless it had come up, quite as much, that one might die. The beauty of the bloom had gone from the old sense of safety—that was distinct: she had left it behind her there for ever. But the beauty of the idea of a great adventure, a big dim experiment or struggle in which she might more responsibly than ever before take a hand, had been offered her instead. It was as if she had had to pluck off her breast, to throw away, some friendly ornament, a familiar flower, a little old jewel, that was part of her daily dress; and to take up and shoulder as a substitute some queer defensive weapon, a musket, a spear, a battle-axe—conducive possibly in a higher degree to a striking appearance, but demanding all the effort of the military posture. (19:248)

No passage in James's fiction better expresses the principle of balance and equivalence at the heart of his idea of tragedy.[32] The idea of loss and gain fused and balanced was inherent in his initial conception of the heroine whose seemingly boundless opportunities augment one's sense of all she must lose and whose awareness of impending death intensifies her awareness of her capacity for life and her sense of life as infinitely precious.

The action of the novel illustrates another idea expressed in the passage quoted above, the idea of the exchange of one value for another. The illustration of this idea, however, requires the presence of a second character, for by itself Milly's death does not exemplify a redemptive sacrifice. In James's words "her stricken state was but half her case, the correlative half being the state of others as affected by her" (19:xi). The image of the wings of the dove symbolizes not only Milly's wealth but her power to work change in the world, as the power of Milton's divine spirit "with mighty wings outspread / Dove-like satst brooding on the vast Abyss / And mad'st it pregnant." Milly's power, which the plot against her enables her to exercise, is revealed most dramatically in the spiritual transformation of Densher, who like Milly comes to know the "strange mixture" that tastes of what is lost and what has been given.

The portrayal of Densher is James's only picture of the mind of a character who is knowingly engaged against his better instincts in a plot to exploit another person. In probing the guilty conscience of

Densher, James does not portray the kind of mental torment that subjects Conrad's Razumov to hallucinations or drives Hawthorne's Dimmesdale to scourge himself and mimic the act of confession. Far more passive than Conrad's or Hawthorne's guilt-ridden sufferers, Densher does not even make a confession but is exposed by another character. He perceives clearly the dramatic shape of the plot: that is, he is always aware when he reaches a turning point in the situation, when he takes the step that involves him more deeply in deception; but he does not allow himself to apprehend the evil of the plot until the end, when Milly's death has released him from bondage to Kate. In the pivotal book 6 he knows that he has reached the point of no return, that "he must break short off if his mind was really made up not to go further"; but as the passive verb indicates, he does not know what he wishes to do, and so long as he is denied union with Kate—the one, overriding desire of which he is certain—his frustrated passion blocks out feelings of guilt. So long as passion binds him, he holds himself a passive agent who does "nothing . . . but what I'm told." Densher reaches his lowest moral point when, assuring himself that Lord Mark alone is responsible for the fatal shock to Milly, he rejoices in his own "comparative innocence, that was almost like purification" (20:86, 91, 265).

If in the following days Densher feels "washed but the more clean" (20:266), his sense of purification is the false illusion that precedes the true experience. His last interview with Milly gives him the sense of being "forgiven, dedicated, blessed"; to recall it in Maud Lowder's company is to stand at the threshold of a sacred place, to sense "the presence within" and feel "the charged stillness" (20:343). The language of the novel indicates that James intended the reader to see Densher's experience as akin to a religious conversion, wrought by the power of Milly's spirit, which like the influx of divine grace illumines what is dark and inspires in Densher the sense of "something deep within him that he had absolutely shown to no one" (20:391). Whether James persuades the reader of the reality of Densher's conversion is another matter. Because James relies mainly on statement to convey the transforming effects of Milly's spirit, his portrayal of Densher's illumination at the end is less convincing than his representation of Densher's indecision and self-deception earlier in the novel. But however one judges the execution of the idea, James's intentions are clear. As he stated in his notebook, Densher's perception of the beauty of Milly's spirit creates for him a new standard of value and breaks his bond to his fiancée: "She is eager, ready to marry now, but he has really fallen in love with the dead girl. . . . In the light of how exquisite the dead girl was he sees how little exquisite is the living."[33]

The choice that Densher places before Kate in the final scene—the sacrifice either of the money or their marriage—is the final act in a drama in which practically every relationship and every decision is presented in terms of loss and gain, payment and price. As the action develops, two kinds of exchange become apparent. The reader is introduced first to the principle of profit and loss which governs Kate and all the members of her family—Lionel Croy and Marian Condrip (Kate's disgraced father and abject sister) as well as Kate's aunt, Maud Lowder, the incarnation of the philistine and a social and financial power in the world of Lancaster Gate, a microcosm of upper middle-class Victorian society. In this world people exist to exploit others or to be exploited. One character is repeatedly described as seeking to *use, show, display, work, do with*, or *place* another. One may simultaneously use and be used by another, as Lord Mark and Maud Lowder exploit each other to their mutual profit. The fullest explanation of the system is given by Kate, who as if exasperated by Milly's ignorance and oppressed by her own position, warns Milly of the mechanism in which they both are caught: "Everyone who had anything to give . . . made the sharpest possible bargain for it, got at least its value in return. The strangest thing furthermore was that this might be in cases a happy understanding. The worker in one connexion was the worked in another; it was as broad as it was long—with the wheels of the system, as might be seen, wonderfully oiled" (19:179).

One's aim is always to get more than one gives, if possible to get without giving anything at all. In any case, as Lord Mark tells Milly, "Nobody here . . . does anything for nothing" (19:160). Kate's relations with her father, her sister, and her aunt, all of whom regard her as a "sensible value" to be exploited for their own profit, have convinced her that life is a fierce struggle in which giving is equivalent to self-destruction: "The more you gave yourself the less of you was left. There were always people to snatch at you, and it would never occur to *them* that they were eating you up." Because she knows herself threatened—"it was perfectly present to Kate that she might be devoured" (19:33, 30), she feels herself justified in manipulating others, including the man she loves, to protect herself: "I use, for the purpose, what I have," she tells Densher. "You're what I have of most precious, and you're therefore what I use most" (20:52).

The existence of another kind of exchange is made explicit in book 7, when Milly reflects that "Sir Luke had appeared indeed to speak of purchase and payment, but in reference to a different sort of cash. Those were amounts not to be named nor reckoned" (20:142). The values are those of the mind and spirit, which Milly ultimately symbolizes for Densher. The payments are made in acts of giving and in suffering, and the rewards cannot be measured in monetary terms. This is not to say that material and spiritual values are mutually antagonistic in this novel.[34] Milly's wealth lifts her above the sordid conditions that trap Kate and enables her in Venice to create the conditions which most enhance her beauty and her power to affect others. Her wealth is such that she can effortlessly pay any sum, however exorbitant the amount demanded for the service to be rendered: "She had been willing, goodness knew, to pay enough for anything, for everything. . . . She was more prepared than ever to pay enough, and quite as much as ever to pay too much" (20:143). The reference here is to her willingness to pay her Italian servant whatever he asks to transform the rented Venetian palace into her court and refuge, but taken in another sense the words are equally true of Milly. For the sense of "having lived" she is ready to pay the price in suffering, to expose herself to exploitation. Kate proposes to give up nothing and "to try for everything" (19:73); Milly sees the power to give as her only resource. "I give and give and give," she tells Lord Mark. "Only I can't listen or receive or accept. . . . I can't make a bargain" (20:161).

At the beginning of the novel Densher is described as one still to be formed and marked by "the final stamp, the pressure that fixes the value" (19:49). So long as he submits to Kate he submits to the law of her society: either one allows oneself to be manipulated for no gain, or one drives a bargain, demanding something in return for what one gives. When Densher, having long endured the rage "at what he wasn't having," finally demands Kate's physical surrender in return for his continued acquiescence in her plan, he thinks of the consummation of their love as his "contract" and "bargain"; Kate's coming to his rooms is "the price named by him" which had been "magnificently paid" (20:175, 237).

Milly can ask no price and make no bargain. Instead her death may be seen as the price of Densher's conversion, in that the beauty of her spirit, by which Densher is transformed, is fully revealed to him only by her dying acts. The money which she gives and he relinquishes thus may be seen to symbolize the nonmaterial payment exacted of both characters. It is the necessity of payment that Kate seeks to evade. When she declares to Densher, "I shall sacrifice nobody and nothing," (19:73) she means that she will reject or injure no one, but the words also imply her will to keep everything and give up nothing. Like every other character of James she is subject to the law of compensation—that every good exacts its price. In her determination to enjoy Densher's love yet "pay no price" (19:61) she ultimately pays the price of the love itself.

The Wings of the Dove has been variously described as tragedy, romance, legend, and social comedy. Critics have seen in the novel likenesses to the morality play and the fairy tale and have compared it to the tragedies of Shakespeare and Ibsen, the symbolic dramas of Maeterlinck, *The Divine Comedy*, and the Arthurian romances.[35] That James regarded Milly's plight as tragic is indicated by the references in his notebooks to Milly as "the tragic girl" and to her "tragic young despair"[36] and by his observation in the novel that Lord Mark, in proposing to Milly, undergoes "his first encounter with a judgement formed in the sinister light of tragedy" (20:157). Although the transformation of Densher gives grounds to argue (as does John O'Neill) that the central action of the novel is religious and transcendent, not tragic,[37] one can also argue that the novel is tragic in its balance of gain and loss. Milly's isolated state, Densher's memory of her "unapproachable terror of the end" (20:341), and the dreary aftermath of Milly's death in which Kate and Densher confront their blighted love—these are impressions that nothing can efface. If Densher is united in spirit to Milly, whose essential likeness to him is several times indicated in the novel, he is separated from every living person. The effect on him of Milly's death seems to preclude not only attachment to any person but any action beyond putting Kate to the test and thus severing their bond.

One would hesitate to offer *The Wings of the Dove* as an example of Hegel's theory of tragedy, to see the novel as a conflict of competing forces both rightful. Clearly Densher in yielding to Kate's manipulation is not choosing the good; and James places Densher's reverence for Milly's spirit higher in the scale of value than his passion for Kate. But if the novel is not a conflict of good with good, it is not a simple conflict of good with unalloyed evil. There is virtue in Kate's effort to free herself from the grasp of her aunt's talons and to resist and rise above the abject collapse of her father and sister "chalk-marked by fate" (19:4). Although Kate sacrifices Densher's love for wealth and position, she is not presented as a mercenary villain, nor does the novel repudiate the "great world" in which Kate is corrupted and Milly perishes. It is true that the callousness and spiritual emptiness of Lancaster Gate are repeatedly revealed. The " 'great,' the dangerous, the delightful world" of which Rowland speaks in *Roderick Hudson* (1:287) seems in this novel tarnished and brutalized. Nonetheless London society, the great country houses like Matcham, the Venetian palace with its priceless art—all that composes "an immemorial, a complex and accumulated, civilisation" (1:334)—is essential to Milly's sense of "having lived." And if it is necessary to the fullness of Milly's life, presumably it is necessary to the fullness of Kate's. Kate's "dire accessibility" (19:28) to pleasure afforded by material things is a moral flaw, as is evident in the brutal acts to which her passion drives her; but the desire for one's place in the world of the privileged was not to James in itself evil, as he indicates in *The*

Princess Casamassima in his sympathy with Hyacinth's conviction that "in this world of effort and suffering life was endurable, the spirit able to expand, only in the best conditions" (5:168). That in one way or another one owes the enjoyment of favoring conditions to the energy of a predatory philistine society is a hard fact of James's world, symbolized in *The Wings of the Dove* by the pervasive force of Maud Lowder. It is part of the romantic character of the novel that the exploitation which presumably produced Milly's immense fortune is never mentioned and that the plot against Milly frees the heiress from any guilt that might attach to her fabulous wealth.

The power of even so corrupt a society as Lancaster Gate to fascinate James's observers and to feed their sense of life is even more fully appreciated if one considers Conrad's pictures of aristocratic society. In every novel and story in which Conrad portrays the European or English upper class—namely "The Return," *The Rescue, The Secret Agent, Chance*, and *The Arrow of Gold*—the prevailing impression is of lifeless forms and exhausted energies. Whereas the characters in *The Golden Bowl*, in learning "the possible heroism of perfunctory things" (24:288), find in their highly organized social existence a source of life-giving order, Conrad in *The Rescue* presents society's "ritual dance of life" (17:412) as a meaningless pattern. Society at its worst in James's novels is vulgar and predatory; in Conrad's novels it is effete and sterile.

Of all Conrad's characters M. George, the innocent and "infinitely receptive" narrator of *The Arrow of Gold* (16:8), comes closest to the experience of James's characters who enter a sophisticated world in ignorance of its conventions and intrigues. Of the society of diplomats, artists, generals, financiers, and politicians who appear in Doña Rita's salon, the narrator observes: "Those people were obviously more civilized than I was. They had more rites, more ceremonies, more complexity in their sensations, more knowledge of evil, more varied meanings to the subtle phrases of their language" (16:70). Such might be the impression of Isabel Archer at Osmond's villa, or of Hyacinth with the princess at Medley, or of Strether at Gloriani's party, or of Milly at Maud Lowder's dinner. But whereas the Princess Casamassima and Gloriani are figures of radiant vitality, the intimates of Doña Rita's circle seem lifeless: "a very superior lot of waxworks . . . with that odd air wax figures have of being aware of their existence being but a sham" (16:69). The artist Henry Allegré, whose "amazing egoism" prompted him to a "mysterious appropriation" of another human being (16:108), reminds one of Osmond. But Osmond is moved by his craving to be envied by the world he affects to disdain. Allegré, motivated by "complete, equable, and impartial contempt for all mankind" (16:73), creates in Rita a figure designed not to compel the world's envy but to stimulate and frustrate men's passions and so to mock human feeling.

With its brilliant visual effects, its portrait of the artist-collector, and its picture of aristocratic society (the most detailed in Conrad's fiction) *The Arrow of Gold* might seem to be the most Jamesian of Conrad's novels. But not only is the sense of ennui and exhaustion foreign to society as James portrayed it; unlike James's central characters the narrator of *The Arrow of Gold* remains an outsider who is initiated into the agonies of frustrated passion but not into the mysteries of the social world, which remains for him simply a brilliant background. The interplay of social forces and human destinies—James's concern in all his important novels—is in Conrad's fiction best studied in *Nostromo*, in which as in *The Wings of the Dove* the impact of material interests upon the relationships of men and women is dramatized through the relation of all the characters to the dominant symbol of economic power.

IV

One might argue that none of the characters of *The Wings of the Dove* has the stature of a tragic hero and still maintain that the novel expresses a tragic sense of life. Similarly one might withhold from Charles Gould, Nostromo, Decoud, Emilia Gould, and Dr. Monygham the appellation *tragic hero* and yet call *Nostromo* a tragic novel. The sources of tragic effect in the two novels, however, are different. *The Wings of the Dove* is dramatic in its concentration on a small group of characters and on one central action.[38] *Nostromo* is epic in its panoramic scope. Instead of a steady focus on one action *Nostromo* presents a multitude of events, sometimes loosely connected, in the lives of many characters. The shifts from character to character and the dislocations in the time framework assure that no one in *Nostromo* shall enjoy the prominence of James's main characters in *The Wings of the Dove*. The characters in Conrad's novel, often dwarfed by the natural setting, seem further diminished when their lives are seen as fragments in the hundred years' history of a country. Much of the tragic feeling in this novel arises from what Monygham calls "the crushing, paralyzing sense of human littleness" (7:433).

As Conrad observed, the central force of *Nostromo* is not a character or an action but a symbol—the silver of the San Tomé mine. "Silver is the pivot of the moral and material events, affecting the lives of everybody in the tale."[39] One might say as much for Milly's fortune in *The Wings of the Dove*. But the kind of power exerted by "material interests" in the two novels is completely different. Although Kate Croy is vivid testimony to the corrupting power of money, *The Wings of the Dove* does not dramatize the "black and merciless things that are behind the great possessions" (25:295), the idea to be developed in *The Ivory Tower*.[40] Not only is the heiress spiritually the most highly developed character in *The Wings of the Dove*, but her fortune is a force for good in that it symbolizes the magnanimity which frees Densher from his bond with Kate. The silver in *Nostromo* is evil in its effects: it corrupts judgment, obsesses the mind, and destroys tenderness and affection. It casts upon those who seek their profit from it a fatal spell, foreshadowed in the first chapter, in the legend of the two gringos who eternally haunt the treasure reputed to lie buried outside the town. The power of Milly's fortune evokes the image of the dove's wings, suggestive of elevation and strength; the victims of the San Tomé mine feel its power as a poison, a deadly disease, and a weight of prison chains.

Charles Gould is humane in his methods in contrast to the first workers of the mine, who mercilessly beat slaves to extract silver, "paid for in its own weight of human bones" (7:52). But the mine under Gould has to some extent transformed the wilderness into a wasteland, destroying a waterfall, killing vegetation, and scarring the hillsides with trenches of refuse. The childless marriage of the Goulds is another sign of the blighting effect of the mine. Although the people of Sulaco extol the mine as a force for stability— "security seemed to flow upon this land from the mountain-gorge"—the immense wealth of the mine is constant provocation to those seeking power, as Monygham implies when he declares that "there is no peace and no rest in the development of material interests" (7:110, 511). Any state sustained by its material wealth alone will be rent by eternal conflict; at the end of *Nostromo* the characters face the prospect of yet another revolution led by the current minister of war. In all periods of Sulaco's history the silver of the mine drives rapacious leaders like Sotillo and Pedro Montero to acts of atrocity. The effects of the mine are tragic in the lives of characters such as the Goulds, Nostromo, and Decoud, whose powers are corrupted or whose hopes of happiness and fulfillment are destroyed by the baneful power of the silver.

The enslaving power of the mine is best observed in Charles Gould, whose corruption is a slow process, manifested at first in apparently trivial signs appearing at widely spaced intervals. Gould is like Densher, a man of decent impulses who, although not seeking wealth, violates his principles in pursuing a scheme the aim of which is material profit. But Gould, whose will to redeem his father's failure ultimately consumes every other impulse, seems at the opposite pole from Densher, betrayed by his fatal indecisiveness. Densher's weakness paradoxically saves him: because he is malleable he is susceptible to the power of Milly's spirit, and the fact that Kate's plot is evil enables him finally to condemn it and free himself. But in working the mine, Gould believes that he serves the interests of peace and justice in his country, and the effort engages his best impulses. If mines stir in him emotions which in another man only human circumstances could arouse—the desolation of abandoned mines, for instance, "appealed to him like the sight of human misery" (7:59), he does not suspect at this point that eventually he will expend all his passion on the San Tomé mine. As he allows himself to compromise his principles to safeguard the mine, however, Gould is driven by the ever-increasing need to succeed and so to justify the compromise. Inevitably the mine itself, rather than the order and justice to be secured by the mine, becomes of all-consuming importance; and by the end of the novel he holds himself ready to dynamite the mine rather than relinquish it to others.

The gradual concentration of his entire being upon one object is revealed most dramatically in his relationship with his wife, in her growing disillusionment and ever-increasing sense of isolation. Early in the novel the grim truth of the statement "the latest phase in the history of the mine . . . was in essence the history of her married life" becomes apparent. As the one character moved by "the wisdom of the heart" (7:66,67), Emilia Gould might be expected to play a part similar to that of Milly Theale. Although she is several times pictured as the good fairy dispensing magic potions, she cannot do as Milly does: she cannot save the man she loves; she cannot defeat the power that robs her of happiness. Whereas the wings of the dove, Milly's spirit, enable others to rise, Emilia initially looks to Gould and to his ambition to give purpose to her life: "Her delight in him, lingering with half-open wings like those birds that cannot rise easily from a flat level, found a pinnacle from which to soar up into the skies" (7:59). Having invested her faith and the force of her idealism in her husband, as he had invested his in the mine, she can only watch helplessly as the silver, which at first seemed justification of their faith, "far-reaching and impalpable, like the true expression of an emotion" gradually becomes a barrier, "a wall of silver-bricks" between herself and her husband. Against "the silent work of evil spirits" her powers fail, and at the end she is the good fairy defeated, "touched by the withering suspicion of the uselessness of her labours, the powerlessness of her magic" (7:107, 222, 520).

Charles Gould never attains his wife's clear perception of the soulless tyranny of the mine, but he too achieves the tragic dignity conferred by that recognition of truth that seems to light the darkest corners of one's life and self. For Gould the moment of tragic knowledge comes not at the end but midway in the action, after the downfall of Ribiera, at the point where the failure of one revolution compels him to back another. Not only does he see as never before the "cruel futility" of all attempts to impose order and peace by financing revolutions; but he perceives for the first time the true nature of the mine and his position in Costaguana. Having long ago resolved to "stoop for his weapons" to safeguard the mine, he now understands that the wealth of the mine is itself his chief weapon, "double-edged with the cupidity and misery of mankind, steeped in all the vices of self-indulgence as in a concoction of poisonous roots, tainting the very cause for which it is drawn, always ready to turn awkwardly in the hand." The effect of recognition, however, is to convince him that the "precipitous path" on which he has ventured compels him to "press forward. At that moment he understood it thoroughly" (7:85, 365, 361–362).

The action which precipitates the sequence of tragic insights—Gould's pledge to the emissary of the bandit Hernandez—also reveals to him the likeness between himself and the outlaw, "equals before the lawlessness of the land" (7:360). Other characters in the novel bear resemblances to Gould—not in personality but in attitude and aim. Holroyd, for instance, in proposing to propagate the faith through economic exploitation, reflects in a crude, exaggerated form Gould's effort to found order and justice on the wealth of the San Tomé mine. The chief engineer perceptively remarks that the two capitalists, who would convert the Gould concession into a spiritual mission, "understand each other's imaginative side . . . they have been made for each other" (7:317). The most important double of Gould, however, is Nostromo, whose corruption by the silver and death by accident at the hands of his adoptive father Giorgio Viola, make him, like Gould and Emilia, one of the chief tragic figures of the novel.

Gould and Nostromo are alike in that both are egoists of tenacious will whose sense of identity is grounded in outward manifestations of their power—Gould's in the mine, Nostromo's in his prestige. Both men are spurred by the words of the dead: Charles Gould by his father's prohibition regarding the mine, Nostromo by Teresa Viola's dying prophecy that the Europeans that Nostromo has served will betray him. Most important both men are bound by the silver, as if fettered to it, by the knowledge that they have forfeited themselves for its sake. Like Gould's history Nostromo's illustrates the failure of a woman's love to break the spell of the silver. The deepest passions of Nostromo are roused not by Giselle Viola, to whom he swears his love and who begs him to carry her away to safety, but by the stolen silver, which he yearns "to clasp, embrace, absorb, subjugate in unquestioned possession." Finally Nostromo, like Charles and Emilia Gould, is tragic by virtue of his awareness: he becomes the "slave of a treasure with full self-knowledge." Once he has begun to steal the silver, which, after it is believed lost in the harbor, Nostromo sees as his "bargain," paid for by his own and others' acts of betrayal, he becomes aware of his moral nature in experiencing its revulsion against the cancer of un-confessed crime: "A transgression, a crime, entering a man's exist-ence, eats it up like a malignant growth, consumes it like a fever. Nostromo had lost his peace; the genuineness of all his qualities was destroyed. He felt it himself, and often cursed the silver of San Tomé" (7:529, 523). One might think that Nostromo, like Haw-thorne's Donatello, becomes fully human only when he commits a crime and suffers. The fact that Nostromo's mind is revealed only in the third part, after he has become Captain Fidanza, suggests transformation, as does the picture of Nostromo awakening "with the lost air of a man just born into the world." But Nostromo's world from the beginning is a fallen world—a "paradise of snakes" (7:411, 105). There are no suggestions of a fortunate fall; no signs that Nostromo is educated and elevated by sin as Donatello is. Nos-tromo feels only torment until he makes his dying confession to Emilia Gould.

That tragic recognition in Conrad's novels rarely brings a sense of relief or reconciliation but instead only intensifies suffering is further demonstrated by the fate of Decoud, the last of the four main tragic figures of Nostromo. Decoud is not corrupted by the silver, nor does he suffer the debasement of an ideal. In Decoud, Conrad created his first important example of the skeptic who questions the motives and value of action and who looks upon the follies and sufferings of mankind, including his own, as a tragicomic

spectacle. As the portrayal of Decoud shows, Conrad saw skepticism as he saw rhetoric—a double-edged gift, a dangerous bless-
ing. Skeptical detachment seems a correlative of intelligence, but
skepticism may corrode one's powers to act and destroy one's sense
of individual existence. Decoud's love for Antonia Avellanos stirs
the "genuine impulses of his own nature" (7:153) to which his habit
of raillery has blinded him, but love also commits him to political
action which his skeptical intelligence condemns as absurd; as if in
reaction his disdain of his own acts and feelings increases, thus
denying him the sustaining power of love. To concentrate the will
upon one purpose alone is to invite madness, but to deny the validity of any action is to court dissolution, for "in our activity alone do
we find the sustaining illusion of an independent existence as
against the whole scheme of things of which we form a helpless
part" (7:497). When Decoud is faced with the supreme test of one's
inner strength, utter solitude, he, like Nostromo, discovers his
inner emptiness.

Given the manifold evidences of the silver's baneful power, Captain Mitchell's judgment of the mine as "a great power . . . for
good and evil" (7:486) seems wide of the mark. What Conrad
dramatizes in *Nostromo* is not the principle of equivalence, the
balance of gain and loss, but the destruction wrought by apparent
success. The mine brings material prosperity, it is true; the province grows "rich swiftly on the hidden treasures of the earth"
(7:504), but the price in wrecked lives makes success a kind of
calamity. Tragedy in Conrad's fiction, as in James's, creates a
paradox; but the paradox is the reverse of that in such novels as *The
Portrait of a Lady*, *The Princess Casamassima*, and *The Wings of
the Dove*. Protagonists like Isabel, Hyacinth, and Milly in suffering
outward defeat or failure achieve a kind of victory simply in the
growth of their understanding or in the efficacy of their spirit, but
Conrad's characters like Gould and Nostromo enjoy material success at the cost of their integrity and peace of mind. In betrayal and
defeat Milly's spirit is triumphant. In his "colossal success" Gould's
spirit is mastered, his life consumed: "a terrible success for the last
of the Goulds." Conrad's emphasis on the wreckage that victory of
whatever kind leaves in its wake extends even to incidental images:

Giorgio Viola, for instance, a relic of an earlier, heroic time, drifts like "a broken spar . . . suffered to float away disregarded after a naval victory" (7:522, 60).

As we have noted, James expresses the idea of equivalence by using such terms as *cash, asset, liability, balance*, and *payment* as metaphors for nonmaterial values. In *The Wings of the Dove* these metaphors suggest not only the superior virtue of the spirit in its contest with the sophisticated world but also the power of the spirit to transform money into an agent of spiritual good. In *Nostromo* where the symbol of material value, the silver, is baneful, turning the profitable working of the mine into a soul-destroying success and betraying the dreams of those like Emilia Gould who once attached spiritual value to the silver, the terms of capitalistic enterprise are rarely used metaphorically to denote moral or spiritual value. References in *Nostromo* to *credit, claims, interest, compensation, fortune, capital, cash*, and *shares* have application only to the operation of the mine. The "inexhaustible treasure" of Dr. Monygham's devotion to Mrs. Gould, "drawn upon in the secret of his heart like a store of unlawful wealth" (7:504) is a rare instance of the expression of spiritual good in terms of material interests.

Because Conrad was at pains in *Nostromo* to create a realistic picture of a South American republic in the nineteenth century, because he fills the novel with topical references to historical figures and to events in the history of his imaginary country, one might think that the "tragic farce" (as Decoud terms the upheaval in Costaguana) is peculiar to that country. But in *Nostromo*, as in *Under Western Eyes*, Conrad intends the plight of characters caught in a particular set of conditions to be universal in its meaning.[41] Isolation such as Decoud realizes when he perceives that between himself and Nostromo struggling together to save the silver "no bond of conviction, of common idea" exists (7:295), is the fate of many of Conrad's characters—Jim and the natives of Patusan; Marlow and the other Europeans in *Heart of Darkness*; Lingard and the Malays in *The Rescue*. A "close-meshed net of crime and corruption" (7:361) lies not only upon Costaguana but upon London of *The Secret Agent* as well. The "moral darkness" against which Avellanos vainly struggles breeds acts of torture in *Heart of*

Darkness, The Secret Agent, Under Western Eyes, and *Victory* as wanton as those which bloody the history of Costaguana.

Acts of physical brutality and torture do not occur in James's novels. The absence of such acts, however, does not lessen the truth of James's statement: "I have the imagination of disaster—and see life indeed as ferocious and sinister."[42] As Conrad perceived, the contests in which James's characters engage are life-and-death struggles for which the imagery of warfare is appropriate. The brutality of antagonists like Kate Croy and Charlotte Stant is no less deadly because it is expressed not in physical violence but in images of shining beasts evoked in their victims' minds. But James gives to his important protagonists the power to survive evil if they cannot destroy it. In his fiction and in his letters to friends he repeatedly affirms that if pain seems overwhelming, one's power to endure is even stronger inasmuch as "it wears us, uses us, but we wear it and use it in return; and it is blind whereas we after a manner see."[43] For James consciousness was the "illimitable power"[44] which in novel after novel he portrayed as his characters' chief defense against indifference, apathy, and despair.

Consciousness in Conrad's novels, on the other hand, often seems the reverse of an "illimitable power," on occasion inducing in characters those very states of indifference and despair from which James's characters are spared. No character of James suffers the kind of existential anguish, the sense of life's absurdity, which besets Decoud and Heyst. The life of the imagination sustains James's characters and gives value to their lives; in Conrad's novels thought often robs characters of the grounds on which they can justify action and vitiates the will to live. At best, awareness is intelligence which enables characters like Monygham and Mrs. Gould and Marlow to understand the forces against which men struggle and to save themselves from self-deceiving optimism. At its most destructive, awareness takes the form of the terrified imagination which paralyzes Jim—or the debilitating skepticism which induces in Heyst and Decoud a deadly weariness. Whereas the source of greatest anguish for James's characters is the sense of deprivation, the fear that they have failed or will fail to live fully, the deepest anguish suffered by Conrad's characters is the blighting conviction that effort is futile, the goals of action illusory.

In the novels of both James and Conrad the sense of tragedy is produced by the corruption of the talents and energies of individual characters, by the corrosion of relationships—marriages, friendships, partnerships—in which characters looked to find their good, and by the protagonist's recognition of evil, within himself and without, which he cannot eradicate. James's characters are enlightened and strengthened by tragic recognition; in contrast Conrad's characters, like Monygham and Gould, merely see more clearly the futility of struggle, the certainty of pain, and the inevitability of failure. What is illimitable in Conrad's world is not the awareness of "we who see," but the cosmic machine, "a tragic accident," made "without thought, without conscience, without foresight, without eyes, without heart" which "knits us in . . . and knits us out."[45]

In general terms, however, the dilemma of James's and Conrad's characters is similar: involvement with others and action in the world lead to betrayal or corruption, disillusionment and suffering; but the price of withdrawal is the atrophy of the will to act and the painful consciousness of a barren life. The chief difference is that James emphasizes the constructive creative powers of the mind, Conrad the enervating or destructive effects of imagination and reflection. James portrays outward defeats in which characters know the sense of having lived fully; Conrad presents outward success that corrupts the victor, as in *Nostromo*, or catastrophe, such as Jim suffers, which cannot be conclusively judged either victory or defeat. Finally James presents characters who through suffering and disillusionment undergo change because something completely new is added to the sum of their experience. Kate's last words to Densher—"We shall never be again as we were"—could be applied to nearly all James's protagonists. Many of Conrad's characters change more dramatically than James's in their physical state and outward circumstances, but what brings change is not the addition of something new but the coming to the surface of what was always latent. In other words time merely unfolds the fate contained within the character from the beginning. Jim longs for a "clean slate," Marlow reflects, "as if the initial word of each our destiny were not graven in imperishable characters upon the face of a rock!" (4:186). What Marlow would say of those he observes is not "We shall never be again as we were" but rather "We can never be other than what we are."

Conclusion

"Life consists of the personal experiments of each of us" (7:172). The words of Gabriel Nash in James's *The Tragic Muse* might stand as an epigraph to the fiction of both James and Conrad. In nearly all their important works the two novelists remove the main characters from familiar surroundings and place them in new environments where they test themselves, try to shape their lives and discover what they are capable of becoming. Some characters like Strether and Marlow and Heyst are forced to examine ideas and principles that they once accepted without question. Others like Jim and Razumov and Maggie Verver, confounded by crises that destroy the security of one life, struggle in new conditions to forge another. Some characters like Willems and Kurtz succumb to the environment while others like Marlow, Newman, Isabel Archer, and Hyacinth Robinson recognize forces against which they are helpless and yet assert their power to choose and act within the limits of their freedom.

Neither James nor Conrad embraced Zola's conception of the novelist as being comparable to a scientist conducting an experiment. Like Zola and Dreiser and their common ancestor Balzac, however, James and Conrad present human development as inseparable from the environment in which it takes place. In the preface to *The Ambassadors* James compares Strether's mind to a fluid which hourly changes color as it absorbs new impressions of the world. James's frequent references, especially in the novels of the 1880s, to characters as organisms, their conditions as the soil in which the organisms grow, remind one of passages in such works as *Père Goriot* and *Sister Carrie*. Conrad's analysis of violent acts, like Winnie's murder of Verloc, as the product of inherited traits and primitive lusts, recalls the pictures of degeneration in *L'Assommoir* or *Germinal*.[1] Although some of Conrad's characters, such as Willems, Almayer and Verloc, seem as much the passive victims of conditions as Gervaise or Hurstwood, other characters, notably Marlow, Razumov, Decoud, Monygham, and Heyst, like most of James's protagonists, exhibit intelligence and powers of observation and analysis that set them apart from the characters of Balzac or Zola or Dreiser. James's criticism of Balzac—that he failed to render the "highest kinds of temper, the inward life of the mind, the *cultivated* consciousness"[2]—marks the vital point which separates both James and Conrad from the European and American naturalists.

In depicting the inward life of intelligent reflective characters, James and Conrad show their most important likenesses to and differences from each other and make their most important contributions to the art of the novel. Both novelists convert images of romantic adventure into metaphors of mental acts and psychological states. Both control the point of view, in first- and third-person narratives, to render experience as the personal impressions of characters. James portrays characters as they move to an ever-fuller knowledge of themselves, their associates, and their conditions; Conrad renders characters suddenly confronted by the unknown and the terrifying, baffled in the presence of persons that cannot be clearly seen, depths that cannot be sounded, and mysteries that cannot be solved. Grotesque realities in James's novels call forth the protagonist's powers of resistance and will to control; in Conrad's fiction the bizarre and sinister either confound characters or force them back to the shelter of illusions. Confidence in the power of the imagination and the reason is reflected in James's novels in the urbanity and detachment of the narrator who satirizes folly. Awareness of uncontrollable evil forces Conrad's narrators to the refuge of bitter irony and sarcasm.

Romantic illusions in James's novels may blind a character to danger and so deprive him of happiness and hope of change; but, at the least, enlightenment affords tragic release, and for a number of characters suffering is essential to the growth of the spirit and to the sense of having lived. In Conrad's novels, on the other hand, moments of recognition rarely afford tragic relief and sometimes merely confirm characters in a disastrous course. Romantic egoists like Kurtz, Gould, and Nostromo, who succeed in worldly enterprises, suffer inward corruption, while the abject in spirit—Verloc, Almayer, Willems, and Lingard—fail even of worldly success. If Marlow in *Heart of Darkness* and Razumov grow in wisdom, their terrible experiences offer little to balance the darkness and corruption of their worlds. It is true of course that James's protagonists in their slow advance to knowledge become increasingly aware of the complexity of character and the mixture of good and evil in human motives that can never be fully sounded. But James's novels, in their structure and patterns of images, reinforce the idea of gradual revelation—of a steady march toward clarification of the obscure and knowledge of the hidden.

In constructing his novels James did not depart radically from the practice of predecessors like Jane Austen or Flaubert or Turgenev. James applied the principle of scenic construction more rigorously than any important novelist before him, but he presents causally connected scenes in chronological sequence, preserves the distinction between the inward and outward lives of characters, and creates characters whose acts spring from motives produced by the interplay of personality and circumstance. What sets James apart from all his predecessors is the importance the imaginative life of his characters assumes in his novels and the fullness with which their impressions are analyzed. In one crowded moment the Jamesian observer may perceive in the silence or the expression or the gesture of another character the attitude of the other person, the extent to which that person's relation to the observer and to other characters has changed since their last meeting, the extent to which the person is aware of the change, and the consequences likely to flow from the perceptions of the change. It is generally agreed that James's creation of the central consciousness is his foremost contribution to the development of the novel. Specifically it is the power to see implications, make connections, and analyze impressions, as a prism refracts light into colors, which confers upon James's central character his value as a subject and as a "compositional resource" (23:vii).

If James showed how to make dramatic the impressions that fill the moments of characters' normal day-to-day lives, Conrad demonstrated how to portray states of shock or fear arising from sudden encounters with the strange and terrible. In first-person narratives, notably in *Heart of Darkness*, the narrator not only indicates that the mind registers different impressions simultaneously and makes obscure associations; his narrative at times, in its broken sentences and abrupt shifts in time, represents the troubled flow of consciousness. Neither James nor Conrad ever shaped a novel from the stream of consciousness of characters as did Joyce and Virginia Woolf and Faulkner, but the interior worlds of Strether and Maggie, Marlow and Razumov are as fully analyzed and as graphically depicted as those of Leopold Bloom or Clarissa Dalloway or Quentin Compson.

Both James and Conrad departed from certain conventions accepted by novelists in the nineteenth century who undertook to present a realistic picture of life. James in his late novels presents characters who converse in stylized dialogues and engage in relationships that create elaborate symmetries such as "clumsy life" capable only of "splendid waste" (10:vi) does not show. Conrad in his most important works not only abandoned the conventional time framework; in *Lord Jim*, *Under Western Eyes*, and *Chance* he replaced the omniscient third-person narrator with a first-person narrator who listens to many characters and pieces together the story from his observations and their accounts. In certain ways, however, Conrad's novels, by their very departure from traditional methods, render life as it is actually experienced. By disrupting chronology Conrad induces in the reader a sense of confusion or frustration such as the characters feel. By portraying a narrator as he listens to others and gathers information, often contradictory and inconclusive, Conrad dramatizes through the method itself the way one in life gains knowledge of other people.

In yet another way both James and Conrad by their break with convention approximate the conditions of our own experience. In depicting ambiguous acts and situations, open to different interpretations, seen by observers who reflect different views, both James and Conrad created characters, like living people, who evoke widely different responses from others and about whom the final word that would resolve the differences is never said. Characters like Emma Woodhouse, Gwendolen Harleth, or Eustacia Vye may be as complex as Conrad's or James's characters, but none has elicited such a diversity of opinion as Rowland Mallet, Isabel Archer, Maggie Verver, Marlow, or Heyst. Although we live in the minds of these characters, they retain the irreducible mysteriousness of human beings. The protagonists in James's novels may eventually apprehend the essential nature of another, as Strether sees Chad, or as Isabel sees Osmond, or as Rowland sees Roderick; but the protagonists themselves remain ambiguous, their motives as open to interpretation as the motives and acts of the persons about whom Marlow speculates. In the novels of both James and Conrad the experience of the reader corresponds to that of the character: the reader, like the character, studies surfaces, weighs evidence, analyzes action, and reaches conclusions which may differ from those of other observers of the situation.

In making perception itself the subject of novels, James and Conrad are perhaps most distinctly "modern." The premises on which such works as *Heart of Darkness*, *Lord Jim*, *The Turn of the Screw*, and *The Sacred Fount* rest—that the reality we perceive is a function of the individual consciousness and that no external standard of truth "out there" is available either to readers or to characters—encourage one to view James and Conrad as precursors of such writers as Nabokov, Gide, and the "new novelists" of France. At least one critic has seen in *The Sacred Fount* likeness to *Last Year at Marienbad*, in which distinctions between real and imagined, present and past, dreaming and waking are impossible to make.[3]

What James and Conrad create in their fiction, however, is closer to the world of Flaubert's novels than to that of Robbe-Grillet's. Both James and Conrad emphasize the opposition of life and art: James in his prefaces stresses the form which art creates; Conrad in his fiction emphasizes the discrepancy between life and the representation of life in words. But neither James nor Conrad calls attention to the fictive nature of the world that he creates or undercuts its reality. Within *Lord Jim* Marlow may dwell on the impossibility of conveying the essence of his experience in words, but the illusion of Marlow and Jim as "real" persons in a "real" world is never broken. One may not know whether the governess in *The Turn of the Screw* sees or imagines ghosts, whether Kurtz in *Heart of Darkness* wins the "moral victory" Marlow says he wins, or whether the characters in *The Sacred Fount* have the motives the narrator thinks that they have. But in all three works the reader is never in doubt that the action presented to him is what the narrator thinks he is seeing. Newmarch is a place in fiction as Middlemarch is; Bly exists for the reader as Udolpho exists for the governess—a "real" place in a world the reader accepts as real. Characters retain their sense of past and present, and the fact that they describe an experience as dreamlike or absurd or unearthly indicates that they have an idea of the normal to which they refer.

In portraying characters who confront the obscure, the unfathomable, the sinister, or the unspeakable, neither James nor Conrad discarded moral principles or espoused moral nihilism. Indeed a number of characters baffled or defeated by the incomprehensible or the uncontrollable cleave ever more firmly to principles of restraint, solidarity, compassion, fidelity, or renunciation. Perception leads to decisions of a moral nature: Strether exhorts Chad to remain in Paris and refuses gain for himself; Milly leaves her fortune to Densher, and he puts Kate to the test; Marlow remains loyal to Kurtz and to Jim; Razumov confesses. The act may fail of its intent; it may affect only the doer and may even work his destruction. Ideals may promote self-deception and feed egotism; they may be debased by the corrupting power of action. The characters of James and Conrad live in a world which dooms people to intolerable alternatives, rewards selflessness with disillusionment and pain, corrupts the weak, and defeats the will of the strong and the weak alike. But because characters like Hyacinth, Milly Theale, Marlow, and Monygham hold to principle when no external authority compels or justifies or rewards them, such characters become themselves a source of values. In their effort to understand their experience and to express its inner meaning, whether to themselves alone or to others, they affirm the importance of that experience as does the novelist who seeks to preserve experience by comprehending it and giving it form.

In conceiving the work of fiction as the development of an action, and in sustaining the illusion that the world of the novel is a reality, self-contained and inviolate, James and Conrad accepted conventions that governed the writing of fiction in the nineteenth century. In analyzing perceptions, in dramatizing the relative nature of truth, and in portraying within the work of fiction characters who are absorbed in defining the nature of the world in which they live, James and Conrad helped to make the conventions of modern fiction.

Notes

CHAPTER ONE

1. Letter to Morton Fullerton, October 2, 1896 (Harvard).

2. *The Letters of Henry James*, Percy Lubbock, 2 vols. (New York: Scribners, 1920), 1:230.

3. *The Works of Joseph Conrad*, Sun-Dial Edition (Garden City, N.Y.: Doubleday, Page, 1920–1928), 2:ix. All references to this edition will be indicated in the text by volume and page numbers.

4. Letter to Marguerite Poradowska, October 29 or November [?] 5, 1894: "I am afraid I am too much under the influence of Maupassant. I have studied *Pierre et Jean*—thought, method, and everything—with the deepest discouragement. It seems to be nothing at all, but the mechanics are so complex that they make me tear out my hair" (*Letters of Joseph Conrad to Marguerite Poradowska: 1890–1920*, trans. and ed. by John A. Gee and Paul J. Sturm, New Haven: Yale University Press, 1940, p. 84).

Letter to Edward Garnett, Saturday, May, 1898: "I've sent you today a copy of . . . that amazing masterpiece *Bel-Ami*. The technique of that work gives one acute pleasure. It is simply enchanting to see how it's done" (*Letters from Joseph Conrad: 1895–1924*, ed. Edward Garnett, Indianapolis: Bobbs-Merrill, 1928, pp. 137–138).

Letter to A. H. Davray, August 22, 1903: "Moi qui suis, sans me vanter, saturé de Maupassant, j'ai été étonné de l'allure maupassantesque que l'on peut donner a la prose anglaise" (*Lettres Françaises*, with an introduction and notes by G. Jean-Aubry, Paris: Paris Librairie Gallimard, 1929, pp. 51–52).

5. Letter to Henry James, December 12, 1908, in G. Jean-Aubry, *Joseph Conrad: Life and Letters*, 2 vols. (Garden City, New York: Doubleday, Page, 1927), 2:91. Hereafter cited as Jean-Aubry.

6. Letter to John Galsworthy (February 11, 1899) Jean-Aubry, 1:270–271.

7. Quoted in Ian Watt, "Conrad, James and *Chance*," in *Imagined*

Worlds, ed. Maynard Mack and Ian Gregor (London: Methuen, 1968), p. 302.

8. Garnett, p. 70.

9. Ibid., p. 74.

10. Jean-Aubry, 1:201, n. 2.

11. Ibid.

12. Garnett, p. 91.

13. Ibid., p. 9.

14. November 30, 1897, *Lettres Françaises*, p. 34.

15. *Conrad: The Critical Heritage*, ed. Norman Sherry (London and Boston: Routledge and Kegan Paul, 1973), p. 75.

16. The fullest discussion of the relation between James and Wells is the introduction by Leon Edel and Gordon N. Ray to their edition of *Henry James and H. G. Wells: A Record of Their Friendship, Their Debate on the Art of Fiction, and Their Quarrel* (Urbana: University of Illinois Press, 1958). The fullest discussion of the relation of Conrad and Wells is in Frederick Karl, "Conrad, Wells, and the Two Voices," *PMLA* 88 (October 1973):1049–1065.

17. Letter of January 20, 1902, in *Henry James and H. G. Wells*, p. 77.

18. Letter of January 8, 1904 (Harvard).

19. *The Legend of the Master*, ed. Simon Nowell-Smith (New York: Scribners, 1948), p. 91.

20. Leon Edel, *Henry James: The Master, 1901–1916* (Philadelphia: Lippincott, 1972), p. 48.

21. Ford Madox Ford, *Return to Yesterday* (London: Victor Gollancz, 1931), p. 23.

22. *South Lodge* (London: Constable, 1943), p. 25.

23. *Thus to Revisit* (London: Chapman and Hall, 1921), p. 58. "Techniques," *Southern Review*, O. S. 1 (July 1935):20–35.

24. Letter to Garnett, December 5, 1897, in Garnett, p. 119.

25. *Hawthorne* (London: Macmillan, 1879), p. 31.

26. H. G. Wells, *Experiment in Autobiography* (New York: Macmillan, 1934), p. 410.

27. Letter to Henry James II, May 23, 1946 (Harvard).

28. Letter of January 6, 1914 (Yale).

29. Letter of November 15, 1902, in *Henry James and H. G. Wells*, pp. 83–85.

30. *The Golden Echo* (London: Chatto and Windus, 1953), p. 64.

31. Letter of October 26, 1903 (Harvard).

32. *Joseph Conrad: Letters to William Blackwood and David S. Meldrum*, ed. William Blackburn (Durham N.C.: Duke University Press, 1958), p. 116.

33. British Museum, Ashley Ms. 4792.

34. Ibid. A grant of £300 to Conrad was made less than three weeks later. On July 11, 1902, James wrote to Gosse: "I rejoice more than I can say in the news that you give me about the grant to J. C.—nor can I tell you, either, how I applaud, esteem, venerate you for the noble energy with which you put these things through" (Colby College Library).

35. Letter to Mrs. David Sargent Curtis, July 17, 1909 (University of Virginia).

36. July 12, 1908. Harvard.

37. October 12, 1909. Harvard.

38. April 2, 1908 (Berg Collection).

39. Berg Collection.

40. Jean-Aubry, 2:91–92.

41. *Lettres Françaises*, p. 77.

42. *Twenty Letters to Joseph Conrad*, ed. G. Jean-Aubry (London: First Edition Club, 1926), 8 pamphlets, pages unnumbered.

43. Letter to Richard Curle, July 14, 1923, in Jean-Aubry, 2:316.

44. Letter of October 13, 1912 (University of Virginia).

45. September 20, 1907, in Jean-Aubry, 2:55–56.

46. Letter of February 27, 1914 (Yale).

47. *Experiment in Autobiography*, p. 525. Several statements in James's letters suggest that he viewed Conrad as a strange unaccountable person. The news that Sidney Colvin had been staying with Conrad moved James to write to Pinker that he was "lost in the wonder of it" (January 2, 1911, Yale). On hearing that Pinker was considering a trip to the United States with Conrad, James marveled at "the courage of your bodily charge of him!" (June 10, 1914, Yale). In a letter to Ford, he remarked Conrad's "great gloom" (October 17, 1908, Yale).

48. Letter to John Galsworthy, June 26, 1910, in Jean-Aubry, 2:112.

49. *Portraits from Memory and Other Essays* (London: George Allen and Unwin, 1956), p. 82.

50. *The English Notebooks*, ed. Randall Stewart (New York: Modern Language Association of America; London: Oxford University Press, 1941, pp. 432–433.

51. Passages are quoted from *Conrad: The Critical Heritage*, pp. 185, 198, 228, 231, 235.

52. B. L. Reid, *The Man from New York: John Quinn and His Friends* (New York: Oxford University Press, 1968), p. 127.

53. *Twenty Letters to Joseph Conrad.*

54. Ibid.

55. Yale.

56. Yale.

57. Berg Collection.

58. *Notes on Novelists* (New York: Scribners, 1914), p. 319. In revising the articles for publication as "The New Novel" in *Notes on Novelists*, James expanded the section on Conrad to twice its original length. The article in the *Times Literary Supplement* is even less favorable to Conrad. The first sentence of the section on Conrad describes *Chance* as "a case of the exhibition of method at any price," and several positive statements in the book do not appear in the newspaper article: e.g., James's reference in "The New Novel" to the "refinement of design" of *Chance* (p. 345), and his statement that "the general effect of *Chance* is arrived at by a pursuance of means to the end in view contrasted with which every other current form of the chase can only affect us as cheap and futile" (p. 346).

59. *Notes on Novelists*, p. 345.

60. Ibid., p. 350. James made the comparison in his letter of February 5, 1914, to Pinker, but omitted it in the article in the *Times Literary Supplement*.

61. *Notes on Novelists*, p. 349.

62. Ibid., p. 351.

63. *Background with Chorus* (London: Hutchinson, 1956), p. 124.

64. May 24, 1916, quoted in Reid, p. 245.

65. July 24, 1915 (Yale). In a letter to Edith Wharton, dated July 19, 1915, James promises to "pass on your earnest prayer at once to the individuals you name. . . . I am a little afraid that some of the eminent persons you direct me to may prove rather arid. I haven't for instance much hope of Conrad, who produces by the sweat of his brow and tosses off, in considerable anguish, at the rate of about a word a month. But I will try, I will do my best" (Yale).

66. "Three Conrad Letters in the Edith Wharton Papers," *Yale University Library Gazette* 44 (January 1970): 148.

67. "Conrad, James and *Chance*," p. 313.

68. Jean-Aubry, 2:278.

69. "Conrad and the Reporters," *New York Evening Post*, May 3, 1923.

70. Reid, p. 245.

71. Letter to Norman Douglas, February 29, 1908, in Jean-Aubry, 2:68.

72. Letter of July 30, 1907 (Berg Collection).

73. The unfinished story, "The Sisters," which Conrad began writing in 1896, has also been cited as showing the influence of James. Although Conrad's description of the artist Stephen, who separates himself from the family business and rejects commercial success in order to seek the secret of artistic genius, can be compared to James's portraits of the artist in *The Tragic Muse* and the tales of the 1890s, the subject of Conrad's work appears to be the relation of Stephen to the two Spanish sisters, Rita and Teresa, both of whom, according to Ford, were to fall in love with the artist. The situation which Ford projects in his introduction to the published text foreshadows the relation of Nostromo to Giselle and Linda Viola in *Nostromo* and the conflict of the two sisters Rita and Therese in *The Arrow of Gold*. See *The Sisters*, with an introduction by Ford Madox Ford (New York: Crosby Gaige, 1928).

74. *Henry James: The Master*, p. 54.

75. Letter to Mrs. Anna E. Bontine, November 22, 1898, in Jean-Aubry, 1:256.

76. *Conrad: The Critical Heritage*, p. 161.

77. Ibid., p. 123.

78. In his essay on *Chance* John Cowper Powys declares that "no work of Conrad has so close an affinity with the art of Henry James as this book." See *A Conrad Memorial Library* (Garden City, N.Y.: Doubleday, Doran, 1929), p. 219. According to Douglas Hewitt, "*Chance* shows the influence of James' own work more than any other of Conrad's books." See *Conrad: A Reassessment*, 2nd ed. (London: Bowes and Bowes, 1969), p. 97.

79. Ibid., p. 274. The phrases Montague quotes are from James's preface to *The Golden Bowl*.

80. *Castles in Spain and Other Screeds* (New York: Scribners, 1927), p. 119.

81. *Joseph Conrad: A Study* (Garden City, N.Y.: Doubleday, Page, 1914), p. 10.

82. "Techniques," p. 25.

83. Edel, *Henry James: The Master*, p. 54; F. W. Dupee, *Henry James* (New York: William Sloane Associates, 1951), p. 281.

84. *Politics and the Novel* (Cleveland: World, Meridian Books, 1957), pp. 79, 76.

85. "James, Conrad and *Chance*," p. 304.

86. *Joseph Conrad: A Critical Biography* (Rpt. 1967, New York: McGraw-Hill, 1960), p. 145.

87. "Conrad in His Historical Perspective," *English Literature in Transition*, 14, no. 3 (1971), 157.

88. E. K. Brown, "James and Conrad," *Yale Review* 35 (winter 1946):265–286; Walter O'Grady, "On Plot in Modern Fiction: Hardy, James, and Conrad," *Modern Fiction Studies* 11 (summer 1965):107–115; Jessie Kocmanova, "The Revolt of the Workers in the Novels of Gissing, James, and Conrad," *Brno Studies in English* 1 (1959):110–139. Ivo Vidan, "*The Princess Casamassima* between Balzac and Conrad," *Studia Romanica et Anglia Zagrabiensia*, nos. 21–22 (July–December 1966):259–276; Roger Ramsay, "The Available and the Unavailable 'I': Conrad and James," *English Literature in Transition* 14, no. 2 (1971):137–145.

89. See, for instance, Frederick Karl, *A Reader's Guide to Joseph Conrad* (New York: Farrar, Straus and Giroux, 1969); R. L. Mégroz, *Joseph Conrad's Mind and Method* (London: Faber and Faber, 1931); Robert Ryf, *Joseph Conrad* (New York: Columbia University Press, 1970).

90. *The Apple Trees: Four Reminiscences* (Waltham Saint Lawrence, Berkshire: Golden Cockrell Press, 1932), p. 56.

CHAPTER TWO

1. See for instance his letter to Warrington Dawson, June 2, 1922. "I now find from repeated attempts that the form of writing consisting in literary appreciation of other men's work, implying analysis and an exposition of ethical and aesthetic values on which all criticism and even a mere panagyric must be based, is not in my way" (Dale B. J. Randall, *Joseph Conrad and Warrington Dawson: The Record of a Friendship*, Durham, N.C.: Duke University Press, 1968, p. 42).

2. *The Novels and Tales of Henry James*, 26 vols. (1907–1919; reprint ed., New York: Scribners, 1962–1965), 2:xv. All references to this edition will hereafter be indicated in the text by volume and page number.

3. *Joseph Conrad: Letters to William Blackwood and David S. Meldrum*, p. 154. The aspect of the method that Conrad stresses in this letter

is the importance of the final incident, in the light of which "the whole story in all its descriptive detail shall fall into its place—acquire its value and its significance."

4. *Joseph Conrad: A Personal Remembrance* (Boston: Little, Brown, 1924), pp. 191–230.

5. Foreword to A. S. Kinkead, *Landscapes of Corsica and Ireland* (London: United Arts Gallery, November–December, 1921).

6. *Partial Portraits* (London: Macmillan, 1888), p. 384.

7. Ibid., p. 406.

8. *The Question of Our Speech and The Lesson of Balzac: Two Lectures* (Boston: Houghton Mifflin, 1905), p. 93.

9. Letter to Louise Colet, September 13,1852, in *Correspondance*, 9 vols. (Paris: Louis Conard, Libraire-Editeur, 1926–1933), 3:21.

10. Letter to H. G. Wells, March 3, 1911, *The Letters of Henry James*, 2:182.

11. Letters to Sidney Colvin, February 27, 1917 (Yale) March 18, 1917, Jean-Aubry, 2:184.

12. Letter to Edward Garnett, November 17, 1906, in *Letters from Joseph Conrad, 1895–1924*, p. 195.

13. *Partial Portraits*, p. 388.

14. *The Notebooks of Henry James*, p. 113.

15. *Partial Portraits*, p. 388.

16. Letter to Edmund Gosse, October 11, 1912 (University of Virginia).

17. *Notes on Novelists*, p. 398; "The Lesson of Balzac," pp. 71–72.

18. *Partial Portraits*, p. 259.

19. Letter to Edward Noble, October 28, 1895, in Jean-Aubry, 1:183.

20. "The Lesson of Balzac," pp. 76–77.

21. In 1895, shortly after he had completed his second novel, Conrad counseled Edward Noble in similar terms: "You must search the darkest corners of your heart, the most remote recesses of your brain—you must search them for the image, for the glamour, for the right expression. And you must do it sincerely, at any cost" (Jean-Aubry, 1:183). In 1920 Conrad advised Edward Garnett, who was beginning a novel: "But before everything switch off the critical current of your mind and work in darkness—the creative darkness which no ghost of responsibility will haunt" (Garnett, p. 273).

22. Letter to Edward Garnett, November 12, 1900, in Garnett, p. 171.

23. Letter to Edward Garnett, August 28, 1908, in Garnett, p. 214.

24. Letter to Mrs. E. L. Sanderson, September, 1910, in Jean-Aubry, 2:116.

25. *Conrad's Eastern World* (Cambridge: University Press, 1966), pp. 270–273. The difference is illustrated by accounts of two young writers of the methods of James and Conrad. After visiting James in Rye in 1906, Hamlin Garland recorded his impressions in his notebook: "His world of fashion, of meetings and partings, is a fine-spun web out of his own brain. He has observed, but merely for the fillip which the objective fact has given to his imagination. . . . He loses concern for the exterior correlation and attends only to the interior unity—the essential interior unity" (quoted from "London Notes 1906," an unpublished notebook in B. R. McElderry, Jr., "Hamlin Garland and Henry James," *American Literature* 23 [January 1952]:443).

Warrington Dawson, in his recollection of Conrad's use of the Humbert case in creating deBarral in *Chance*, describes a practice the opposite of James's: "Conrad in his great artistic conscientiousness always wanted more and more information until he felt so completely sure of his ground that he felt as much at home there as in his own house" (Randall, p. 42).

26. *Notes on Novelists*, p. 192.

27. Letter to Mrs. Humphry Ward, September 30, 1909 (University of Virginia).

28. Letter of June 20, 1913, in Randall, p. 159.

29. *Joseph Conrad and the Fiction of Autobiography* (Cambridge: Harvard University Press, 1966), p. 137 and passim. For another detailed study of this idea of truth in Conrad's works, see James Guetti, *The Limits of Metaphor: A Study of Melville, Conrad, and Faulkner* (Ithaca, N.Y.: Cornell University Press, 1967), esp. pp. 46–68, 139–148.

30. *Conrad's Manifesto: Preface to a Career: The History of the Preface to the Nigger of the Narcissus*, with facsimiles of manuscripts, ed. David R. Smith (Philadelphia: Philip H. and A.S.W. Rosenbach Foundation, 1966), p. 67.

31. Letter of March 23, 1896, in Garnett, p. 46.

32. Letter to Richard Curle, July 14, 1923, in Jean-Aubry, 2:317.

33. Letter to F. M. Hueffer, June, 1901 (Yale).

34. Letter of October 9, 1899, in Jean-Aubry, 1:280.

35. Letter to Richard Curle, April 24, 1922, *Letters of Joseph Conrad to Richard Curle* (Garden City, N.Y.: Doubleday, Doran, 1928), letter no. 89.

36. Letter to Mrs. E. L. Sanderson, September, 1910, in Jean-Aubry, 2:118.

37. *Partial Portraits*, pp. 227–228.

38. "The Lesson of Balzac " pp. 97–98.

39. *Essays in London and Elsewhere* (New York:Harpers, 1893),p. 265.

40. "The Lesson of Balzac," p. 97.

41. Ibid., p. 100.

42. Letter of April 24, 1894, in *Letters of Joseph Conrad to Marguerite Poradowska, 1890–1920*, p. 66.

43. *Joseph Conrad and the Fiction of Autobiography*, pp. 58–63 and passim.

44. *Principles of Art* (Oxford: Clarendon Press, 1938), pp. 118–119.

45. "The Lesson of Balzac," p. 84.

46. *Notes on Novelists*, p. 57.

47. *Partial Portraits*, pp. 57–58.

48. Letter of November 1, 1906, in *Twenty Letters to Joseph Conrad*.

49. "Ivan Turgenieff," in *The Portable Henry James*, ed. Morton Dauwen Zabel (New York: Viking, 1951), p. 461. One may note that whereas Conrad stresses the bonds that unite all men, James, although never denying the importance of such bonds, stresses instead the uniqueness of each writer's vision: "Humanity is immense and reality has a myriad forms" (*Partial Portraits*, pp. 387–388).

50. In his notes to *The Ivory Tower* James vividly expressed his satisfaction in the form packed to bursting: "I seem to see already how my action, however tightly packed down, will strain my Ten Books, most blessedly, to cracking. That is exactly what I want, the tight packing *and* the beautifully audible cracking; the most magnificent masterly little vivid economy, with a beauty of its own equal to the beauty of the donnée itself, that ever was" (25:278).

51. Letter to Edward Garnett, June 19, 1896, in Garnett, p. 59; to Mr. and Mrs. E. L. Sanderson, August 31, 1898, in Jean-Aubry, 1:247; to Edward Garnett, Good Friday, 1899, in Garnett, p. 153.

52. Letter to F. M. Hueffer, March 29, 1911 (Berg Collection).

53. *The Notebooks of Henry James*, pp. 111, 134.

54. Letters to E. L. Sanderson, February 2, 1897 (Yale); October 12, 1899, Jean-Aubry, 1:283; to Arthur Symons, August 29, 1908, in Arthur Symons, *Notes on Joseph Conrad with Some Unpublished Letters* (London: Meyers, 1925), p. 18.

55. Letter of August 10, 1898, in *Letters to William Blackwood and David S. Meldrum*, p. 27.

56. James's phrase in *Hawthorne*, p. 65.

57. Letter to Maxime du Camp, April, 1846, in *Selected Letters of Gustave Flaubert*, trans. and ed. Francis Steegmuller (New York: Farrar, Straus and Young, 1953), p. 43.

58. Letter to Louise Colet, September 18, 1846, in *Selected Letters*, p. 76. See also letter to Louise Colet, April 24, 1852: "We must . . . live for our vocation, climb into our ivory tower, and dwell there along with our dreams" (p. 135).

59. The fullest discussion of the relation of Conrad to Flaubert is Donald Yelton, *Mimesis and Metaphor: An Inquiry into the Genesis and Scope of Conrad's Symbolic Imagery* (The Hague: Mouton, 1967), pp. 104–106 and passim. Similarities between the preface to *The Nigger of the Narcissus* and Maupassant's preface to *Pierre et Jean* (1888) are noted by G. J. Worth in "Conrad's Debt to Maupassant in the preface to *The Nigger of the Narcissus*," *Journal of English and Germanic Philology* 54 (October 1955):700–704. The parallels between James's "The Art of Fiction" (1884) and Maupassant's preface of four years later are noted by Philip Grover in *Henry James and the French Novel* (New York: Barnes and Noble, 1973), pp. 117–121.

60. Pater, *Appreciations, with an Essay on Style* (London: Macmillan, 1931), p. 6.

61. Ibid., p. 235.

62. *Partial Portraits*, p. 388.

63. *The Renaissance* (London: Macmillan, 1925), p. 238.

64. Ibid., p. 236.

65. Ibid., p. 235.

66. This point of resemblance is noted by Alan M. Rose, "Conrad and the Sirens of Decadence," *Texas Studies in Literature and Language* 11 (spring 1969):804–805. See also J. J. Duffy, "Conrad and Pater: Suggestive Echoes," *Conradiana* 1 (summer 1968):45–47.

67. *The Renaissance*, p. 235.

68. Letter to Henry Adams, March 21, 1914, in *Letters of Henry James*, 2:361.

69. *The Theory of the Novel in England* (New York: Columbia University Press, 1959), esp. pp. 222–224.

70. "Is There a Life After Death?" in F. O. Matthiessen, *The James Family* (New York: Knopf, 1947), pp. 611–613.

CHAPTER THREE

1. Letter to Edward Noble, October 28, 1895, in Jean-Aubry 1:183.

2. "Eugene Pickering," *The Complete Tales of Henry James*, ed. Leon Edel, 12 vols. (Philadelphia: Lippincott, 1961–1964), 3:315.

3. Conrad develops the idea that situations like characters have physiognomies to be analyzed, in the manuscript of *Chance*, in a passage deleted from the published novel: "Events like beings have their aspect, their character and features, their figure, and even their drapery of circumstances in which they acquire something of an air of mystery as they move across our line of vision into the past" (MS, p. 308, Berg Collection).

4. Letter to Violet Paget, May 10, 1885, in *The Selected Letters of Henry James*, p. 206.

5. Letter to Edward Noble, November 2, 1895, in Jean-Aubry 1:184.

6. *Partial Portraits*, pp. 387–388.

7. See for instance Jocelyn Baines, *Joseph Conrad: A Critical Biography*, pp. 242–243; Frederick Karl, *A Reader's Guide to Joseph Conrad*, pp. 50–55; Donald Yelton, *Mimesis and Metaphor*, p. 111.

8. "Conrad, James and Chance," in *Imagined Worlds*, p. 306.

9. *Conrad the Novelist* (Cambridge, Mass.: Harvard University Press, 1958), p. 140.

10. *The Notebooks of Henry James*, p. 257.

11. *Notes on Novelists*, p. 441.

12. For illustration of Marlow's analytical power, see Janet Burstein, "On Ways of Knowing in *Lord Jim*," *Nineteenth-Century Fiction* 26 (March 1972):456–468.

13. *Chance* (London: Methuen, 1914), p. 76.

14. See J. E. Tanner, "The Chronology and the Enigmatic End of *Lord Jim*," *Nineteenth-Century Fiction* 21 (March 1967): 369–380.

15. For fuller discussion of this aspect of Marlow's experience, see Bruce Johnson, "Names, Naming, and the 'Inscrutable' in Conrad's *Heart of Darkness*," *Texas Studies in Literature and Language* 12 (winter 1971):675–688; and William F. Zak, "Conrad, F. R. Leavis, and Whitehead: *Heart of Darkness* and Organic Holism," *Conradiana* 4 (1972):5–24.

16. J. Hillis Miller, in his essay on Conrad in *Poets of Reality* (Cambridge, Mass.: Harvard University Press, 1965), points out a number of instances in *Heart of Darkness* and *The Rescue* when characters experience a state in which "the ordinary qualities of time and space disappear,

a state in which they are no one and nowhere because they are everywhere at once" (p. 32).

17. "Conrad in His Historical Perspective," p. 159.

18. "'The Beast in the Jungle': An Analysis of James's Late Style," *Modern Fiction Studies* 16 (summer 1970):187. Seymour Chatman, in *The Later Style of Henry James* (Oxford: Basil Blackwell, 1972), discusses James's use of verbs of mental action, intransitive verbs, and metaphors and his use of psychological verbs and adjectives as nouns, as part of his effort to "catch the mind at work in all its uncertainty" (p. 41).

19. *The Sacred Fount* (New York: Scribners, 1901), p. 13.

20. *The Bostonians* (London: Macmillan, 1886), p. 410.

21. Peter K. Garrett, *Scene and Symbol from George Eliot to James Joyce* (New Haven: Yale University Press, 1969), p. 177.

22. For detailed discussions in which different kinds and classes of images are identified and the functions of images analyzed see Robert L. Gale, *The Caught Image: Figurative Language in the Fiction of Henry James* (Chapel Hill: University of North Carolina Press, 1964); Alexander Holder-Barrell, *The Development of Imagery and Its Functional Significance in Henry James's Novels*, Cooper Monographs no. 3 (Bern: Francke Verlag, 1959); Austin Warren, "Symbolic Imagery in the Later Novels," *Rage for Order* (Chicago: University of Chicago Press, 1948).

23. *Scene and Symbol*, pp. 102–103. See also Warren, p. 149.

24. The same process is dramatized in "The Jolly Corner," in which the protagonist Spencer Brydon initially wonders what would have been his destiny had he remained in America, then conceives "a strange *alter ego* deep down somewhere within me" (17:449). As he broods on his conception, the idea becomes "the presence" whom he stalks in the empty night hours in his ancestral house; as if his imagination had created in the alter ego a consciousness and imbued him with physical reality, the presence seems to watch and wait for Brydon, and at the end a figure confronts him animated by "the roused passion of a life larger than his own" (17:477).

25. See, for example, Peter J. Conn, "Seeing and Blindness in 'The Beast in the Jungle,'" *Studies in Short Fiction* 7 (summer 1970):472–475; Courtney Johnson, "John Marcher and the Paradox of the Unfortunate Fall," *Studies in Short Fiction* 6 (winter 1969):121–135.

26. Yelton, *Mimesis and Metaphor*, p. 46. The parallels between *Victory* and Villiers d l'Isle Adam's *Axel* are developed in detail in Katherine Haynes Gatch, "Conrad's Axel," *Studies in Philology* 48 (January 1951):98–106.

27. Yelton, p. 30.

28. *The Major Phase*, p. 72.

29. *Hawthorne*, p. 119.

30. Michael Egan, *Henry James: The Ibsen Years* (London: Vision Press, 1972), pp. 120, 131. Warren also emphasizes the importance to James of Ibsen, in *Rage for Order*, pp. 142–144.

31. *Essays in London and Elsewhere*, pp. 230, 237, 239, 243.

32. *Notes and Reviews*, p. 25.

33. *Notes on Novelists*, p. 427.

34. *The Notebooks of Henry James*, p. 228.

35. Marlow's effort in *Chance* to enter into the feelings of the main characters is discussed in Royal Roussel, *The Metaphysics of Darkness* (Baltimore: Johns Hopkins Press, 1971), pp. 87, 170ff.

36. Marlow's assumption of the novelist's omniscience in *Chance* is discussed by Carl H. Grabo, in *The Technique of the Novel* (New York: Scribners, 1928), pp. 69–70; and by William York Tindall in "Apology for Marlow," *From Jane Austen to Joseph Conrad*, ed. Robert C. Rathburn and Martin Steinman, Jr. (Minneapolis: University of Minnesota Press, 1958), pp. 274–285. Roussel points out occasions when Marlow misjudges characters and fails to foresee the effects of their actions (*The Metaphysics of Darkness*, p. 177).

37. In Marlow's words Jim "stood there for all the parentage of his kind" (4:43); "he was like a figure set up on a pedestal, to represent in his persistent youth the power, and perhaps the virtues, of races that never grow old, that have emerged from the gloom. I don't know why he should always have appeared to me symbolic" (4:265). Marlow reminds his audience that Jim is "one of us."

38. *Essays in London and Elsewhere*, p. 227.

CHAPTER FOUR

1. "The Art of Fiction," *Partial Portraits*, p. 393.

2. *The Castle of Otranto: A Gothic Story*, ed. W. S. Lewis (London: Oxford University Press, 1969), p. 7.

3. *The Progress of Romance Through Times, Countries and Manners* (New York: Garland Press, 1970), p. 111.

4. *Notes and Reviews*, p. 10.

5. *The Miscellaneous Prose Works of Sir Walter Scott*, 6 vols. (Edinburgh: Robert Cadell, 1834,) 6:129.

6. "Emma: A Novel," *Quarterly Review* 14, in *Sir Walter Scott on Novelists and Fiction*, ed. Ioan Williams (New York: Barnes and Noble, 1968), pp. 227, 232, 235.

7. Letter to Violet Paget, April 27, 1890 (Colby College Library).

8. "The Art of Fiction," *Partial Portraits*, p. 390.

9. Letter to Sidney Colvin, March 18, 1917, in Jean-Aubry, 2:185.

10. Letter of March 10, 1902, in Jean-Aubry, 1:303.

11. Preface to *The Leather-Stocking Tales, The Complete Works of J. Fenimore Cooper*, 32 vols. (New York: Putnam [1893?] 1:vii.

12. Edward Garnett, "Romantic Biography" (review of F. M. Ford's *Joseph Conrad*), *Nation and Athenaeum* 36, no. 10 (December 6, 1924):366.

13. "Emma: A Novel," in *Sir Walter Scott on Novelists and Fiction*, p. 230.

14. Letter to J. B. Pinker, January 6, 1902 (Berg Collection).

15. "The Art of Fiction," *Partial Portraits*, p. 402.

16. Samuel Hynes, "The Spirit of Romance," *Edwardian Occasions* (London: Routledge & Kegan Paul, 1972), p. 72.

17. *Anatomy of Criticism: Four Essays* (Princeton, N.J.: Princeton University Press, 1957), p. 151.

18. Conrad, letter to William Blackwood, July 4, 1901, *Letters to William Blackwood and David S. Meldrum*, p. 130.

19. Preface to *The House of the Seven Gables, The Writings of Nathaniel Hawthorne*, 22 vols. (Boston: Houghton Mifflin, 1900), 7:xxii.

20. Preface to *The Blithedale Romance, The Writings of Nathaniel Hawthorne*, 8:xxix–xxx.

21. *The Anatomy of Criticism*, p. 186.

22. *La Préface de Cromwell*, ed. Maurice Sourian (Paris: Société française d'imprimerie et de libraire, 1897), pp. 191ff.

23. Appendix, A Note on "Romance," in *The Nature of a Crime* by Joseph Conrad and Ford Madox Ford (Garden City, N.Y.: Doubleday, Page, 1924), p. 95.

24. For discussion of the motifs of the fairy tale and Gothic romance in *The American*, see George Knox, "Romance and Fable in James's *The American*," *Anglia*, 83, no. 3 (1965):308–323. Other detailed studies of Gothic elements in James's fiction are Martha Banta, *Henry James and the Occult* (Bloomington: Indiana University Press, 1972), esp. pp. 169–178; 183–194; Richard Chase, *The American Novel and Its Tradition* (Garden City, N.Y.: Anchor Books, 1957), pp. 117–137; Leon Edel, Introduction to *The Ghostly Tales of Henry James* (New Brunswick, New

Jersey: Rutgers University Press, 1948); Manfred Mackenzie, "Ironic Melodrama in *The Portrait of a Lady*," *Modern Fiction Studies* 12 (spring 1966): 7–23. James's fullest discussion of Gothic writers is his early review "Miss Braddon," published in the *Nation*, November 9, 1865, and reprinted in *Notes and Reviews*.

25. *The Comic Sense of Henry James* (New York: Oxford University Press, 1960), esp. pp. 27–43.

26. *Quentin Durward*, Border Edition, 2 vols. (London: John C. Nimmo, 1894), 2:121.

27. See for instance Mutlü Blasing, "Double Focus in *The American*," *Nineteenth-Century Fiction* 28 (June 1973):74–84; John Robert Moore, "An Imperfection in the Art of Henry James," *Nineteenth-Century Fiction* 13 (March 1959):351–356; George Saintsbury, review of *The American* in the *Academy*, July 1877, in *Henry James: The Critical Heritage*, ed. Roger Gard (London: Routledge and Kegan Paul, 1968), p. 46.

28. *Partial Portraits*, p. 166.

29. "The Language of Adventure in Henry James," *American Literature* 32 (November 1960):291–301.

30. Stevenson, "A Gossip on Romance," *The Travels and Essays of Robert Louis Stevenson* (New York: Scribners, 1924), 13:333.

31. *Washington Square* (New York: Harper, 1881), p. 62. All subsequent references are to this edition and will be given parenthetically in the text.

32. *The Comic Sense of Henry James*, p. 166.

33. Ibid., p. 167.

34. Leon Edel, *Henry James: The Conquest of London, 1870–1881* (Philadelphia: Lippincott, 1962), p. 394.

35. Ibid., p. 421.

36. *The Castle of Otranto*, p. 88.

37. "Tradition and the Individual Talent," *Selected Essays*, new ed. (New York: Harcourt, Brace, 1950), p. 4.

CHAPTER FIVE

1. *Biographia Literaria*, ed. John Calvin Metcalf (New York: Macmillan, 1926), p. 191.

2. "A Note on 'Romance,'" *The Nature of a Crime* (New York: Doubleday, Page, 1924), pp. 96–97.

3. *Conrad's Measure of Man* (Madison: University of Wisconsin Press, 1954), p. 174.

4. Thomas Moser, in "The Rescuer Ms: A Key to Conrad's Development—and Decline," *Harvard Library Bulletin* 10 (autumn 1956):325–355, gives the history of the composition of the novel, analyzes the differences between "The Rescuer" ms and the completed novel, and analyzes the relation of "The Rescuer" to Conrad's other works, especially *Lord Jim*.

5. Bruce Johnson, *Conrad's Models of Mind* (Minneapolis: University of Minnesota Press, 1971), pp. 178–179; Moser, *Joseph Conrad: Achievement and Decline*, p. 150.

6. September 6, 1897, *Letters to William Blackwood and David S. Meldrum*, p. 10.

7. Jean-Aubry, 2:212. *The Rescue* was serialized in America not in *Cosmopolitan* but in *Romance*, November 1919–May 1920; in England, in *Land and Water*, January–July 1919.

8. Letter to J. B. Pinker, February 15, 1919 (Berg Collection). Conrad made his most favorable statements about *The Rescue* in his letters to Pinker. To Thomas Wise, who bought the manuscript, Conrad made a modest claim for the novel. "I myself, without being elated, think fairly well of the story. The romantic feeling is certainly there; but whether I can manage to keep the interest of the tale going—that's another question" (February 16, 1919, Ashley 492, British Museum). Hugh Walpole quoted Conrad as saying of the novel, "Of course, *mon cher*, it is not very good. I did my best work long ago" (quoted in Rupert Hart-Davis, *Hugh Walpole: A Biography*, London: Macmillan, 1952, p. 195).

9. John D. Gordan shows that Rajah James Brooke, to whom Conrad pays tribute at the beginning of *The Rescue*, was a model for Lingard as well as for Jim ("The Rajah Brooke and Joseph Conrad," *Studies in Philology* 35, October 1938:618–625).

10. The likenesses between the two characters are noted by Johnson, pp. 179, 190–194, and Wiley, p. 134.

11. September 6, 1897, *Letters to William Blackwood and David S. Meldrum*, p. 10.

12. See also the scene in chap. 24 of *Roderick Hudson* in which Sam Singleton appears in the distance greatly magnified by the setting sun.

13. Wiley, p. 187.

14. Johnson, pp. 195–196.

15. Royal Roussel makes this point about Jim in *The Metaphysics of Darkness* (Baltimore: Johns Hopkins University Press, 1971), p. 81.

16. *Ninety Three* (Boston: Little, Brown, 1899), p. 459.

17. "Victor Hugo's Romances," *The Travels and Essays of Robert Louis Stevenson*, 14:52.

18. *Ninety-Three*, p. 522.

19. Letter to Mrs. E. L. Sanderson, June 27, 1897 (Yale).

20. "*Lord Jim:* The Romance of Irony," *Critical Quarterly* 8 (autumn 1966):240.

21. "Marlow and *Chance:* A Reappraisal," *Texas Studies in Literature and Language* 10 (spring 1958):91–105. See also John A. Palmer, *Joseph Conrad's Fiction: A Study in Literary Growth* (Ithaca, N.Y.: Cornell University Press, 1968), pp. 211–217; Wiley, pp. 144–145.

22. Albert Guerard, in *Conrad the Novelist*, p. 264, and Douglas Hewitt, in *Joseph Conrad: A Reassessment*, pp. 89–102, quote passages in which Marlow idealizes Anthony. Hewitt notes Conrad's use of romantic clichés in the climactic scene where Anthony at last realizes Flora's love for him.

23. Manuscript of *Chance*, p. 488 (Berg Collection).

24. Ibid., pp. 489–490.

25. Letter to J. B. Pinker, April 1912 (Berg Collection). The original manuscript ends with the words, spoken by Powell: "Pah! Foolishness. You ought to know better, he said" (p. 1089). Conrad added the last six pages, about 1400 words, in April 1912.

26. Letter to J. B. Pinker, October 11, 1913 (Berg Collection).

27. Letter to J. B. Pinker, June 12, 1913 (Berg Collection).

28. Letter to J. B. Pinker, June 1, 1913 (Berg Collection).

29. For discussion of this theme in James's fiction, see Leon Edel, Introduction, *The Sacred Fount* (New York: Grove Press, 1953), pp. xxv–xxix.

30. The fullest discussions of Conrad's treatment of romantic love are Bernard Meyer, *Joseph Conrad: A Psychoanalytic Study* (Princeton: Princeton University Press, 1967), esp. pp. 221–247; Thomas Moser, *Joseph Conrad: Achievement and Decline*, esp. chap. 2.

31. *The Romantic Novel in England* (Cambridge, Mass.: Harvard University Press, 1972), p. 250.

32. This discussion of the romance plot is based on Northrop Frye's "Theory of Myths" in *Anatomy of Criticism*.

33. See "Henry James's Metaphysical Romances," *Nineteenth-Century Fiction* 9 (June 1954):1–21.

34. Frye, *Anatomy of Criticism*, p. 190.

35. The parallel is fully developed by Lillian Feder, "Marlow's De-

scent into Hell," *Nineteenth-Century Fiction* 9 (March 1955) :280–292.

36. See especially Dorothy Van Ghent, Introduction, *Nostromo* (New York: Rinehart, 1961). Claire Rosenfield devotes a chapter to *Nostromo* in her book *The Paradise of Snakes: An Archetypal Analysis of Conrad's Political Novels* (Chicago: University of Chicago Press, 1971), the fullest study of myth and legend in Conrad's fiction.

37. "Is There a Life After Death?" *The James Family*, p. 610.

38. *Victory: The Rhetoric of Shifting Perspectives*, Pennsylvania State Studies, no. 32 (University Park, Pa., 1971). Secor discusses the ways in which *Victory* inverts the situations and relationships in *The Tempest* and *Comus* (pp. 63–68).

CHAPTER SIX

1. *Notes by Mr. Henry James on a Collection of Drawings by Mr. George du Maurier*, exhibited at the Fine Arts Society, 148 New Bond Street, 1884, p. 12.

2. *The Complete Tales of Henry James*, 9:413.

3. Ibid., 12:431.

4. *Washington Square*, pp. 12–13.

5. Poirier, *The Comic Sense of Henry James*, pp. 21ff.

6. *Henry James and the Modern Reader* (Edinburgh: Oliver and Boyd, 1964), p. 77.

7. "Crapy Cornelia," *The Complete Tales of Henry James*, 12:348. Rich vulgar women are the chief targets of James's attack in the late fiction. Mrs. Worthingham ("Crapy Cornelia") is "ignorant as a fish" and exhibits a "bright pampered confidence which would probably end by affecting one's nerves as the most impertinent stroke in the world" (12:347). Mrs. Drack ("Julia Bride") has a face like a "featureless desert in a remote quarter of which the disproportionately small eyes might have figured a pair of rash adventurers all but buried in the sand" (12:171). Gussy Bradham (*The Ivory Tower*) "was naturally never so the vulgar rich woman able to afford herself all luxuries as when she was most stupid about the right enjoyment of these and most brutally systematic . . . for some inferior and desecrating use of them" (25:45).

8. J. A. Ward, *The Imagination of Disaster: Evil in the Fiction of Henry James* (Lincoln: University of Nebraska Press, 1961), p. 27.

9. *The Bostonians* (London: Macmillan, 1886) p. 100. Subsequent page references, shown parenthetically, are to this text.

10. *The Ambiguity of Henry James* (Urbana: University of Illinois Press, 1971), p. 105.

11. *Modern Satire* (New York: Harcourt, Brace and World, 1962), p. 167. Stanton de Voren Hoffmann analyzes scenes of low comedy as symbolic of disorder in *Heart of Darkness* (*Comedy and Form in the Fiction of Joseph Conrad*, pp. 19–27, 42–45).

12. Ms *Razumov*, pp. 583, 585, 451–452 (Yale).

13. Ibid., p. 450.

14. Ibid., p. 483.

15. Ibid., pp. 444, 888.

16. Avrom Fleishman, in *Conrad's Politics: Community and Anarchy in the Fiction of Joseph Conrad* (Baltimore: Johns Hopkins University Press, 1967), p. 170, discusses Holroyd as a satire on Theodore Roosevelt and his rationalization of imperialism.

17. See Juliet McLauchlan, *Conrad: Nostromo* (London: Arnold, 1969), pp. 19–20.

18. Letter of May 10, 1885, *Selected Letters of Henry James*, p. 206.

19. Letter to Conrad, November 22, 1912, *Letters of Arnold Bennett*, ed. James Hepburn, 3 vols. (London: Oxford University Press), 2:321.

20. *A Conrad Memorial Library*, p. 176. Poirier calls attention to James's opinion that Turgenev's fiction was marred by "excessive irony" (*The Comic Sense of Henry James*, pp. 202–203).

21. *The Complete Tales of Henry James*, 12:433.

22. *Partial Portraits*, pp. 273–274. Of *Bel-Ami*, which Conrad called "that amazing masterpiece," James observed: "The world represented is too special, too little inevitable . . . a world in which every man is a cad and every woman a harlot. . . . His [the main character's] colleagues and his mistresses are as depraved as himself, greatly to the injury of the ironic idea, for the real force of satire would have come from seeing him engaged and victorious with natures better than his own" (p. 277).

23. Ibid., p. 266.

CHAPTER SEVEN

1. *English Literature in the Sixteenth Century* (Oxford: Clarendon Press, 1954), p. 415.

2. *The Painter's Eye: Notes and Essays on the Pictorial Arts*, ed. John L. Sweeney (Cambridge, Mass.: Harvard University Press, 1956), pp. 60–61, 93, 230–231, 323.

3. *The Bostonians*, p. 46.

4. Ibid., p. 59.

5. *The Stones of Venice*, 3 vols. (Boston: Estes and Lauriat, 1897), 3:126).

6. Wolfgang Kayser, *The Grotesque in Art and Literature*, trans. Ulrich Weisstein (Bloomington: Indiana University Press, 1963), p. 184.

7. *The Complete Tales of Henry James*, 3:290.

8. *The Bostonians*, p. 63.

9. *The Letters of Henry James*, 1:116.

10. *The Notebooks of Henry James*, p. 262.

11. *The Comic Sense of Henry James*, pp. 215–216.

12. Ibid., p. 216.

13. See for instance Bruce Johnson, *Conrad's Models of Mind*, pp. 169–173; Frederick Karl, *A Reader's Guide to Joseph Conrad*, pp. 258–260; John A. Palmer, *Joseph Conrad's Fiction*, pp. 178–179.

14. Kayser, pp. 184–185.

15. *The Reign of Wonder* (Cambridge: Cambridge University Press, 1965), pp. 282–286.

16. *Henry James and the Modern Reader*, pp. 218–219. Ruth Yeazell, in " 'The New Arithmetic' of Henry James," *Criticism* 16 (spring 1974):109–119, analyzes the dialogues of the Assinghams as grotesque exaggerations of the elaborations and indirections of James's late style and shows how the Assinghams "simultaneously provide relief from the tremendous tensions of the rest of the novel and grotesquely mirror those same tensions"; (p. 109).

17. *La Préface de Cromwell*, pp. 191, 195.

18. Kayser, p. 197.

19. In the dramatized version of *The Secret Agent* the assistant commissioner describes the existence of a secret agent as "the nearest thing to living under a curse" (21:81).

20. For a full discussion of the theme see David L. Kubal, "*The Secret Agent* and the Mechanical Chaos," *Bucknell Review* 15 (December 1967):65–77.

21. *The Imagination of Disaster*, p. 72.

22. Letter to Edmund Gosse, October 12, 1898 (Duke University).

23. December 9, 1898, *Henry James and H. G. Wells*, p. 56.

24. Letter to Ford Madox Ford, n.d. (Yale).

25. See, respectively, Joseph J. Firebaugh, "The Ververs," *Essays in Criticism* 4 (October 1954):401, 407; Quentin Anderson, *The American Henry James*, p. 318; Francis Fergusson, "*The Golden Bowl* Revisited,"

Sewanee Review 63 (winter 1955):13–28; H. K. Girling, "The Function of Slang in the Dramatic Poetry of *The Golden Bowl*," *Nineteenth-Century Fiction* 11 (September 1956):133; Caroline G. Mercer, "Adam Verver, Yankee Businessman," *Nineteenth-Century Fiction* 22 (December 1967):255.

CHAPTER EIGHT

1. Letter to Hugh Clifford, January 25, 1919, in Jean-Aubry, 2:217.

2. *Literary Reviews and Essays*, ed. Albert Mordell (New York: Twayne, 1957), p. 208. See also James's letter to Howells, March 30, 1877: "I suspect it is the tragedies in life that arrest my attention more than the other things and say more to my imagination; but, on the other hand, if I fix my eyes on a sun-spot I think I am able to see the prismatic colors in it" (*Selected Letters*, pp. 69–70).

3. Ellen Douglass Leyburn makes this observation about James and illustrates it in *The Strange Alloy: The Relation of Comedy to Tragedy in the Fiction of Henry James* (Chapel Hill: University of North Carolina Press, 1968), p. xiv.

4. *Letters to R. B. Cunninghame Graham*, pp. 70–71.

5. *Ford Madox Ford: The Critical Heritage*, ed. Frank MacShane (London: Routledge and Kegan Paul, 1972), p. 22.

6. Letter to Galsworthy [1908], in Jean-Aubry, 2:78.

7. Each of the mythological figures with whom Roderick's statue is compared—Hylas, Narcissus, Paris, and Endymion (1:17)—is a beautiful youth who dies having inspired, or succumbed to, a fatal passion.

8. The point is developed by Oscar Cargill in *The Novels of Henry James* (New York: Macmillan, 1961), pp. 30–32.

9. Philip Weinstein, in *Henry James and the Requirements of the Imagination* (Cambridge, Mass.: Harvard University Press, 1971), pp. 25–26, discusses Rowland's role as a scapegoat.

10. Leyburn, p. xvi.

11. Henry James, *Autobiography*, p. 560.

12. For a full discussion of the principle of equivalence, see Henry Alonzo Myers, *Tragedy: A View of Life* (Ithaca, N.Y.: Cornell University Press, 1956).

13. See for instance, Frederick Karl, *A Reader's Guide to Joseph Conrad*, p. 102; Walter Wright, *Romance and Tragedy in Joseph Conrad* (Lincoln: University of Nebraska Press, 1949), p. 131.

14. *Romance and Tragedy in Joseph Conrad*, p. 154.

15. Clifford Leech, *Tragedy* (London: Methuen, 1969), p. 69.

16. See for instance Murray Krieger's discussion of Kurtz as a "tragic visionary" and "God's angry man" who sees man alone in a world without sanctions or moral order and who "seizing upon nothingness, is alone bold enough to take the existential consequences of his godlessness" (*The Tragic Vision: Variations on a Theme in Literary Interpretation*, New York: Holt, Rinehart, and Winston, 1960, p. 16).

17. *Anatomy of Criticism*, p. 40.

18. For excellent analyses of the structure of *The Princess Casamassima*, see John L. Kimmey, "*The Princess Casamassima* and the Quality of Bewilderment," *Nineteenth-Century Fiction* 22 (June 1967):47–63; John O'Neill, *Workable Design: Action and Situation in the Fiction of Henry James* (Port Washington, N.Y.: Kennikat Press, 1973), pp. 49–69; and J. A. Ward, *The Search for Form* (Chapel Hill: University of North Carolina Press, 1967), pp. 117–122, 136–140.

19. Manuscript, *Razumov*, p. 1321 (Yale). The addition alters the meaning of the statement "perdition is my lot," as it appeared in the manuscript: ". . . The real truth is that in giving your brother up it was myself that I have betrayed most basely. It was seeing you that—I understand this. Most basely. And therefore perdition is my lot."

20. *Literary Reviews and Essays*, p. 191.

21. Ibid., p. 192. Conrad shared James's view of Neshdanoff. In a letter to Galsworthy, 1908, he refers to the "two incapables that come to one's mind, the loquacious and the nervous, Rudin and Nejdanov," in Jean-Aubry, 2:80.

22. *Anatomy of Criticism*, p. 212.

23. Letter to Mary Ward, October 24, 1912 (University of Virginia).

24. *Modern Tragedy* (London: Chatto and Windus, 1966), pp. 32–42.

25. *The Philosophy of Fine Art by G. W. F. Hegel*, trans. F.P.B. Osmaston, 4 vols. (London: G. Bell, 1920), 4:321.

26. *The World as Will and Idea*, trans. J. Kemp, 8th ed. (London: Kegan Paul, Trench, Trübner, n.d.), 1:326.

27. Ibid., p. 327.

28. Hegel, 4:318.

29. See, for instance, Joseph Firebaugh, "A Schopenhauerian Novel: James's *The Princess Casamassima*," *Nineteenth-Century Fiction* 13 (December 1958):177–197; Bruce Johnson, *Conrad's Models of Mind*, pp. 41–53; 208–209.

30. Hegel, 4:295–296.

31. *Workable Design*, pp. 106, 118–120.

32. James often defined the artistic process in terms of equivalence. Of the subject of *The Wings of the Dove* he observed: "It might have a great deal to give, but would probably ask for equal services in return, and would collect this debt to the last shilling" (19:v). In an entry in his notebook on February 14, 1895, after reference to "the subject of the dying girl who wants to live" James reflected on the gain to be derived from the bitter years spent in the vain effort to succeed as a dramatist: "My infinite little loss is converted into an almost infinite little gain" (*The Notebooks of Henry James*, p. 188).

33. Ibid., p. 173. The case against Densher is convincingly argued by Sallie Sears, in *The Negative Imagination: Form and Perspective in the Novels of Henry James* (Ithaca, N.Y.: Cornell University Press, 1968), pp. 93ff.

34. See John Goode, "The Pervasive Mystery of Style: *The Wings of the Dove*," *The Air of Reality: New Essays on Henry James* (London: Methuen, 1972), pp. 257–266; Laurence Bedwell Holland, *The Expense of Vision: Essays on the Craft of Henry James* (Princeton: Princeton University Press, 1964), pp. 323–324.

35. For discussion of the literary sources and allusions in the novel see Oscar Cargill, *The Novels of Henry James*, pp. 338–382.

36. *The Notebooks of Henry James*, pp. 169–170.

37. *Workable Design*, p. 107.

38. In his notebook, November 7, 1894, James stressed the dramatic nature of the situation: "I seem to get almost a little 3 act play. . . . I get, at any rate, a distinct and rather dramatic *action*" (*The Notebooks of Henry James*, p. 173).

39. Letter to Ernst Bendz, March 7, 1923, in Jean-Aubry, 2:296.

40. Robert Gale notes that in *The Ivory Tower* James rarely uses money as a metaphor for spiritual value (*The Caught Image: Figurative Language in the Fiction of Henry James*, pp. 202–205).

41. In his letter of July 17, 1923, to Richard Curle, who had sent Conrad the manuscript of an essay to be published in the *Times Literary Supplement*, Conrad suggested that the article begin with "a couple of short paragraphs of general observation on authors and their material, how they transform it from particular to general, and appeal to universal emotions by the temperamental handling of personal experience" (*Conrad to a Friend: 150 Selected Letters from Joseph Conrad to Richard*

Curle, Garden City, N.Y.: Doubleday, Doran, 1928, p. 155). The first paragraph of Curle's essay incorporates with little change the statement in Conrad's letter.

42. Letter to A. C. Benson, June 29, 1896, *Henry James: Letters to A. C. Benson and Auguste Monod*, ed. E. F. Benson (London: Elkin Mathews and Marrot; New York: Scribners, 1930), p. 35.

43. Letter to Grace Norton, July 28, 1883, *The Letters of Henry James*, 1:101.

44. Ibid., p. 100.

45. Letter to R. B. Cunninghame Graham, December 20, 1897, in Jean-Aubry, 1:216.

CONCLUSION

1. See James Walton, "Conrad and Naturalism: *The Secret Agent*," *Texas Studies in Literature and Language* 9 (1967):289–301.

2. *Notes on Novelists*, p. 157.

3. Giorgio Melchiori, "Cups of Gold for the Sacred Fount: Aspects of James's Symbolism," *Critical Quarterly* 7 (winter 1965):305.

Bibliography

I · WORKS BY HENRY JAMES

Autobiography: A Small Boy and Others; Notes of a Son and Brother; The Middle Years. Edited by F. W. Dupee. New York: Criterion Books, 1956.

The Bostonians. London and New York: Macmillan, 1886.

The Complete Tales of Henry James. 12 vols. Edited by Leon Edel. Philadelphia: Lippincott, 1961–1964.

Essays in London and Elsewhere. New York: Harper, 1893.

French Poets and Novelists. London: Macmillan, 1884.

Hawthorne. London: Macmillan, 1879.

Henry James and Robert Louis Stevenson: A Record of Friendship and Criticism. Edited by Janet Adam Smith. London: Rupert Hart-Davis, 1948.

Henry James Letters. Vols. 1, 2. Edited by Leon Edel. Cambridge: Harvard University Press, 1974–1975.

The Letters of Henry James. Edited by Percy Lubbock. 2 vols. New York: Scribners, 1920.

Letters to A. C. Benson and Auguste Monod. Edited by E. F. Benson. London: Elkin Mathews and Marrot; New York: Scribners, 1930.

Letters of Henry James to Walter Berry. Paris: The Black Sun Press, 1928.

Literary Reviews and Essays. Edited by Albert Mordell. New York: Twayne, 1957.

The Notebooks of Henry James. Edited by F. O. Matthiessen and Kenneth B. Murdock. New York: Oxford University Press, 1947.

Notes (no. 15 of Series) by Mr. Henry James on a Collection of Drawings by Mr. George du Maurier, exhibited at the Fine Art Society, 148 New Bond Street, 1884.

Notes and Reviews. With a preface by Pierre de Chaignon la Rose. Cambridge, Mass.: Dunster House, 1921.

Notes on Novelists. New York: Scribners, 1914.

The Novels and Tales of Henry James. 26 vols. New York: Scribners, 1907–1917. Reprint, 1962–1965.

The Painter's Eye: Notes and Essays on the Pictorial Arts. Edited with an introduction by John L. Sweeney, Cambridge, Mass.: Harvard University Press, 1956.

Partial Portraits. London: Macmillan, 1888.

The Question of Our Speech and The Lesson of Balzac: Two Lectures. Boston: Houghton Mifflin, 1905.

The Sacred Fount. New York: Scribners, 1901.

Selected Letters. Edited by Leon Edel. New York: Farrar, Straus and Cudahy, 1955.

Theory of Fiction: Henry James. Edited by James E. Miller, Jr. Lincoln: University of Nebraska Press, 1972.

Three Letters from Henry James to Joseph Conrad. Edited by G. Jean-Aubry. London: First Edition Club, 1926. One of eight pamphlets in *Twenty Letters to Joseph Conrad*.

Views and Reviews. Introduction by Le Roy Phillips. Boston: Ball, 1908.

Washington Square. New York: Harper, 1881.

Within the Rim and Other Essays, 1914–15. London: W. Collins, 1919.

II · WORKS BY JOSEPH CONRAD

Conrad to a Friend: 150 Selected Letters from Joseph Conrad to Richard Curle. Garden City, N.Y.: Doubleday, Doran, 1928.

Conrad's Manifesto: Preface to a Career: The History of the Preface to the Nigger of the 'Narcissus,' with facsimiles of manuscripts. Edited by David R. Smith. Philadelphia: The Philip H. and A.S.W. Rosenbach Foundation, 1966.

Foreword to A. S. Kinkead, *Landscapes of Corsica and Ireland*. London: The United Arts Gallery. November–December 1921.

Joseph Conrad: Letters to William Blackwood and David S. Meldrum. Edited by William Blackburn. Durham, N.C.: Duke University Press, 1958.

Joseph Conrad's Letters to R. B. Cunninghame Graham. Edited by C. T. Watts. London: Cambridge University Press, 1969.

Letters from Joseph Conrad, 1895–1924. Edited by Edward Garnett. Indianapolis: Bobbs-Merrill, 1928.

Letters of Joseph Conrad to Marguerite Poradowska, 1890–1920. Translated and edited by John A. Gee and Paul J. Sturm. New Haven: Yale University Press, 1940.

Lettres Françaises. With an introduction and notes by G. Jean-Aubry. Paris: Paris Librairie Gallimard, 1929.

The Sisters. With an introduction by Ford Madox Ford. New York: Crosby Gaige, 1928.

The Works of Joseph Conrad. Sun-Dial Edition. 22 vols. Garden City, New York: Doubleday, Page, 1920–1928.

III · WORKS ABOUT HENRY JAMES

Anderson, Quentin. *The American Henry James*. New Brunswick, New Jersey: Rutgers University Press, 1957.

Banta, Martha. *Henry James and the Occult*. Bloomington: Indiana University Press, 1972.

Beach, Joseph Warren. *The Method of Henry James*. New Haven: Yale University Press, 1918.

Bell, Millicent. *Edith Wharton and Henry James: The Story of Their Friendship*. New York: G. Braziller, 1965.

Bewley, Marius. *The Complex Fate: Hawthorne, Henry James, and Some Other American Writers*. With an introduction and 2 interpolations by F. R. Leavis. London: Chatto and Windus, 1952.

Bowden, Edwin T. *The Themes of Henry James: A System of Observation Through the Visual Arts*. New Haven: Yale University Press, 1956.

Buitenhuis, Peter. *The Grasping Imagination: The American Writings of Henry James*. Toronto: University of Toronto Press, 1970.

Cargill, Oscar. *The Novels of Henry James*. New York: Macmillan, 1961.

Chase, Richard. *The American Novel and Its Tradition*. Garden City, New York: Anchor-Doubleday, 1957.

Chatman, Seymour. *The Later Style of Henry James*. Oxford: Basil Blackwell, 1972.

Crews, Frederick C. *The Tragedy of Manners: Moral Drama in the Later Novels of Henry James*. New Haven: Yale University Press, 1957.

Dupee, F. W. *Henry James*. New York: William Sloane Associates, 1951.

Dupee, F. W., ed. *The Question of Henry James: A Collection of Critical Essays*. New York: Henry Holt, 1945.

Edel, Leon. *Henry James: The Conquest of London, 1870–1881*. Philadelphia and New York: Lippincott, 1962.

———. "Henry James: The Dramatic Years," *The Complete Plays of Henry James*. Philadelphia and New York: Lippincott, 1949.

———. *Henry James: The Master, 1901–1916*. Philadelphia and New York: Lippincott, 1972.

———. *Henry James: The Middle Years, 1882–1895*. Philadelphia and New York: Lippincott, 1962.

———. *Henry James: The Treacherous Years, 1895–1901*. Philadelphia and New York: Lippincott, 1969.

———. *Henry James, The Untried Years, 1843–1870*. Philadelphia and New York: Lippincott, 1953.

———, ed. *Henry James: A Collection of Critical Essays*. Englewood Cliffs, New Jersey: Prentice-Hall, 1963.

——— and Ray, Gordon N., eds. *Henry James and H. G. Wells: A Record of Their Friendship, Their Debate on the Art of Fiction, and Their Quarrel*. Urbana: University of Illinois Press, 1958.

Egan, Michael. *Henry James: The Ibsen Years*. London: Vision Press, 1972.

Gale, Robert L. *The Caught Image: Figurative Language in the Fiction of Henry James*. Chapel Hill: University of North Carolina Press, 1964.

Gard, Roger, ed. *Henry James: The Critical Heritage*. London: Routledge & Kegan Paul, 1968.

Goode, John, ed. *The Air of Reality: New Essays on Henry James*. London: Methuen, 1972.

Grover, Philip. *Henry James and the French Novel*. New York: Barnes & Noble, 1973.

Holder-Barrell, Alexander. *The Development of Imagery and Its Functional Significance in Henry James's Novels*. The Cooper Monographs, No. 3. Bern: Francke Verlag, 1959.

Holland, Laurence Bedwell. *The Expense of Vision: Essays on the Craft of Henry James*. Princeton, New Jersey: Princeton University Press, 1964.

Isle, Walter. *Experiments in Form: Henry James's Novels, 1896–1901*. Cambridge, Massachusetts: Harvard University Press, 1968.

Jefferson, D. W. *Henry James and the Modern Reader*. Edinburgh: Oliver and Boyd, 1964.

Krook, Dorothea. *The Ordeal of Consciousness in Henry James*. Cambridge: University Press, 1962.

Lebowitz, Naomi. *The Imagination of Loving: Henry James's Legacy to the Novel*. Detroit: Wayne State University Press, 1965.

Leyburn, Ellen Douglass. *The Strange Alloy: The Relation of Comedy to Tragedy in the Fiction of Henry James*. Chapel Hill: University of North Carolina Press, 1968.

McElderry, Bruce R., Jr. *Henry James*. New York: Twayne, 1965.

Matthiessen, F. O. *Henry James: The Major Phase*. London and New York: Oxford University Press, 1944.

———. *The James Family*. New York: Knopf, 1947.

Maves, Carl. *Sensuous Pessimism: Italy in the Work of Henry James*. Bloomington: Indiana University Press, 1973.

Nowell-Smith, Simon. *The Legend of the Master*. New York: Scribners, 1948.

O'Neill, John. *Workable Design: Action and Situation in the Fiction of Henry James*. Port Washington, New York: Kennikat Press, 1973.

Poirier, Richard. *The Comic Sense of Henry James: A Study of the Early Novels*. New York: Oxford University Press, 1960.

Powers, Lyall H. *Henry James and the Naturalist Movement*. Lansing: Michigan State University Press, 1971.

Putt, S. Gorley. *Henry James: A Reader's Guide*. Ithaca, New York: Cornell University Press, 1966.

Richardson, Lyon N., ed. *Henry James: Representative Selections*. New York: American Book Company, 1941.

Samuels, Charles T. *The Ambiguity of Henry James*. Urbana: University of Illinois Press, 1971.

Sears, Sallie. *The Negative Imagination: Form and Perspective in the Novels of Henry James*. Ithaca, New York: Cornell University Press, 1968.

Stone, Donald David. *Novelists in a Changing World: Meredith, James, and the Transformation of English Fiction in the 1880's*. Cambridge, Massachusetts: Harvard University Press, 1972.

Tilley, Wesley H. *The Background of the Princess Casamassima*. University of Florida Monographs, No. 5. Fall, 1960. Gainesville, Florida.

Trilling, Lionel. Introduction to *The Princess Casamassima*. 2 vols. New York: Macmillan, 1948.

Ward, Joseph A. *The Imagination of Disaster. Evil in the Fiction of Henry James*. Lincoln: University of Nebraska Press, 1961.

———. *The Search for Form: Studies in the Structure of James's Fiction*. Chapel Hill: University of North Carolina Press, 1967.

Wegelin, Christof. *The Image of Europe in Henry James*. Dallas: Southern Methodist University Press, 1958.

Weinstein, Philip. *Henry James and the Requirements of the Imagination*. Cambridge, Massachusetts: Harvard University Press, 1971.

Weisenfarth, Joseph. *Henry James and the Dramatic Analogy*. New York: Fordham University Press, 1963.

Winner, Viola Hopkins. *Henry James and the Visual Arts*. Charlottesville: University Press of Virginia, 1970.

Zabel, Morton D., ed. *The Portable Henry James*. Revised by Lyall H. Powers. New York: Viking, 1968.

IV · WORKS ABOUT JOSEPH CONRAD

Baines, Jocelyn. *Joseph Conrad: A Critical Biography*. New York: McGraw-Hill, 1960.

Busza, Andrzej. *Conrad's Polish Literary Background and Some Illustrations of the Influence of Polish Literature on His Work*. Rome: Polish Historical Institute, 1964.

Conrad, Jessie. *Joseph Conrad and His Circle*. New York: Dutton, 1935.
———. *Joseph Conrad: As I Knew Him*. Garden City, New York: Doubleday, 1926.

Crankshaw, Edward. *Joseph Conrad. Some Aspects of the Art of the Novel*. London: John Lane, 1936.

Curle, Richard. *Joseph Conrad: A Study*. London: Kegan Paul, Trench, and Trübner, 1914.

Fleishman, Avrom. *Conrad's Politics: Community and Anarchy in the Fiction of Joseph Conrad*. Baltimore: The Johns Hopkins Press, 1967.

Gillon, Adam. *The Eternal Solitary: A Study of Joseph Conrad*. New York: Bookman, 1960.

Gordan, John Dozier. *Joseph Conrad: The Making of a Novelist*. Cambridge, Massachusetts: Harvard University Press, 1940.

Graver, Lawrence. *Conrad's Short Fiction*. Berkeley and Los Angeles: University of California Press, 1969.

Guerard, Albert. *Conrad the Novelist*. Cambridge, Massachusetts: Harvard University Press, 1958.

Guetti, James. *The Limits of Metaphor: A Study of Melville, Conrad, and Faulkner*. Ithaca, New York: Cornell University Press, 1967.

Gurko, Leo. *Joseph Conrad: Giant in Exile*. London: F. Muller, 1962.

Hay, Eloise Knapp. *The Political Novels of Joseph Conrad: A Critical Study*. Chicago: University of Chicago Press, 1963.

Hewitt, Douglas. *Conrad: A Reassessment*. 2nd edition. London: Bowes and Bowes, 1969.

Hoffman, Stanton de Voren. *Comedy and Form in the Fiction of Joseph Conrad*. The Hague: Mouton, 1969.

Jean-Aubry, G. *Joseph Conrad: Life and Letters*. 2 vols. Garden City, New York: Doubleday, Page, 1927.

Johnson, Bruce. *Conrad's Models of Mind*. Minneapolis: University of Minnesota Press, 1971.

Karl, Frederick. "Conrad, Wells, and the Two Voices." *PMLA*, 88 (October, 1973), 1049–1065.

———. "Joseph Conrad's Literary Theory." *Criticism*, 2 (Fall, 1960), 317–335.

———. *A Reader's Guide to Joseph Conrad*. New York: Farrar, Straus and Giroux, 1969.

———. "Three Conrad Letters in the Edith Wharton Papers." *Yale University Library Gazette*, 44 (January, 1970), 148–151.

Keating, John. *A Conrad Memorial Library*. Garden City, New York: Doubleday, Doran, 1929.

Kirschner, Paul. *Conrad: The Psychologist as Artist*. Edinburgh: Oliver and Boyd, 1968.

McLauchlan, Juliet. *Conrad: Nostromo*. London: Arnold, 1969.

Mégroz, R. L. *Joseph Conrad's Mind and Method*. London: Faber and Faber, 1931.

Meyer, Bernard. *Joseph Conrad: A Psychoanalytic Study*. Princeton, New Jersey: Princeton University Press, 1967.

Miller, J. Hillis. *Poets of Reality*. Cambridge, Massachusetts: Harvard University Press, 1965.

Moser, Thomas. *Joseph Conrad: Achievement and Decline*. Cambridge, Massachusetts: Harvard University Press, 1957.

Mudrick, Marvin, ed. *Conrad: A Collection of Critical Essays*. Englewood Cliffs, New Jersey: Prentice-Hall, 1966.

Najder, Zdzislaw, ed. *Conrad's Polish Background: Letters to and from Polish Friends*. Translated by Halina Carroll. London: Oxford University Press, 1964.

Palmer, John A. *Joseph Conrad's Fiction: A Study in Literary Growth*. Ithaca, New York: Cornell University Press, 1968.

Randall, Dale B. J. *Joseph Conrad and Warrington Dawson: The Record of a Friendship*. Durham, North Carolina: Duke University Press, 1968.

Rosenfield, Claire. *The Paradise of Snakes: An Archetypal Analysis of Conrad's Political Novels*. Chicago: University of Chicago Press, 1967.

Roussel, Royal. *The Metaphysics of Darkness: A Study in the Unity and Development of Conrad's Fiction*. Baltimore: The Johns Hopkins Press, 1971.

Ryf, Robert. *Joseph Conrad*. New York: Columbia University Press, 1970.

Said, Edward. *Joseph Conrad and the Fiction of Autobiography*. Cambridge, Massachusetts: Harvard University Press, 1966.

Secor, Robert. *Victory: The Rhetoric of Shifting Perspectives*. The Pennsylvania State Studies, No. 32. University Park, Pennsylvania, 1971.

Seltzer, Leon F. *The Vision of Melville and Conrad: A Comparative Study*. Athens: Ohio University Press, 1970.

Sherry, Norman. *Conrad and His World*. London: Thames and Hudson, 1972.

————. *Conrad's Eastern World*. Cambridge: University Press, 1966.

————. Conrad's Western World. Cambridge: University Press, 1971.

————, ed. *Conrad. The Critical Heritage*. London and Boston: Routledge and Kegan Paul, 1973.

Stewart, J.I.M. *Joseph Conrad*. New York: Dodd, Mead, 1968.

Symons, Arthur. *Notes on Joseph Conrad with Some Unpublished Letters*. London: Meyers, 1925.

Tanner, Tony. *Conrad: Lord Jim*. London: Arnold, 1963.

Thorburn, David. *Conrad's Romanticism*. New Haven: Yale University Press, 1974.

Wiley, Paul L. *Conrad's Measure of Man*. Madison: University of Wisconsin Press, 1954.

Wright, Walter. *Romance and Tragedy in Joseph Conrad*. Lincoln: University of Nebraska Press, 1949.

Yelton, Donald. *Mimesis and Metaphor: An Inquiry into the Genesis and Scope of Conrad's Symbolic Imagery*. The Hague: Mouton, 1967.

Zabel, Morton D. Introduction to *Under Western Eyes*. Garden City, New York: Anchor-Doubleday, 1963.

————. *The Portable Conrad*. Revised by Frederick Karl. New York: Viking, 1969.

V · COMPARATIVE STUDIES OF
JAMES AND CONRAD

Brown, E. K. "James and Conrad." *Yale Review*, 35 (Winter 1946), 265–285.

Kocmanová, Jessie. "The Revolt of the Workers in the Novels of Gissing, James, and Conrad." *Brno Studies in English*, 1 (1959), 119–139.

O'Grady, Walter. "On Plot in Modern Fiction: Hardy, James, and Conrad." *Modern Fiction Studies*, 11 (Summer 1965), 107–115.

Ramsay, Roger. "The Available and the Unavailable 'I': Conrad and James." *English Literature in Transition*, 14 (1971), 137–145.

Vidan, Ivo. "*The Princess Casamassima* between Balzac and Conrad." *Studia Romanica et Anglia Zagrabiensia*, Nos. 21–22 (July–December 1966), 259–276.

Watt, Ian. "Conrad, James and *Chance*." *Imagined Worlds*, edited by Maynard Mack and Ian Gregor. London: Methuen, 1968.

VI · WORKS BY AND ABOUT FRIENDS AND
ACQUAINTANCES OF JAMES OR CONRAD

Bellamy, William. *The Novels of Wells, Bennett and Galsworthy, 1890–1910*. New York: Barnes and Noble, 1971.

Bennett, Arnold. *Letters of Arnold Bennett*. 2 vols. Edited by James Hepburn. London: Oxford University Press, 1970.

Benson, A. C. *Memories and Friends*. London: John Murray, 1924.

Cassell, Richard A. *Ford Madox Ford: A Study of His Novels*. Baltimore: Johns Hopkins Press, 1961.

Ford, Ford Madox. *Joseph Conrad: A Personal Remembrance*. Boston: Little, Brown, 1924.

———. *Letters of Ford Madox Ford*. Edited by Richard M. Ludwig. Princeton, New Jersey: Princeton University Press, 1965.

———. *Memories and Impressions: A Study in Atmospheres*. New York and London: Harper, 1911.

———. *Portraits from Life*. Boston: Houghton Mifflin, 1937.

———. *Return to Yesterday*. London: Victor Gollancz, 1931.

———. "Techniques." *Southern Review*, 1 (July 1935), 20–35.

———. *Thus to Revisit*. London: Chapman and Hall, 1921.

Galsworthy, John. *Castles in Spain and Other Screeds*. New York: Scribners, 1927.

Garnett, David. *The Golden Echo*. London: Chatto and Windus, 1953.

Goldring, Douglas. *The Last Pre-Raphaelite: A Record of the Life and Writings of Ford Madox Ford*. London: Macdonald, 1948.

————. *South Lodge*. London: Constable, 1943.

Hart-Davis, Rupert. *Hugh Walpole*. London: Macmillan, 1952.

Hynes, Samuel. *Edwardian Occasions*. New York: Oxford University Press, 1972.

Lucas, E. V. *The Colvins and Their Friends*. New York: Scribners, 1928.

MacShane, Frank. *The Life and Work of Ford Madox Ford*. New York: Horizon Press, 1965.

————. ed. *Ford Madox Ford: The Critical Heritage*. London and Boston: Routledge and Kegan Paul, 1972.

Meixner, John A. *Ford Madox Ford's Novels: A Critical Study*. Minneapolis: University of Minnesota Press, 1962.

Mizener, Arthur. *The Saddest Story: A Biography of Ford Madox Ford*. New York and Cleveland: World, 1971.

Morrell, Ottoline. *Memories of Lady Ottoline Morrell: A Study in Friendship, 1873–1915*. Edited by Robert Gathorne-Hardy. New York: Knopf, 1964.

Moser, Thomas C. "From Olive Garnett's Diary: Impressions of Ford Madox Ford and His Friends, 1890–1906." *Texas Studies in Literature and Language*, 16 (Fall 1974), 511–533.

Mottram, R. H. *For Some We Loved: An Intimate Portrait of Ada and John Galsworthy*. London: Hutchinson, 1956.

Ohmann, Carol. *Ford Madox Ford: From Apprentice to Craftsman*. Middletown, Connecticut: Wesleyan University Press, 1964.

Reid, B. L. *The Man from New York: John Quinn and His Friends*. New York: Oxford University Press, 1968.

Rothenstein, William. *Men and Memories: Recollections of William Rothenstein*. 3 vols. New York: Coward-McCann, 1931–1940.

Russell, Bertrand. *Portraits from Memory and Other Essays*. London: George Allen and Unwin, 1956.

Swinnerton, Frank L. *Background with Chorus*. London: Hutchinson, 1956.

Walpole, Hugh. *The Apple Trees: Four Reminiscences*. Waltham Saint Lawrence, Berkshire: The Golden Cockrell Press, 1932.

Wells, H. G. *Experiment in Autobiography*. New York: Macmillan, 1934.

Wiley, Paul L. *Novelist of Three Worlds: Ford Madox Ford*. Syracuse, New York: Syracuse University Press, 1962.

VII · WORKS ON MODERN LITERATURE

Allen, Walter. *The Modern Novel in Britain and the United States*. New York: Dutton, 1964.
Beach, Joseph Warren. *The Twentieth Century Novel: Studies in Technique*. New York: Appleton-Century, 1932.
Beebe, Maurice. *Ivory Towers and Sacred Founts: The Artist as Hero in Fiction from Goethe to Joyce*. New York: New York University Press, 1964.
Bogan, Louise. *Selected Criticism: Prose, Poetry*. New York: Noonday Press, 1955.
Booth, Wayne C. *The Rhetoric of Fiction*. Chicago: University of Chicago Press, 1961.
Bowden, Edwin. *The Dungeon of the Heart: Human Isolation and the American Novel*. New York: Macmillan, 1961.
Clayborough, Arthur. *The Grotesque in English Literature*. Oxford: Clarendon Press, 1965.
Eagleton, Terence. *Exiles and Emigres: Studies in Modern Literature*. New York: Schocken Books, 1970.
Engelberg, Edward. *The Unknown Distance: From Consciousness to Conscience: Goethe to Camus*. Cambridge, Massachusetts: Harvard University Press, 1972.
Friedman, Alan. *The Turn of the Novel*. New York: Oxford University Press, 1966.
Garrett, Peter K. *Scene and Symbol from George Eliot to James Joyce*. New Haven: Yale University Press, 1969.
Gindin, James J. *Harvest of a Quiet Eye: The Novel of Compassion*. Bloomington: Indiana University Press, 1971.
Goldknopf, David. *The Life of the Novel*. Chicago: University of Chicago Press, 1972.
Grabo, Carl H. *The Technique of the Novel*. New York: Scribners, 1928.
Howe, Irving. *Politics and the Novel*. Cleveland and New York: World, Meridian Books, 1957.
Kayser, Wolfgang. *The Grotesque in Art and Literature*. Tr. by Ulrich Weisstein. Bloomington: Indiana University Press, 1963.

Kiely, Robert. *The Romantic Novel in England*. Cambridge, Massachusetts: Harvard University Press, 1972.

Krieger, Murray. *The Tragic Vision: Variations on a Theme in Literary Interpretations*. New York: Holt, Rinehart and Winston, 1960.

Leavis, F. R. *The Great Tradition: George Eliot, Henry James, Joseph Conrad*. New York: George Stewart, 1949.

Lubbock, Percy. *The Craft of Fiction*. New York, Scribners, 1921.

McCullough, Bruce. *Representative English Novelists: Defoe to Conrad*. New York: Harper, 1946.

Michel, Laurence A. *The Thing Contained: Theory of the Tragic*. Bloomington: University of Indiana Press, 1970.

Stewart, J.I.M. *Eight Modern Writers*. Oxford: Clarendon Press, 1963.

Swinden, Patrick. *Unofficial Selves: Character in the Novel from Dickens to the Present Day*. London: Macmillan, 1973.

Tanner, Tony. *The Reign of Wonder: Naivety and Reality in American Literature*. Cambridge: University Press, 1965.

Thomson, Philip. *The Grotesque*. London: Methuen, 1972.

Tindall, William York. *Forces in Modern British Literature, 1885–1956*. New York: Knopf, 1947.

Van Ghent, Dorothy. *The English Novel: Form and Function*. New York: Rinehart, 1953.

Williams, Raymond. *Modern Tragedy*. London: Chatto and Windus, 1966.

Zabel, Morton D. *Craft and Character in Modern Fiction*. New York: Viking, 1957.

Index

DATE			